George Eliot

Godless Woman

Brian Spittles

150th YEAR

M

MACMILLAN

First published 1993 by
THE MACMILLAN PRESS LTD
Houndmills, Basingstoke, Hampshire RG21 2XS
and London
Companies and representatives
throughout the world

ISBN 0–333–57217–3 hardcover
ISBN 0–333–57218–1 paperback

A catalogue record for this book is available
from the British Library

Printed in Hong Kong

For Matthew, Edmund and Brian

Contents

Acknowledgements

I wish firstly to thank Professor Norman Page for his initial encouragement and subsequent help. This book would certainly not have been written without his enthusiasm and assistance. I also wish to thank Cathryn Tanner, Doreen Alig, Rosemary M. Thornely, Professor Emma Harris, Dr David Grylls, Joyce Alied, and the staffs of Ruskin College, the University of Oxford English Faculty, and Bodleian, Libraries for their invaluable assistance in many diverse ways. I record my thanks, too, to Dr Stephen Regan for his cheerful support as my main colleague during the wearisome periods of toil we have been through together, and which threatened at times to swamp even the resilient George Eliot.

It is absolutely impossible to overstate my debt to Dr Ruth Whittaker, who literally made it possible for me to write this book. I value highly both her academic integrity and personal friendship. Her own future book will I'm sure shed exciting new light on George Eliot, as her past work on Sterne and Lessing have enlightened my teaching. Finally all credit must go to Margaret Wickett, who helped me out of errors and difficulties with grace and humour, and contributed many ideas that would otherwise not appear in this book.

Abbreviations

Page references to Eliot's novels are to the following Penguin editions:

Adam Bede (1985)
Daniel Deronda (1986)
Felix Holt (1987)
Middlemarch (1985)
The Mill on the Floss (1985)
Romola (1980)
Silas Marner (1985)

Compilations of other writing by Eliot are referenced by the following coding:

GEL   Gordon S. Haight (ed.), *The George Eliot Letters*
           Volumes I-III (London: Oxford University Press, 1954)
           Volumes IV-VII (London: Oxford University Press, 1956)
           Volumes VIII-IX (New Haven: Yale University Press, 1978)

LIFE   J. W. Cross (ed.), *George Eliot's Life as Related in Her Letters and Journals*, New Edition (Edinburgh: William Blackwood and Sons, 1887)

POEMS   Lucien Jenkins (ed.), *George Eliot: Collected Poems* (London: Skoob Books Publishing Ltd, 1989)

SEP   A. S. Byatt and Nicholas Warren (eds), *George Eliot: Selected Essays, Poems and Other Writings* (Harmondsworth: Penguin, 1990)

SL   Gordon S. Haight (ed.), *Selections from George Eliot's Letters* (New Haven: Yale University Press, 1985)

General Editor's Preface

In recent years many critics and teachers have become convinced of the importance of recognizing that works of literature are grounded in the conditions of their production in the widest possible sense of that phrase – in the history, society, ideas and ideologies of their time, the lives and careers of their authors, and the prevailing circumstances of the literary market-place and the reading public. To some extent this development reflects both a disenchantment with the 'practical criticism' approach that held sway for so long in school, college and university teaching of literature and a scepticism towards the ahistorical biases encouraged by some more recent schools of critical theory.

It is true that lip-service has long been paid to 'background': the English Tripos at Cambridge, for instance, embodied the 'life, literature and thought' formula from its early years. Such an approach, however, tended to treat 'background' as distinct and detachable from literary works and as constituting a relatively minor, marginal and even optional element in the study of a text. What is now perceived to be in question is something more vital and more central: not a loosely defined relationship between certain novels, plays and poems on the one hand and 'history' or 'ideas' on the other, but an intimate informing and shaping of the one by the other. Colonialism in Conrad or Kipling, Christian theology in Milton or Bunyan, scientific discovery in Tennyson or Hardy, politics in Yeats or Eliot: these are not background issues against which the texts can be foregrounded but crucial determinants of the very nature of the texts themselves without which they would be radically different and which profoundly affect the way we understand and value them.

At the same time, as most teachers are ready to attest, even a basic knowledge of the historical and cultural conditions of past including recently past, generations cannot be taken for granted. To many students, periods as recent as the 1930s or the Great War are largely a closed book, while key concepts of earlier generations such as Darwinism or Puritanism, and major movements such as the spread of literacy and the growth and decline of imperialism, are known in the sketchiest outline if at all.

This series is intended to provide in an accessible form materials that will make possible a fuller and deeper understanding of the work of the major authors by demonstrating in detail its relationship to the world, including the intellectual world, in which it was produced. Its starting-point is not a notion of 'background' but a conviction that many, perhaps most, great writers are in an integral sense *in* and *of* their time. Each volume will look afresh at the primary texts (or a selection of them) in relation to the ways in which they have been informed and shaped by both the external and the ideological conditions of their worlds. Historical, political, scientific, theological, philosophical and other dimensions will be explored as appropriate. By understanding more fully the contexts which have made particular works what they are and not otherwise, students and others will be able to bring new understanding to their reading of the texts.

NORMAN PAGE

1

Obscurity to Eminence

A party-game list of the three most eminent Victorian women might read: the Queen, Florence Nightingale and George Eliot. Another trio, of the period's most important novelists, could reasonably consist of Charles Dickens, Thomas Hardy and George Eliot. The specific names in both cases can be argued about, but it is virtually impossible to get any other name but Eliot's into both trinities of eminence. That in itself is part of the remarkableness of the Eliot phenomenon, but her achievement is perceived as even more extraordinary in the light of her background and upbringing. Even a cursory summary of her life reveals fascinating areas of enigma and paradox. Grasping those is part of the challenging, and exciting, process of understanding Eliot's fiction.

Eliot was born on 22 November 1819 into an obscure family living in a quiet provincial, unsophisticated agrarian backwater of England. She died on 22 December 1880, and among many illustrious people who attended her funeral were the poet Robert Browning and the scientist T. H. Huxley, illustrating both Eliot's status and its breadth: literary and intellectual. She was born the youngest daughter of five surviving children. Her father, Robert Evans, had a son and daughter living from his first marriage in 1801 – their mother had died in 1809 – so that her half-brother and half-sister were both in their teens by the time Eliot was born. Robert Evans remarried in 1813 and Eliot was born with a sister, Chrissey, who was five years old, and a brother, Isaac, who was three. After Eliot's birth there were also twin brothers who died in infancy, not an uncommon event at the time. Eliot was born into a lower middling-class rural family, in the English Midlands, during a period when little formal education was available for such a person, and the highest aspiration she might have was to become the wife of a relatively prosperous farmer.

Eliot's father had begun his working life as a carpenter, but by the time of her birth had risen to the position of agent for a large rural estate. His social mobility was also manifested in the second marriage into a farming family. The most thorough Eliot scholar,

Gordon Haight, has observed of the Pearson family into which Evans married: 'There is little doubt that Robert Evans was made aware that he had raised himself socially by this match'.[1] Evans' career represents both the social dynamic that was a central feature of the nineteenth century, and which came to inform Eliot's own vision of community and history, and the essentially conservative values that often underlie such achievement.

However, instead of submitting to the fate that appeared to await her, respectable marriage into the agrarian community and a parochial life of unliterate worldly obscurity, Eliot gained notoriety by living openly with a man married to another woman; became the internationally respected translator of German theological and philosophical works; and in addition mastered French, Italian, Latin, Hebrew, and ancient Greek; worked as an influential journal editor; was an essayist of note, a quite prolific poet and a leading novelist; and was accepted as one of the great intellectual figures of her day. All those features contribute to the enigma and paradox that form Eliot's life and work, making both an absorbing study.

In some respects Eliot's childhood and youth were not typical for a female of her region and social class. As a child receiving basic schooling Eliot quickly proved herself an able scholar and linguist. She was consequently given a good elementary education at local private schools. At the age of thirteen she was sent to a school in the nearest large town, Coventry, run by Mary and Rebecca Franklin, who were sisters still in their twenties – well-educated and sophisticated for the provincial culture in which they lived. They were clearly very good teachers, liberal and broad-minded within a Baptist framework. Eliot read widely, learned passionately and became an Evangelical enthusiast. She retained two of these characteristics all her life, but lost the last one – and all orthodox belief – in her early twenties.

In her Coventry life Eliot read avidly, intelligently and eclectically, gaining the admiration and friendship of the literary and intellectually influential people of the city. One of them, Charles Bray, for instance, wrote a book on the *Philosophy of Necessity*; and he was related through marriage to the London based Charles Hennell who in 1838 published *An Inquiry into the Origins of Christianity*. Those were the kind of subjects that fascinated Eliot, and eventually it was indirectly through Hennel and his sister Sara, who remained a life-long friend of Eliot's, that she was asked to translate Strauss' *Das Leben Jesu*. Through that circle Eliot gained access to the world of writing and publishing, and ultimately her career in London: as translator, editor, essayist and novelist.

One area in which George Eliot's personal experience connected with public aspects of her society was, of course, her status as a woman. She was concerned with the problems of being female, and the theme recurs through the novels – but it is important to appreciate the elusiveness of her thinking and attitudes. Her writing is sometimes celebrated as progressive early feminist, yet it is also condemned for its conservatism. It is ultimately too enigmatic to categorize facilely, and her own life too paradoxical for the drawing of simplistic conclusions. Eliot, for instance, lived for twenty-four years with a man who was unable to marry her, but never attacked the institution of marriage. She was also a woman who suffered fairly frequent debilitation, often being severely ill with rheumatism, headaches and toothache, for example, yet she travelled many times to, and extensively across, the continent of Europe in a period in which such journeys were neither comfortable nor fast. Despite her constitutional weakness she also learnt the vigorous and quite newly invented game of lawn tennis at the age of fifty-seven. These actions demonstrate the paradoxical nature of the woman, a feature of her personality that became embodied in her work.

Eliot's whole personality was somewhat enigmatic. Growing up at a time when girls and young women were required to be physically attractive within the conventions of the day, and possess the graces society considered feminine – and not to be inconveniently intelligent – she had all the wrong attributes. Her physical appearance, for instance, was not immediately prepossessing. In 1869 an American visitor, Charles Norton, described meeting Eliot: 'one rarely sees a plainer woman; dull complexion, dull eyes, heavy features'.[2] A few months later another trans-Atlantic visitor, Henry James, exercised his embryonic skills as a novelist in an account of her to his father:

> she is magnificently ugly – deliciously hideous. She has a low forehead, a dull grey eye, a vast pendulous nose, a huge mouth, full of uneven teeth and a chin and jaw-bone *qui n'en finissent pas* [which are endless] ... [a] great horse-faced blue-stocking.[3]

Although Eliot was approaching fifty years of age when these descriptions of her were written she had not changed fundamentally, and was aware from an early age that she was not considered a great beauty. When she was twenty years old, for instance, Eliot felt some attraction towards Joseph Brezzi, who was teaching her Italian. Nothing developed and she wrote to a friend, Martha Jackson, in October 1840:

> Every day's experience seems to deepen the voice of foreboding that has long been telling me 'The bliss of reciprocated affection is not allotted to you under any form. Your heart must be widowed in this manner from the world . . .'. Time only will prove the prophetic character of my presentiment.
>
> (SL, p. 14)

There is maybe a fear expressed here that having the wrong attributes would cause Eliot to live a life unfulfilled romantically.

In the event the 'magnificently ugly' Eliot was not entirely without admirers and desirers. In 1845 she received an unaccepted proposal of marriage from a painter who remains anonymous. In 1851 Eliot was lodging in London in the house of the publisher John Chapman, and their relationship caused some jealousy on the part of Chapman's wife which led to Eliot having to find new lodgings. This, however, was an enigmatic episode: no details of the physical relationship (if any) between Chapman and Eliot emerged, although he was known to be a philanderer, and already had a mistress, Elisabeth Tilley, living in the house. Eliot also met the political philosopher Herbert Spencer. Writing of him to her friends the Brays in April of the following year she claimed 'we are not in love with each other', but that Spencer: 'is a good, delightful creature and I always feel better for being with him' (SL, p. 95). At the same time Spencer wrote, to his friend Edward Lott, praising Eliot's 'womanly qualities and manner' and revealing: 'We have been for some time past on very intimate terms . . . I had frequently . . . the pleasure of her companionship'.[4] Two months later Eliot confided to the Brays of herself and Spencer that 'all the world is setting us down as engaged' (SL, p. 98). Many years later Spencer confirmed that there had been: 'reports that I was in love with her, and that we were about to be married'.[5] Yet ultimately they remained simply friends, with Eliot probably being the more disappointed of them.

It was in 1854, when Eliot was thirty-four years old, that she began living with George Lewes, whom she had known for almost three years as part of the London intellectual circle. They stayed together happily until his death in 1878. Subsequently Eliot, then sixty years of age, produced perhaps the greatest surprise of even her unpredictable life by marrying John Cross, who had been a friend of Eliot and Lewes for some years. The event was a double shock to some of her contemporaries: that Eliot, who had lived so long without benefit of clergy should marry at all; and that her chosen husband was twenty years younger than her. The feminist critic Jennifer Uglow has commented that the marriage was: 'a further blow to her free-thinking and Unitarian friends ... the town buzzed with rumour'.[6] Whatever her limitations in attractiveness were considered to be Eliot clearly had qualities that did attract, and it was partly the unconventional nature of these that made them difficult for some people to appreciate.

In fact the young Henry James whilst recording Eliot's 'delicious hideousness' also perceived her virtues: 'in this vast ugliness resides a most powerful beauty which ... charms the mind ... a delightful expression, a voice soft and rich ... sagacity and sweetness ... a great feminine dignity and character'.[7] This perception confirms an earlier one by William Hale White, who himself wrote six fine novels later under the name of Mark Rutherford. Writing in *The Bookman* in 1902 White remembered working with Eliot fifty years earlier when they were both lodging at Chapman's house:

> If there was any sincerity (an indispensable qualification) in the person with whom she came into contact, she strove to elicit his best.... I have never seen anybody whose search for the meaning and worth of persons and things was so unresting as hers.[8]

Spencer's memory affirms the validity of this assessment, for he recalled that although Eliot's head: 'was larger than is usual in women ... her face was remarkably transfigured by a smile'.[9] Of her voice and general demeanour Spencer remembered: 'Its tones were always gentle, and, like the smile, sympathetic.... Conscientious and just in all relations and consequently indignant against wrong, she was nevertheless so tolerant of human weakness as to be quickly forgiving'.[10] Eliot was generous morally, emotionally and financially. She had an attractiveness of personality which, for the discerning, overcame the more superficial aspects of her appearance.

These facets of her personal experience were worked through the novels. Marriage is certainly a recurring concern, both in its social and emotional aspects: the novels analyse ideas of total compatibility, and diverse kinds of incompatibility. Eliot explores the complexities, and possible paradoxes, of physical and sexual attractiveness, eschewing the uncomplicated stereotypes of popular literature. Dorothea Brooke in *Middlemarch*, for example, has yearnings which were both 'rational and ardent' (p. 112) – paradoxical within the conventions of the day that saw a dichotomy between head and heart, intellect and blood. It takes the artist's perception of the German Naumann to realize that Dorothea has a 'sensuous force controlled by spiritual passion' (p. 221). Dorothea's husband, Casaubon, is clearly unable to embrace such an enigma.

In Eliot's novels physical plainness sometimes appears to be associated with intelligence, honesty and sincerity, whilst overt sexual attractiveness can connote a shallowness of feeling and intellect, although that is not invariably the case. In the structure of *Middlemarch* the character of Dorothea is flanked by those of Mary Garth and Rosamond Vincy. When Mary and Rosamond are together looking into a mirror:

> Mary Garth seemed all the plainer standing at an angle between the two nymphs – the one in the glass, and the one out of it, who looked at each other with eyes of heavenly blue ... most men in Middlemarch ... held that Miss Vincy was the best girl in the world, and some called her an angel. Mary Garth, on the contrary, had the aspect of an ordinary sinner: she was brown; her curly dark hair was rough and stubborn; her stature was low.
>
> (pp. 139–40)

If there is an element of stereotyping the contrast here between plainness/sincerity and beauty/deviousness there is also, in the novel's broader context, an artistic finesse and a complexity that goes beyond mere representational characterization. The linking of Rosamond's 'heavenly blue' eyes with her reputation as 'an angel' creates an ironic prolepsis, for she manipulates their angelic qualities at moments of crisis. When, later in the novel, Lydgate has determined not to become emotionally involved with her: 'she felt that the tears had risen, and it was no use to try to do anything else than let them stay like water on a blue flower' (p. 335). The effect on Lydgate is immediate, striking at him where he was most vulnerable: 'the ambitious man who was looking at those Forget-me-nots under the water was very warmhearted and rash' (ibid.). Although the narrative presents Rosamond as having no control over her tears she is not unaware of their affect. The episode ends with Lydgate 'bound' (p. 336) to Rosamond; and the word is used in both the conventional sense of being engaged to, and with the connotation that he had lost his free will to her.

Rosamond's essential narcissism is expressed in the earlier passage by the fact that she and her reflection 'looked at each other', there were 'two nymphs' – the self-regarding is active rather than merely passive mirroring. That attribute of character is also expressed by the reiterated description of her hair, with its 'infantile fairness' (pp. 139ff.). Rosamond is as egocentric as an infant, but without that being's innocence. Any common stereotyping is denied by the sexually alluring Rosamond being in reality emotionally cold, whilst it is the plain Mary who has the emotional warmth.

Mary's qualities are 'honesty, truth-telling fairness' (p. 140). The pun on the meanings of fair, with such close juxtaposition, is obviously intentional – but perhaps there is slightly more complexity in the portraits than an approach through stereotyping suggests. For the novel does show an awareness of the limitations of Rosamond's education, and Mary is not without defects:

> Plainness has its peculiar temptations and vices quite as much as beauty; it is apt either to feign amiability, or, not feigning it, to show all the repulsiveness of discontent. . . . Her shrewdness had a streak of satiric bitterness continually renewed.
>
> (ibid.)

Eliot is usually exploring the complexities of character and situation, rather than writing within predetermined, simplistic conventions about them. In one form of reading this ability to project the

parodoxes and enigmas of her own experience into her art provides one of the great strengths of the novels.

A different interpretive approach, however, sees Eliot denying
fundamental aspects of her own experience. In some respects, it
can be argued, she was an early feminist, continuing a tradition
taken from Mary Wollstonecraft and her 1792 publication *Vindica-
tion of the Rights of Woman*. Eliot, indeed, was a close friend of
Barbara Leigh Smith – later known as Barbara Bodichon – who
founded the magazine *The Englishwoman's Journal* – which subsequently became *The Englishwoman's Review* – in 1857 partly in
order to provide a platform for feminist polemic, and to which
Eliot subscribed. Also, Eliot's own very unconventional, socially
shocking, liaison with George Lewes, with whom she lived for
twenty-four years between 1854 and 1878, may be taken to
confirm the view of her as a feminist.

Yet she never wrote against marriage, and in her novels seems
to deny the ideal of female independence. Another feminist critic,
Gillian Beer, has observed that: 'George Eliot has been a knot of
controversy for feminist critics'.[11] Kate Millett, as an example of
the more militant aspects of feminism, conclusively dismissed
Eliot ideologically: '"Living in sin", George Eliot lived the revolution . . . but she did not write of it'.[12] There is much truth in this
verdict. Mary Garth, for instance, marries happily, and so too does
the widowed Rosamond after her initial disappointment with
Lydgate. Dorothea, after a long struggle to achieve a degree of
self-assertion, ends the novel happy and fulfilled in domestic
circumstances:

> she never repented that she had given up position and fortune
> to marry Will Ladislaw . . . that she should give him wifely help.
> . . . and be only known in a certain circle as a wife and mother.
>
> (pp. 893-4)

Some critics see this as a betrayal of feminist ideas, and also of
Eliot's own experience, since by the time she wrote it she had
been living with Lewes for eighteen years. Millett finds the novel
contradictory:

> Dorothea's predicament in *Middlemarch* is an eloquent plea that
> a fine mind be allowed an occupation; but it goes no further
> than petition. She marries Will Ladislaw and can expect no

more of life than the discovery of a good companion whom she can serve as secretary.[13]

The answer may be in the novel itself when the narrator touches on the fact that some characters were not happy about Dorothea's marriage to Will: 'But no one stated exactly what else that was in her power she ought rather to have done' (p. 894). It may be argued broadly that such a lack of choice implicitly criticizes the society that narrows actions down so much, and there is explicit criticism too, a reminder that the character was 'struggling amidst the conditions of an imperfect social state' (p. 896). However, the tone of regret in the novel's Finale is diluted – and the argument does not satisfy critics who want characters to lead by example. Dorothea does accept the traditional female role, and is presented as happy in it.

Light can be thrown on the apparent contradiction between the novel's polemic and the author's experience by considering the latter more closely. Eliot realized that not all marriages were entirely the result of free and independent choice by both partners. As early as 1841, at the age of twenty-one, according to her friend Mary Sibree, Eliot thought that many: 'young people being brought together, and receiving intimations that mutual interest was desired and expected, were apt to drift into connections on grounds not strong enough for the wear and tear of life' (LIFE, p. 58). Eliot's view on marriages of this type was of a compassionate rather than purely ideological nature:

> The conception of the union of two persons by so close a tie as marriage, without a previous union of minds as well as hearts, was to her dreadful. 'How terrible it must be,' she once said to me, 'to find one's self tied to a being whose limitations you could see, and must know were such as to prevent your ever being understood!'
>
> (ibid.)

Both Rosamond and Lydgate are disappointed in, and by, their marriage. Both married without truly knowing the other, although thinking they did. In a world in which the process of divorce was extraordinarily expensive and slow, errors were mostly paid for until the death of one of the partners. Eliot, of course, was involved in another solution, as Lewes had a wife with whom he did not live. She also knew the social and emotional price of that way out.

The social situation was complicated because although emotion, passion and love were private feelings marriage was a public contract (although these factors remain true attitudes to the contract, and its legal status, have become much more tenuous). When the experiences of love and marriage were compatible no problems arose, but difficulties did occur if one partner's feelings changed, or in the case of a more or less arranged wedding the individuals involved could not be happy together. Parental, particularly patriarchal, influence was powerful – and could even take the form of actual control. That affected sons as well as daughters, but was especially strong in the case of the latter. Even the indulgent Vincy in *Middlemarch* has a moment of rebellion against his daughter's choice: 'I don't believe Lydgate has got a farthing. I shan't give my consent to their marrying. . . . The sooner the engagement's off, the better' (p. 378). His objection is mainly financial, and is overcome by: 'a demand that Lydgate should insure his life – a demand immediately conceded' (p. 389). Nevertheless for the original reader the threat Vincy makes to veto the marriage of his daughter was real. In *The Mill on the Floss* Maggie Tulliver's father forbids her to meet Philip Wakem, and she has to comply. After a not entirely chance, clandestine meeting with Philip in which he reveals his continued interest in her:

> Maggie went home . . . with a mental conflict. . . . Here suddenly was an opening in the rocky wall which shut in the narrow Valley of Humiliation, where all her prospect was the remote unfathomed sky. . . . She might have books, converse, affection . . . *must* she always live in this resigned imprisonment?
>
> (p. 424)

Maggie's choice is between duty to her father's wishes, which entails an apparently perpetual loneliness, and a life of love and companionship that requires defiance of the prohibition against the potential husband. The italicization of '*must*' emphasizes the sharpness of the dilemma, and the fact that Maggie has no real choice. Even after Tulliver's death she is not free, as the power of patriarchy passes in effect to her brother, and he is no less rigid in its application. Tom's, 'inward criticism of his father's faults did not prevent him from adopting his father's prejudice' (p. 579).

Eliot experienced the weight of fraternal disapproval herself, as many of her readers must have too since it reflects not uncommon Victorian attitudes.

Despite all this personal experience and intellectual analysis Eliot, apparently paradoxically, undeviatingly subscribed to the idea of the institution of marriage. In the year after her union with Lewes had begun Eliot wrote to an old Coventry friend, Cara Bray, who disapproved of the liaison:

> Assuredly if there be any one subject on which I feel no levity it is that of marriage and the relation of the sexes – if there is any one action or relation of my life which is and always has been profoundly serious, it is my relation to Mr. Lewes. . . . Light and easily broken ties are what I neither desire theoretically nor could live for practically.
>
> (SL, pp. 151–2)

The emphaticness of the syntax – 'any one subject', 'any one action', the later negatives – expresses a great depth of feeling. The validity of the emotion was ultimately proved by the fact that the relationship with Lewes lasted twenty-four years, and was broken only by his death. At its beginning Eliot was afraid that disapproval sprang in part from the idea that she had chosen to live with Lewes *in order* to flout convention and the laws of marriage. Those who see a discrepancy between Eliot's actions and her fiction appear to fall into the error.

Before her friendship with Lewes developed in the way it did Eliot was translating the contemporary German philosopher Ludwig Feuerbach's *The Essence of Christianity*. He considered that religion emanated from human love, and went on to argue, in the final chapter, 'Concluding Application', of Eliot's 1854 translation:

> marriage – we mean of course, marriage as the free bond of love – is sacred in itself. . . . That alone is a religious marriage, which is a true marriage, which corresponds to the essence of marriage – of love. And so it is with all moral relations. Then only are they moral . . . only as the free bond of love.[14]

With hindsight this can be read as prophetic of Eliot's own attitude to Lewes and their circumstances.

She did not *choose* to challenge legal marriage, the choice she

had was to live with Lewes, to undertake an illicit and secret
affair with him, or to renounce any form of intimate friendship
with him. Lewes' marriage had already broken down in all but
name, and his wife had given birth to the child of another man,
but because of the complexity of the divorce laws he was unable
to obtain legal freedom to remarry. As Eliot explained in an 1857
letter to Vincent Holbeche: 'He is unable at present to contract a
legal marriage, because, though long deprived of his first wife by
her misconduct, he is not legally divorced' (SL, p. 175). Since Eliot
did not approve of 'Light and easily broken ties' – she had written
to Cara Bray in the letter quoted above: 'Women who are satisfied
with such ties do *not* act as I have done – they obtain what they
desire and are still invited to dinner' (SL, p. 152) – the idea of an
affair would have been anathema. Her only real option was love
and social ostracism, or loneliness. At the age of thirty-four in the
Victorian period the latter may have been a choice for life. The
former option had its own price, of not being 'invited to dinner',
and all that implied.

The marriage theme is explored through Esther Lyon in *Felix
Holt*. She realizes her love for Felix, but recognizes that marriage
to him would entail an enormous material sacrifice:

> There was something which she now felt profoundly to be the
> best thing that life could give her. But – if it was to be had at all –
> it was not to be had without paying a heavy price for it, such as
> we must pay for all that is greatly good. A supreme love, a
> motive that gives a sublime rhythm to a woman's life, and exalts
> habit into partnership with the soul's highest needs, is not to be
> had where and how she wills. . . . It is not true that love makes all
> things easy: it makes us choose what is difficult. . . . still there
> was the dread that after all she might find herself on the stony
> road alone.
>
> (p. 591)

The religious nature of the diction in the extract indicates the
importance of love in the novel. It is a profound experience,
'sublime' and exalting, fulfilling 'the soul's highest needs'. Yet
there is no conventional sentimentality, as the insistence on
'paying', 'price', 'pay' shows that nothing is 'easy'.

Having paid the price herself Eliot considered herself married,
more so than those people who were simply bound by a legality

that lacked emotional substance. In letters to her brother Isaac and half-sister Frances in 1857 she referred to Lewes as 'My husband' (GEL, II, pp. 331 and 333). There may indeed have been some deliberate linguistic equivocation. The length of time that elapsed, almost three years, between the start of the intimate relationship, and Eliot informing her closest living relatives of it, suggest that she was wary of their reactions. Events justified Eliot's fears, for not only did Isaac break off relations with her, but also exercised his prerogative as Victorian head of the nuclear family by pressuring their sister Chrissey, as well as Frances, to renounce her. Part of Eliot's own price for love was to be exorcised from her family, and it hurt her deeply. Nevertheless she insisted to her brother's solicitor, 'Our marriage is not a legal one, though it is regarded by us both as a sacred bond' (SL, p. 175). This echoes the Feuerbach concept she had translated in 1854. That passage goes on to compare the idea of the true marriage Eliot and Lewes contracted with the kind of relationship many people were trapped into:

> a marriage the bond of which is merely an external restriction, not the voluntary, content self-restriction of love, in short, a marriage which is not spontaneously concluded, spontaneously willed, self-sufficing, is not a true marriage, and therefore not a truly moral marriage.[15]

It was not Eliot's liaison that was immoral, but the hypocrisy of loveless, socially-conventional marriages. Such a notion is indeed a fundamental challenge to, if not an actual attack upon, a commonly accepted form of marriage – but it is also a defence of the ideal of marriage.

Eliot's attitudes to marriage were consistent throughout her life and work. After all, she eventually married John Cross, a friend of eleven years standing, and the happy marriages of Dinah and Adam in *Adam Bede*, Eppie and Aaron in *Silas Marner*, Esther Lyon and Felix in *Felix Holt*, Dorothea and Will, Mary and Fred, in *Middlemarch*, and Mirah and Daniel in *Daniel Deronda* are expressions of Eliot's deep belief that private emotions could be fulfilled in 'spontaneously concluded, spontaneously willed, self-sufficing ... true marriage'. The emphasis on spontaneity – originally Feuerbach's, but clearly endorsed by Eliot through her activity of translation – reflects the idea that marriage must be through the

free mutual choice of the individuals involved, not family pressures, financial considerations or social expectations, or mere sexual attraction: 'unions formed in the maturity of thought and
feeling, and grounded only on inherent fitness and mutual attraction' (SEP, p. 11). Eliot wrote these words in an article entitled
'Woman in France: Madame de Sablé', which appeared in the
Westminster Review, just after her liaison with Lewes had begun. A
key word is certainly 'maturity' – for it is only through maturity
that self-knowledge and discernment about others are attained. It
is the lack of these qualities that lead Rosamond and Lydgate, and
initially Dorothea and Casaubon, into disastrous marriages; also
Molly and Godfrey in *Silas Marner,* and Gwendolen and Grandcourt in *Daniel Deronda*; and Hetty Sorrel's catastrophic mistake in
Adam Bede springs partly from the same cause, as in part does
Maggie Tulliver's destructive relationship with Stephen Guest
too.

It was not marriage as a way of living in itself that worried
Eliot, but misconceived liaisons. She knew that women were
generally the more vulnerable gender in such cases, but her
feminism was qualified by personal experience – the knowledge
that Lewes was financially, and to some extent emotionally,
abused by his wife for over twenty-five years, until his death.
Indeed, Lewes contributed to the financial upkeep of four children fathered by another man. Over the course of his relationship
with Eliot that increasingly meant in practice that, as his income
tended to fall and hers increased, she was contributing money to
Lewes' wife's extravagant household. Eliot was always aware of
the paradoxes and complexities of circumstances and people, and
that merely theoretical approaches to problems were likely to be
simplistic. That is an important factor in the fiction's interest. The
analysis and development of themes is usually immediately relevant to the initial reader, and yet has a value too for different
readers in diverse conditions.

The view that Eliot was untrue to her own experience by
apparently deriding marriage in life whilst condoning it in her
novels, has also been applied to her choice of a male pseudonym.
At one end of the spectrum of this argument a psycho-analytic
commentator, Michael Ginsburg, referring to Freud's theories,
concludes: 'Writing is the process by which a woman – Mary Ann
Evans – becomes a man ... the symbolic way by which a woman
produces herself a phallus'.[16] At the simpler sociological edge

there is an idea that in the nineteenth century male authors had almost a monopoly on publication. Whatever Eliot may have thought of the former idea, had it been presented to her, she certainly knew that women novelists abounded. Marilyn Butler has written that in the early years of the nineteenth century: 'Maria Edgeworth was easily the most celebrated and successful of practising English novelists. . . . The public bought her novels in large numbers',[17] whilst David Grylls has observed: 'At the end of the nineteenth century the most popular novelist in Great Britain was probably Marie Corelli'.[18] Eliot's century began and ended dominated by female novelists, and between those two there were many more women, including such contemporaries of Eliot as Harriet Martineau, Margaret Oliphant, Rosa Nouchette Carey, Charlotte Elizabeth Tonna, Frances Trollope, the phenomenally successful Charlotte Yonge, who wrote over one hundred and fifty books, and Mary Braddon, whose novels sold well over a million copies – all of whom, and a great many more, published under their own names. In addition there were the Brontë sisters who assumed androgynous names, Marie Louise Ramé who adopted the name Ouida; and writers who used the married form of their names – Mary Ward who wrote as Mrs Humphrey Ward, the intellectually respected Mrs Gaskell, and perhaps the most read of all Victorian novelists, who published over fifty titles, Mrs Henry Wood.

Throughout her life Eliot was notoriously diffident as an author, and it was natural for her to write articles and essays anonymously. Even her translation of Strauss' *The Life of Jesus*, which she worked on for over two years, was published in 1846 without her name being credited; although her 1854 translation of Feuerbach's *The Essence of Christianity* did carry her pre-Eliot name, Marian Evans. When Eliot began to write fiction a name of some kind could not be avoided, and it was unsurprising in view of her earlier diffidence that she chose a pseudonym. Her first story, *Amos Barton*, was published in 1857 and Eliot's identity concealed from everyone except George Lewes for over a year, and was not revealed even to the publisher until after the appearance of the book edition of *Scenes of Clerical Life* in 1858. Eliot wrote to the publisher, John Blackwood, in February 1857: 'I shall be resolute in preserving my incognito, having observed that a *nom de plume* secures all the advantages without the disagreeables of reputation' (SL, p. 165). This letter was signed 'George Eliot'.

Her own explanation of the choice of pseudonym was simple: 'George was Mr Lewes's Christian name, and Eliot was a good mouth-filling, easily-pronounced word' (LIFE, pp. 212–3). Perhaps there is a measure of disingenuousness in this disarming claim, but no one has yet produced actual evidence against Eliot's recorded version. It does appear to be a matter of purely personal nervous self-effacement rather than gender politics.

In fact Eliot had a life-long, enigmatic relationship with names. At her baptism her Christian names were registered as Mary Anne – her family name, of course, being Evans. A school notebook dated 1834 is inscribed Marianne Evans, and three years later she signed her sister's registration of marriage, at which Eliot was a bridesmaid, Mary Ann; in 1849 she changed to Marian, a form Eliot was still using in 1880. There were also various nick-names that Eliot accepted. Clematis was one, and Polly a child-hood name that Eliot signed personal letters with even after becoming an author. From that name her friend Sara Hennell punned Pollian – on the basis of Apollyon, the 'angel of the bottomless pit' in the Book of Revelation (Ch. 9, v.11); and the 'foul fiend' Bunyan's Christian meets in the 'Valley of Humiliation'.[19] It was obviously a mutually enjoyed joke, for as late as 1877 Eliot signed a letter to Sara 'Pollian' (SL, p. 492). George Lewes had four sons within his marriage, and with whom he retained life-long contact. Eliot became known to them by the German form Mutter, and remained so even after their father's death and her marriage to Cross. After Eliot had begun to live with Lewes she wrote forcefully to her friend Bessie Parks:

> you must please not call me *Miss Evans* again. I have renounced that name, and do not mean to be known by it in any way. It is Mr. Lewes's wish that the few friends who care about me should recognize me as Mrs. Lewes, and my Father's Trustee sends me receipts to sign as Marian Lewes, so that my adoption of the name has been made a matter of business.
>
> (SL, p. 178)

This may be interpreted as cowardice before the pressures of social prejudice, or as a manifestation of the seriousness with which Eliot viewed her relationship with Lewes. In any event she signed personal letters variously Marian Lewes, Marian E. Lewes, M. E. Lewes, and M.E.L. After Eliot's late marriage to John Cross she frequently signed herself M. A. Cross, but also occasionally produces a hybrid form, Mary Ann Cross, combining early versions of the Christian names with her ultimate surname.

Names are signifiers, at least in part projecting an image of the bearer. Jennifer Uglow has nominated the form M. E. Lewes as 'the most significant pseudonym of all',[20] emphasizing the point that it was an adopted, rather than married, name despite Eliot's claim that it was 'a matter of business'. Eliot did perhaps use diverse names as a defensive strategy against a world of curiosity and potential hostility. She was fully aware of the signifying value of names, as their emblematic use in the fiction testifies.

Not all the fictional names are used emblematically, of course, but *Middlemarch*, for instance, provides a number of examples. The emblematic tradition is very long and respectable, and perhaps Bunyan's overt use of it provided one of the influences on Eliot. She adopted the nickname Apollyon from Sara Hennell's usage of it in the early 1840s, and in *Middlemarch* there are several references to 'immortal Bunyan' (p. 881) and his works, perhaps the main one in this respect being the epigraph to Chapter 85. Eliot's technique is more covert than Bunyan's, but extends nineteenth-century verisimilitude into emblemism. Lydgate, for example, is an archaic spelling of lychgate, the entrance into a churchyard burial ground – so that he is from the beginning associated with death, not only professionally as a doctor, but in a metaphoric sense in that he contracts a dead marriage and his ambitions to do 'great work' (p. 178) die, as he too literally dies 'when he was only fifty' (p. 892). Rosamond suggests perhaps a rose of the world, a flower that attracts with its delicate beauty but is also a worldly rose that entraps the naive and unworldly. One etymological meaning of garth is garden, and the Garth family are a kind of garden in which traditional values of honesty, humanity and tolerance flower – and indeed the last numbered chapter of the novel mainly takes place in the Garths' garden: 'Mary saw Fred at the orchard-gate' (p. 887), and they discuss their marriage. Even this extremely brief explication – and the concept can be taken a great deal further – brings out the point that Eliot was interested in the signifying value of names, whether her own or that of her characters.

Like all writers Eliot was in part a product of her time. Her work reflects many of the major concerns of her historical period and, more subtly, refracts the issues of her day by exploring them in a slightly oblique manner: often by setting them back in time. Eliot and her readers were aware that they were living through probably the most dynamic period of change Britain, and more particularly England, had ever experienced.

Her birth occurred in 1819, the year in which Victoria, eventual queen who gave her name to the period, was also born. Eliot died nine days before the end of 1880, giving her life an almost perfect symmetry across the middle sixty-one years of the century. The world into which Eliot was born was entirely different from that in which she died.

The population of mainland Britain in 1819 was about 14 million, at the time of Eliot's death it had more than doubled to around 30 million. Perhaps more importantly the balance of the population had shifted from agrarian work and rural living to industrialism and urban life. Eliot was born into an economic society in which agriculture was by far the most important activity in producing wealth and employing labour. By 1880 factory work and other forms of industrial activity had become dominant. In 1819, for example, the railway had not even been invented, but by 1880 over 14,000 miles of track existed in Britain alone, and the railway had become the great nineteenth-century symbol of economic, scientific and technological progress across almost the whole globe. Heavy engineering had emerged from virtually nothing to become a major industrial and economic force. There was also an enormous increase in lighter industries such as the manufacture of textiles.

With the fundamental change in the nature of wealth and work there was a concomitant expansion of towns. During the course of the century as a whole the population of London, for instance, increased from just under one million to about four and a half million, but of even more significance was the growth of the great provincial industrial centres. Birmingham grew by over seven times; Manchester by a factor larger than nine; and such places as Blackburn, Glasgow, Leeds and Leicester by more than tenfold. One of the most dramatic illustrations concerns the Teesside community of Middlesbrough. As late as the 1831 census it was a village consisting of a mere 383 people, but with the development of large-scale furnace technology its population was over 40,000 by the time of Eliot's death.

The demographic and economic changes that occurred during Eliot's lifetime were probably the fastest and most dynamic internally-produced movements any nation in the world had ever undergone. Such developments cannot be self-contained, and they caused the central struggle in Britain of the nineteenth century: that for political power.

In the year of Eliot's birth out of a total population of about fourteen million less than half a million were entitled to vote in parliamentary elections. Even allowing for the fact that the overall population includes children the proportion to whom the franchise extended was still very small – less than 4 per cent. By 1886, within a few years of Eliot's death, there were nearly five million electors in a population of approximately thirty million, a rise to about 17 per cent. This reflects an extremely hard fought, and at times bitter and actually violent, process that was crystallized during Eliot's life in the two parliamentary Reform Acts of 1832 and 1867 – which paved the way for a further extension of the franchise in 1884. In 1819 parliament was dominated by the traditional ruling classes, largely the landed gentry and their nominees, but with economic ascendancy increasingly passing to the middling classes – those with commercial, mercantile, industrial and manufacturing interests – it was obvious that a widening schism existed between the political/parliamentary and financial power bases.

That conflict was made more complex by the existence of the vast majority of the people who had no power, except their vital occupational skills and labour. Those variously designated the masses, the labouring classes or the common people were at some periods very dissatisfied with their circumstances, and were at times courted for their support by both the landed gentry and bourgeoisie, and at other times reviled by their erstwhile political friends.

An illustration of the political turmoil occurred in the very year of Eliot's birth. In 1819 economic recession had led to unemployment or reduced wages for many workers, and a demonstration was organized to take place at St Peter's Fields in Manchester. The peaceful gathering was violently and bloodily dispersed by armed troops. The historians Cole and Postgate retrospectively described the scene:

> suddenly forces of yeomanry and soldiers rode in upon the crammed demonstrators.... The yeomanry began to charge in earnest at the helpless crowd, which fled in panic. Eleven

persons were killed and many hundreds injured, some by sabre
cuts and some by being trampled underfoot by the horses of
the yeomanry or by the fleeing crowd. Two women and a child
were left among the dead. Among decent-minded people, this
horrible massacre, known in derision as 'The Battle of Peterloo',
provoked an immediate revulsion of feeling.[21]

The name commemorating the suppresion of unarmed citizens in
St Peter's Fields came from a satiric reference to the glorious
defeat of Napoleon at Waterloo only four years earlier. It was a
popular reminder to the government, representing the landed
gentry, that a debt to the common people had apparently been
forgotten.

The twin events of the year in which Eliot was born – the birth
of Victoria and the Peterloo massacre – symbolically ran through
the period of her life. Victoria was eventually to become the
emblem of British domination over the globe, whilst the other
occurrence was remembered by radicals throughout the reign as a
symbol of social injustice and vicious political oppression.

Three years before Eliot died Queen Victoria was proclaimed
Empress of India, celebrating Britain's imperial status. A newspaper described the ceremony in glowing terms: 'magnificent
memorial banners ... the vast amphitheatre was filled with foreign embassies and the native nobility. ... The whole presented a
scene of unprecedented brilliancy and splendour' (*The Daily Tele-
graph*, 2 January 1877). The respect shown to the British Crown,
according to the report, by 'foreign' dignatories emphasizes the
importance of the international acceptance of Britain's role as a
world power. Whilst the attendance – and therefore, presumably,
support – of 'the native nobility' demonstrated the non-
oppressive, welcomed nature of British rule. That was certainly
the way in which the British ruling classes liked to see their
leadership, and to have it perceived by those they led.

The massacre of Peterloo in the year of Victoria's birth, however, was never forgotten by radicals. It had been commemorated,
for example, by Shelley in his poem *The Mask of Anarchy*, 'Written
on the Occasion of the Massacre at Manchester'.[22] Shelley ironically describes the 'Freedom' vaunted by the ruling classes from
the view of the lower classes:

'Tis to see your children weak
With their mothers pine and peak,
When the winter winds are bleak, —
They are dying whilst I speak.

'Tis to hunger for such diet
As the rich man in his riot
Casts to the fat dogs that lie
Surfeiting beneath his eye.[23]

It was into that duality of the supremacy of Britain and the
struggle within the nation over power and justice, epitomized in
those two events of 1819, that Eliot was born, and through which
she wrote. Eliot was well aware of all these factors of the dynamic
of her age, and refracted them through the issues explored in her
novels.

Adam Bede, which was published in 1859, opens 'in the year of
our Lord 1799' (p. 49) and ends 'in 1807' (p. 581) – it is set
specifically in the period before the greatest changes of the
nineteenth century occurred, and the contemporary reader
brought a knowledge of the difference between past and current
styles of life to interpretations of the novel. *Silas Marner*, published 1861, takes place over a longer time span which covers the
same period. The opening statement of the novel clearly invites
the reader to identify a period of about 60 years earlier: 'In the
days when spinning-wheels hummed busily in the farmhouses'
(p. 51). The time is later defined a little more closely as 'the early
years of this century' (p. 52) and is measured by Eppie's growing
up, concluding in or after 1817 when 'Mant's Bible' (p. 214) that
Mary reads was published. To some extent these novels have
been seen as merely nostalgic, looking back sentimentally to a
past, and implicitly better, age – and the books do contain such an
element; but there is also a more serious thematic purpose. Again
the reader is required to bring a sense of historical perspective to
the process of comprehension. It is partly by knowing where, in
history, we have come from that we understand where we are.
That is a particularly vital axiom in times of rapid change.

Romola, which appeared in 1862–3, is Eliot's only truly historical
novel. It is set in fifteenth-century Renaissance Florence, another
period and place of dynamic change and conflict, a time that
produced an artistic and intellectual crucible for Europe. World

leadership emanated then from Italy, as it did from Britain by the 1860s. Both civilizations were creating great wealth and exciting new ideas, and each too rested uneasily on tensions and doubts. On an individual level the novel is concerned with the betrayal of love and hope; and in public life with the degeneration of ideals into cynical pragmatism. These were themes close to Victorian experiences and fears.

It is not insignificant that *Felix Holt* and *Middlemarch* are both set immediately before the first Reform Act of 1832. Although it does not explore that specific theme, *The Mill on the Floss* (1860) is also set around that time. The novel does make reference to political historical events – as when, for instance, Tulliver and Deane: 'exchange their views concerning the Duke of Wellington whose conduct in the Catholic Question had thrown such an entirely new light on his character' (p. 132). Wellington, the hero of Waterloo, became prime minister in 1828 and in the following year passed the Roman Catholic Emancipation Act, which amongst other reforms removed restrictions that existed on Catholics holding public offices. It was particularly unpopular in the Protestant provinces of the country, raising a fear – felt to be real, however unjustified – that eventually a Catholic dominated parliament could put mainland Britain back under Papal authority. The fact that the worst fears of the anti-reformers had not been borne out in the subsequent 30 years are part of the novel's interpretive perspective.

The same is true of *Felix Holt*, published in 1866 during the struggle that preceded the second Reform Act of 1867 and starting 'Five-and-thirty years ago' (p. 75). *Middlemarch* appeared in 1871–2. The initial readers had experience of the actual consequences of the 1867 Reform Act, and could bring that perspective to bear on the conflicts and fears the 1832 Act caused. The 1876 *Daniel Deronda* is set in the period 1864–6, and although not dealing directly with the political build-up to the 1867 Reform Act again presents a view of a pre-Reform age to a post-Reform readership.

Even when she was not dealing with specific political concerns Eliot was always involved in broad social and intellectual considerations. All the major novels at least touch on, and some explore in great detail, the issues of education, religion and science.

When Eliot was born no State provision for education existed; by the time she died elementary education was compulsory for all children, and a system of State schools had been developed to help provide it. Eliot's own basic education had taken place in very good small private establishments, but in most advanced studies she was virtually self-taught. She was also given a different education, in separate institutions, from her brother Isaac. Her concern about education, especially for females, sprang in part from her own experience; but it was a central social issue too throughout the Victorian era.

In the early part of the nineteenth century orthodox Christian thought had encountered little fundamental challenge. Eliot's upbringing as a member of the Church of England was typical, and the schools she attended as a girl were mainly run by unmarried women of Protestant Evangelical persuasion. As a girl she taught in a local Sunday school, and went through a period of religious enthusiasm. At the age of 22, however, Eliot declared a rejection of orthodoxy, causing a bitter conflict with her father which resulted in her writing to him, although they were living in the same house, in an attempt to explain her attitudes to the scriptures:

> I regard these writings as histories consisting of mingled truth and fiction, and while I admire and cherish much of what I believe to have been the moral teaching of Jesus himself, I consider the system of doctrines built upon the facts of his life . . . to be most dishonourable.
>
> (SL, p. 21)

This shows Eliot to be moving in the mainstream of Victorian philosophic agnosticism, and towards a form of humanism that became increasingly the sanctuary of people unable to live within Christian theology, but unable to live without some moral and ethical guidance. Her translations from the German of Strauss' *The Life of Jesus, Critically Examined*, started two years after the letter quoted above, and later Feuerbach's *The Essence of Christianity* illustrate that tendency. Eliot's own life again mirrors the movement of her age.

The mid-century threat to religious thought was crystallized by Charles Darwin's *The Origin of Species*, published in 1859. Theories of the evolution of life, which were often seen to be contrary to the Christian concept of a sudden six-day Creation, although Darwin himself remained a Christian, gained credence from about the 1830s. As scientific knowledge and understanding expanded throughout the century forms of humanism became increasingly intellectually popular. Eliot's work on Strauss in her mid-twenties illustrates her early awareness of this process, and later she actively contributed to the development of scientific thought. Her artistic interest in science is manifested in various references through the novels, and in *Middlemarch* it is related to the theme of perception:

> Even with a microscope directed on a water-drop we find ourselves making interpretations which turn out to be rather coarse; for whereas under a weak lense you may seem to see a creature exhibiting an active voracity into which other smaller creatures actively play ... a stronger lense reveals to you certain tiniest hairlets which make vortices for these victims while the swallower waits passively.
>
> (p. 83)

The development of lenses was a vital aspect of nineteenth-century technology and science: they literally change the way things are seen and reveal even phenomena that no one knew existed. In the passage quoted there is a fusion of the importance of the technical act of changing lenses and its philosophic implications. The fact that Lewes was a scientist was obviously influential in Eliot's scientific interests, although she always had a keen intellectual curiosity in new concepts.

In very many areas Eliot's own life parallels the major movements and concerns of the middle decades of the nineteenth century. Her work was not a mere reflection of the turmoil, but was centrally involved in it and on occasions at the forefront of the processes. From humble provincial origins, intellectually and artistically unpromising, Eliot did indeed become the eminent woman of her time.

2

The Female Thinker

Although Eliot is best known as a novelist she came to that literary form comparatively late in her career. Her first short story, *The Sad Fortunes of the Rev. Amos Barton*, was published in *Blackwood's Magazine* in 1857, by which time she was 37 years old. Two other stories followed: *Mr Gilfil's Love Story* and *Janet's Repentance*. In 1858 they were published in book form under the title *Scenes of Clerical Life*. It was a modest introduction to prose fiction for an author who was to become a seminal novelist. She had, though, already written a good deal in other fields.

Eliot's first published piece, as early as 1840, in the *Christian Observer*, was the poem known by the title *Farewell*. It is a late teenager's poem on the imminence of death and the awaiting joy of heaven, conventional poetry and sentiment of the period. However, Eliot went on to find her own poetic voice, and in addition to magazine publication produced two reputable volumes: *The Spanish Gypsy* in 1868, and the 1874 book *The Legend of Jubal and Other Poems*.

The former is a long narrative – over 7000 lines – that reworks some of the themes of the novels. The heroine, Fedalma, grows up in a different culture from that to which she belongs by birth. Eppie in *Silas Marner*, Esther of *Felix Holt* and Daniel Deronda all experience a similar fate. In all these instances the works are concerned in part with the discovery of true roots and values. The action of the poem is set at the same time as *Romola*: 'The fifteenth century ... Is near its end' (POEMS, p. 204). The story takes place in Spain rather than Italy, but the idea that European civilization is at a crossroads is again strong:

> The Moslem faith, now flickering like a torch
> In a night struggle on this shore of Spain,
> Glares.
>
> (ibid.)

The conflict is between the 'Moslem' Moors of North Africa and the European Christians of Spain. The imminence of change in medieval history parallels the experience of it in recent history, in relation to reform of the franchise and the other aspects of the nineteenth-century dynamic.

The public events, as in all Eliot's fiction, provide a background into which individual lives are integrated. Fedalma has grown up among high-born characters, and is about to marry into the nobility when she is reclaimed by her true father, a gypsy whose culture brings him into conflict with aristocratic society. Fedalma, like other of Eliot's characters, renounces material wealth and status in order to pursue a destiny involving self-sacrifice with a deeper, more personal, reward. Fedalma describes herself:

> as one who sees
> A light serene and strong on one sole path
> Which she will tread till death.
>
> (p. 449)

The idea of the renunciation of the individual ego's claims in order to merge it into a greater, and communal, good is a recurring one, and is one way in which Eliot fuses the lives of her characters with great public and historical developments.

Armgart, in the collection *The Legend of Jubal and Other Poems*, is composed in a dramatic, nominally theatrical form. It explores basically similar themes, although without a particular historical background, but perhaps with a more overt contemporary feminist debate. Armgart is a singer who rejects a proposal of marriage that is made in peculiarly patriarchal terms – her suitor declaring:

> Men rise the higher as their task is high,
> The task being well achieved. A woman's rank
> Lies in the fulness of her womanhood.
>
> (p. 128)

Armgart replies as both an artist – an operatic singer – and as a woman who refuses to make her art subservient to domesticity:

> What! leave the opera . . .
> Sing in the chimney-corner to inspire
> My husband reading news? . . .

> ... I am an artist by my birth –
> By the same warrant that I am a woman.
>
> (p. 129)

The word 'inspire' is clearly ironic in the context of a *prima donna* singing to a man who is simultaneously reading a newspaper. The juxtaposition of the ideas of the enormity and artistic freedom of the opera-house and the narrow, confined domestic 'chimney-corner' powerfully conveys the choice. It is hardly surprising that Armgart chooses a public career.

The poem, however, develops beyond that simple dichotomy. The artist, Armgart can be interpreted as representing all creators, is constantly in danger of becoming isolated from the mass of humanity, of being trapped in a creative egocentricity that, although it is different from, has the same result as a materialistic egotism. Armgart's rejection of the proposal of marriage is, within Eliot's thinking, morally equivocal:

> Oh, I can live unmated, but not live
> Without the bliss of singing to the world,
> And feeling all my world respond to me.
>
> (p. 134)

The 'bliss' she is mainly concerned with is Armgart's own, not the world's; and she slips from 'the world' to 'my world', suggesting that to her the two are synonymous. The emphasis of 'my' and 'me' also reveals the singer's egotism.

Armgart becomes bitter about fate after suffering an illness that ends her operatic career, and her female cousin points out:

> you smiled
> From your clear height on all the million lots
> Which yet you brand as abject.
>
> (p. 146)

Whilst defending her own rights as a woman, from the position of strength granted by her talent, Armgart had despised those women who were less fortunate. Her salvation lies in the acceptance of service rather than applause, as she comes to recognize:

> I am a broken thing ...
> I would take humble work and do it well –
> Teach music, singing.
>
> (p. 150)

Teaching signifies a 'humble' involvement in community, assisting others, as against the ego seeking its own individual 'bliss'. Providing help has its value too, and Armgart is able to mend her 'broken' life.

The concept of accepting limitations, coming to realistic terms with expectations, recurs in the novels. Most obviously in regard to the signifier of music it occurs in *Daniel Deronda*. Gwendolen's insufficient singing talent parallels the inadequacy of her judgement. She marries Grandcourt in the egoistic expectation that she could manipulate him, only to discover that she is the one manipulated and abused. Gwendolen pays dearly for her egoism. Mirah, though, has both talent and humility, and it is thematically appropriate that Daniel and Mirah should accept the idea of service to others together.

Perhaps Eliot's most influential poem during the Victorian period was 'O May I Join the Choir Invisible', written in 1867 and included in the 1874 collection. It returns to her first poetic theme of death, although with an entirely different vision. Long before 1867 Eliot had lost faith in the idea of a conventional Christian after-life, and the poem grapples with the problem of how life can have meaning if it simply ends in oblivion. Eliot writes in celebration:

> Of those immortal dead who live again
> In minds made better by their presence: live
> In pulses stirred to generosity.
>
> (p. 49)

Immortality consists of being remembered for good qualities, and having had an influence that was comforting and inspiring. The poet yearns for such reward:

> May I reach
> That purest heaven, be to other souls
> The cup of strength in some great agony,
> Enkindle generous ardour, feed pure love.
>
> (p. 50)

The poem uses such religious imagery as 'heaven' and 'souls', but in a context of celebrating 'the multitude/Divinely human' (p. 49). Because of this, and its lyricism, the poem was adopted by the Positivists. They were a humanist religious sect that grew from the work of the French philosopher Auguste Comte in the 1830s. It was an attempt to create a Religion of Humanity based on scientific method.

Although Eliot was never a Positivist as such she was very interested in Comte's ideas. It is perhaps not insignificant that Lewes translated Comte's *Philosophy of the Sciences*, and that Eliot read the proofs of that book in 1853, the year before Lewes and Eliot began life together. In 1867 she wrote to her friend Maria Congreve about Comte's intellectual influence: 'My gratitude increases continually for the illumination Comte has contributed to my life' (SL, p. 325). Eliot's husband recorded that almost at the end of her life: 'During her illness I read aloud . . . Comte. . . . For all Comte's writing she had a feeling of high admiration, intense interest, and very deep sympathy' (LIFE, p. 620). That interest and sympathy dated back to the 1840s, Eliot's loss of orthodox Christian faith and the beginning of her intellectual reputation.

Her intellectual standing emanated from the translation of *The Life of Jesus, Critically Examined*, by the German philosopher David Friedrich Strauss, which was published in 1846. Although it appeared without the translator's name the intellectual coterie who read the book also knew of its source. Eliot's reputation as a scholar of German humanist metaphysics led to a translation of Ludwig Feuerbach's *The Essence of Christianity*, which was published in 1854, and was followed by an unpublished version of Spinoza's *Ethics*.

It was in the period around the middle of the century that Eliot established herself as a literary intellectual. In 1851 she became the anonymous editor – although again acknowledged within influential circles – of John Chapman's *Westminster Review*, an important radical and free-thinking quarterly journal. Eliot began writing for it as a book reviewer, but during the 1850s wrote a number of long articles on a variety of subjects: from Ancient Greek tragedy, through Milton's attitudes to divorce, to contemporary issues. She also contributed to *The Leader*, a weekly newspaper Lewes had co-founded in 1850, filling in for him when he was ill.

One of those articles dealt with an issue touched on in chapter 1 of this book – the status of female novelists. In 1854 Eliot wrote:

> Although it is quite true that lady-novelists are, if not the best, among the best, it is equally true that the female pen is capable of writing a very bad novel, when wilful women set their wits that way.
>
> (*The Leader*, 15 April 1854)

It was the quantity, as well as the quality, of bad novels being turned out by women, and the affect they had, that concerned Eliot. Two years later, in the process of reviewing some novels in the *Westminster Review*, she took up the theme again at more length. In 'Silly Novels by Lady Novelists' Eliot castigates the producers of 'Women's silly novels' for being isolated from the common experiences of life:

> The fair writers have evidently never talked to a tradesman except from a carriage window; they have no notion of the working-classes except as 'dependants'. . . . It is clear that they write in elegant boudoirs, with violet-coloured ink and a ruby pen . . . inexperienced in every form of poverty except poverty of brains.
>
> (SEP, p. 142)

Eliot always saw herself as a professional writer, and one of the problems of the 'silly' novelists was that most of them were dilettantes. Her own novels usually avoid the kind of traps outlined in the quotation. The social range of her characters, for example, stretches from Hetty Sorrell the dairymaid of *Adam Bede* to the baronetcies of Lydgate's family and Sir Hugo Mallinger. Her two long, final novels in particular each encompass a broader portrayal of English society than any other work of the time.

The inadequacies manifested by the 'fair writers' were in themselves partly a result of class factors. Eliot argued:

> Where there is one woman who writes from necessity, we believe there are three women who write from vanity; and, besides, there is something so antiseptic in the mere healthy fact of working for one's bread, that the most trashy and rotten kind of feminine literature is not likely to have been produced under such circumstances. 'In all labour there is profit'; but

ladies' silly novels, we imagine, are less the result of labour than of busy idleness.

(SEP, p. 162)

This was exactly the three-quarters of female novelists Eliot did not want to be associated with when she started to publish fiction. Those women who were comfortably off, and had sufficient education to be literate – although not literary, in Eliot's terms – lacked the virtues of the true writer/artist: 'those moral qualities that contribute to literary excellence – patient diligence, a sense of the responsibility involved in publication, and an appreciation of the sacredness of the writer's art' (p. 161). That 'sacredness' granted privilege and status, but it also carried enormous responsibility.

Eliot perceived that the type of novels she was reviewing damaged the whole female cause. Although Eliot had in some ways been fortunate in her schooling she had, as a lower middling-class female, been denied the kind of formal education she might have liked. She was, therefore, much concerned with the nature, and purpose, of young women's learning. If those with education misuse it in order to write silly novels it undermines the case for its expansion:

If, as the world has long agreed, a very great amount of instruction will not make a wise man, still less will a very mediocre amount of instruction make a wise woman. And the most mischievous form of feminine silliness is the literary form, because it tends to confirm the popular prejudice against the more solid education of women.

(p. 154)

Two points are being made here: silly women novelists are harmful to the cause of female education in general; but the nature of the instruction provided encourages that kind of product, because it is 'mediocre' rather than 'solid'.

Real education, for men and women, does not encourage the kind of display of learning that, in the article, is characteristic of the 'fair writers' who are: 'encouraged by the extremely false impression that to write *at all* is a proof of superiority in a woman' (p. 162). True learning both creates a sense of perspective, and is manifested in a grasp of proportion: 'A really cultured woman, like a really cultured man, is all the simpler and the less obtrusive for her knowledge; it has made her see herself and her opinions in something like just proportions' (p. 155). Eliot is wary of women, and men too of course, who display book learning as a simple accoutrement, something with which to impress those with less academic education. It is a form of egotism that true culture, as opposed to a veneer, will overcome. One problem with intellectual ostentation is that it defeats its object – particularly in gender terms, for female novelists who indulge in it do not impress intelligent readers, but make themselves, and by association other women writers, appear ridiculous. In the article Eliot concludes: 'Fiction is a department of literature in which women can ... fully equal men. ... women can produce novels not only fine, but among the very finest' (p. 162). Clearly Eliot was neither an ideological feminist, arguing the superiority of women writers, nor, despite the article's deliberately provocative title, was she doctrinally against female novelists, only 'silly' ones.

The essay unconsciously provides something of a manifesto for Eliot's own later artistic attitudes and ambitions. It is also an illustration of her polemical method. In conducting argument she was always concerned to present differing points of view, and to reach a balanced conclusion based on a pragmatic, realistic acceptance of reality. For instance, her argument that women novelists did not have to prove themselves superior by a display of empty learning – which in fact merely made them look silly – and her belief that by subscribing to the moral qualities required to produce art they could achieve a worthwhile goal. At the same time Eliot recognized that the kind of education provided for literate women actually encouraged many of them to lack a sense of true proportion – and that was largely a social responsibility. Eliot was also aware of the importance of class, both as a determinate in social relations and a factor in literature. All these features of her polemical work inform her fiction.

They were, indeed, recurring elements in her thought. In 1856 Eliot wrote, for the *Westminster Review*, what was ostensibly a review of two books written by the German social scientist Wilhelm Heinrich von Riehl. In that essay, 'The Natural History of German Life', Eliot praises Riehl for not being: 'a man who looks at objects through the spectacles either of the doctrinaire or the dreamer' (SEP, p. 127). Riehl is presented as a practical thinker, and his ideas on politics and society are implicity endorsed by Eliot.

She perceives that Germany is going through an earlier stage of the same socio-economic development that Britain, and particularly England, had already experienced. That dynamic had not ceased in the mid-1850s, and indeed continued throughout Eliot's lifetime – as she was prophetically aware it would. Riehl's observations were converted into Eliot's own polemic of history.

It was a period in which theories of social organization abounded. For example, the socialism of the Chartists, and the utopianism of Robert Owen were not long dead; whilst newly emerging for the future were the projected Communism of Karl Marx, the collectivism of the Co-operative movement and the fraternal hopes of the new form of trade unionism. Eliot found all these unpractical because based on idealism rather than reality:

> The thing for mankind to know is, not what are the motives and influences which the moralist thinks *ought* to act on the labourer or the artisan, but what are the motives and influences which *do* act on him.
>
> (p. 111)

The italicization of the juxtaposed *'ought'* and *'do'* emphasizes the difference between theory and practice, desire and actuality.

For Eliot that actuality involved acknowledging the essential conservatism of the common people. Riehl writes of peasants, and Eliot tends to expand the meaning of that word – which in a technical sense had no real application to nineteenth-century England – to cover all labourers, artisans, and even small farmers such as Dagley in *Middlemarch*; and when she writes of 'the peasant's inveterate habit of litigation' (p. 118) the idea immediately conjures an image of Tulliver, respectable miller and farmer, who is ruined by his predilection for litigation in *The Mill on the Floss*. Such men, in Eliot's view, are dominated by traditional attitudes, manners and behaviour: *'Custom with him holds the place of sentiment, of theory, and in many cases of affection.* ... The peasant never questions the obligation of family-ties – he questions *no custom'* (SEP, pp. 119–20). This creates continuity, but acts against change. Tom Tulliver's fierce defence of his family's good name, his hard work and abstemious prudence in slowly building up the funds with which to pay off his father's debts, are presented as virtues. Tom does not have to think about his actions in this regard, he simply behaves that way because it is the only course that occurs to him.

Change, however, is in the nature of history, and the 'peasant's' obduracy can be a limitation. When the railway agents arrive in the area of Middlemarch they are set upon by: 'six or seven men in smock-frocks with hay-forks in their hands' (p. 601). The historical perspective indicates how small-minded this action is – for although it was not uncommon in 1831, when the railways were developing, by 1871–2, when the novel was being read, the country was covered with railways and everyone knew that 'hay-forks' could not halt the processes of science, technology, economics and history. That form of change Eliot accepted as inevitable: it could sometimes be described as progress, as improving the conditions of life, but it was not necessarily good, and could cause casualties. Her response was to look for amelioration of the harm rather than oppose the processes.

The doctrinaires and dreamers, in Eliot's definition of them, either wanted to prevent change, which was impossible; or to force transformation, or the pace of it. Eliot had two main objections to the latter. Firstly, it affronted the notion of inevitable historical processes: 'What has grown up historically can only die out historically, by the gradual operation of necessary laws' (SEP, p. 127). Forcing change destroyed continuity, causing cultural fragmentation. Secondly, it was not actually desired by the majority of the common people, because of their essential conservatism: 'A system which disregards the traditions and hereditary attachments ... is simply disintegrating and ruinous' (p. 122). Such systems emanate from 'abstract democratic and socialistic theories' (p. 129), which do not take into account 'the organic structure of society' (pp. 133–4). Riehl explicates that very point, and Eliot approves of his reasoning. In summarizing his position: 'It is the conservatism of a clear-eyed, practical, but withal large-minded man' (p. 139), she implies her own.

The eponymous Adam Bede's process, and progress, from employee to employer, and owner of Jonathan Burge's erstwhile timber-yard, epitomizes the best of change for Eliot. It represents a gradual, and organic, growth: evolution without disruption – a fundamentally conservative, but not reactionary, vision. The fact that *Adam Bede* is set between 1799 and 1807, in the early days of the Industrial Revolution, may make it appear to be an exercise in mere nostalgia, a longing to recapture something that has been irrevocably lost. On the other hand, by showing organic growth in implicit contrast to the faster pace of change in the late 1850s Eliot may have been encouraging the reader to think about the nature of change. Eliot approached the problem again in *Felix Holt*, and overtly in the ensuing essay – 'Address to Working Men, by Felix Holt' – published by *Blackwood's Magazine* in 1868. It was considered of sufficient importance to be reprinted in Eliot's last major publication, in 1879, the collection *Impressions of Theophrastus Such* (and is reprinted as Appendix A in the edition of *Adam Bede* referred to throughout this book, and to which the following page numbers relate).

Felix Holt's address is concerned with the potential power and responsibility for working men created by the 1867 Reform Act. For the first time many, although in fact still a minority, of working *men* faced the possibility of being able to vote. 'Holt the Radical' outlines some of the public evils of the day: 'commercial lying and swindling, the poisonous adulteration of goods, the retail cheating, and the political bribery which are carried on' (p. 610). The blame for these activities, however, does not rest entirely with the perpetrators. Working men have been silently acquiescent, and now that they have an electoral voice they also have a: 'heavy responsibility; that is to say, the terrible risk we run of working mischief and missing good, as others have done before us' (p. 611). A tone of conservatism enters the Address, and there follows an attack on 'our Trades-unions' for 'cutting away the timbers of our ship' (p. 614). Felix echoes Riehl when he argues in favour of 'the common estate of society' and that: 'the security of this treasure demands, not only the preservation of order, but a certain patience on our part' (p. 621). The idea of organic growth, of continuity being embodied in change, is central: 'I expect great changes, and I desire them. But I don't expect them to come in a hurry, by mere inconsiderate sweeping' (p. 620). This summarizes Eliot's own view of cautious optimism. There is no fear of change as such, but of the wrong kind of destructive transformation. Felix Holt does not acknowledge the limitations of the Reform Act – the facts that ballots were still (until 1872) held in public rather than being confidential, that most men, and all women, were left unenfranchised. Despite her own female status Eliot refused to actively support the movement for female suffrage. Although in favour in principle she was more concerned at controlling its momentum than increasing it.

The dichotomy is between revolution and evolution. Eliot's scientific interests perhaps persuaded her towards the latter form of social development. She lived in an age when scientific advances were rapid, broad and fundamental. Eliot's long-standing interest in science was intensified when her friendship with Lewes began. In 1856, for instance, they spent three months working together, at Ilfracombe and Tenby, studying natural life for a series of articles Lewes was to write for *Blackwood's Magazine*, under the title 'Sea-Side Studies'. She wrote to Bray with enthusiasm of their 'zoological expeditions on the rocks' from which they 'gained a large influx of new ideas' (SL, p. 156), and that was by no means their only extended field trip.

In 1859 Eliot read Darwin's *The Origin of Species* within weeks of its publication, and retained a keen interest in scientific, especially physiological, ideas throughout her life. In 1879, the year after Lewes' death, she donated £5000 to the creation of the George Lewes Studentship in Physiology at Cambridge. The specific choice of subject was a recognition for posterity of a mutual scientific passion. Although Lewes was the professional scientist Eliot was not a passive, or entirely junior, partner. Lewes died leaving a book, *Problems of Life and Mind*, unfinished and Eliot was knowledgeable enough to complete the work. Indeed, the critic Sally Shuttleworth has commented: 'Eliot was so conversant with Lewes' philosophy that, in preparing the final series of *Problems of Life and Mind* for publication after Lewes' death, she substantively rewrote some of the sections'.[1] The central concept in that volume was organicism, and can be related back to the 1850s: specifically to Eliot's appreciation of Riehl's ideas on the organic nature of society, and to the work she and Lewes did on the structure of organisms in marine biology. Eliot's theoretical belief in the importance of continuity within development and change was manifested in practice in her own intellectual life.

That life was both more extensive, and deeper, than that of almost any other man or woman of her time. In reading the novels it is essential to grasp that the range of allusions, sometimes exceedingly erudite, are not a manifestation of vanity, an attempt to display her own learning in order to establish that characteristic she refers to in the essay on 'Silly Lady Novelists' as 'superiority'. Eliot's references spring from an understanding of many disciplines, which is the result of genuine intellectual eclecticism: quotations from Ancient Greek tragedy, *The Holy Bible*,

Dante, Shakespeare, Wordsworth; other novelists; references to mythology, historical events, scientific theories, theological argument, etc. – add an actual depth to the texture of the texts. The very brief discussion, in chapter 1 above, of the way in which even the verisimilic detail of names may be linked to an emblematic tradition illustrates this; and the explication of an almost random reference indicates a similar artistic fineness. For example, in *Romola* there is the Biblical allusion: 'there are strong suspicions that his handsome son would play the part of Rehoboam' (p. 49). This is not an arrogant display of the author's learning. Particularly at that time she might have expected her readers to have some knowledge of the *Old Testament*, and understand that Rehoboam was the son of Solomon who, becoming king after his father's death, ignored good advice and became a tyrant, announcing to his subjects: 'My father made your yoke heavy, and I will add to your yoke: my father also chastised you with whips, but I will chastise you with scorpions' (I *Kings* XII, 14). Not surprisingly Rehoboam's subjects rebelled against his tyranny, and an opportunity for creating harmony and progress ended in disaster. This reference informs the mood of the whole novel, and is one of the ways in which that historical story is also made a parable for Eliot's own day.

In her 'Notes on Form in Art' Eliot shows clear artistic self-consciousness: 'things must be recognized as separate wholes before they can be recognized as wholes composed of parts, or before these wholes again can be regarded as relatively parts of a larger whole' (SEP, p. 232). The relationship between the complete text and the components that comprise it is deliberate and critical, not accidental or purposeless. Each detail contributes to the whole. All are worth pursuing for the enlightenment they give, for Eliot never wrote down to her readers, and the reader must always make the effort to achieve Eliot's own extremely high level of comprehension. It is a formidable task, but one of abundant reward.

3

The Female Novel

The development of the railways was perhaps, somewhat surprisingly, the first important influence on early Victorian reading habits. By the 1840s railway travel was expanding very rapidly. In 1838 only 500 miles of track were in operation, by 1848 5000 miles were in use, and most of the increase was due to passenger rather than freight transport. The change was so dramatic, the potential effects sufficiently widespread, for the issue to be raised in Parliament:

> ... the House must be fully aware that the present was a very important era in the history of railroads ... this was the proper time and fitting opportunity to refer the matter to a committee to investigate the subject.
>
> (*Hansard*, 5 February 1844)

The importance of the phenomenon is indicated by the fact that the speaker was not a backbench MP of no particular consequence, but William Gladstone, a future prime minister, and one of the most powerful political figures of the Victorian period. Railways were faster, cheaper and more comfortable than horse-drawn coaches – although comfort is a relative concept, which in this context emphasizes the awful discomfort of most coach journeys. Despite their comparative speed trains were still quite slow, and journey times therefore long – but it was generally possible to read in order to alleviate the boredom of travel. This factor opened up new markets for novels. It is not coincidental, either, that W. H. Smith's railway station bookstalls, stocked with journals and magazines carrying stories and serializations of novels, became a feature of the traveller's culture from the 1840s.

During Eliot's writing lifetime perhaps the two strongest influences on the writer's market-place were the circulating libraries, and the many magazines and journals that serialized fiction. Books were relatively expensive and one way of reading them was through the services of a private library, the largest of which,

Mudie's Select Library, was founded, significantly during the railway boom, in 1842.

In Eliot's period the most common, although not the only, form of novel publication was in three volumes at a price of half a guinea each, which meant a complete novel cost thirty-one shillings and sixpence (£1.52½p.). All prices are, of course, significant only in relation to incomes. The two largest single groups of employees were agricultural workers, who accounted for approximately 20% of the working male population; and domestic servants, who comprised over a tenth of female employees. At the time Mudie set up his Select Library the pay of agricultural labourers, according to the statistics researched by the historian J. H. Clapham, was not generous: 'In ten northern counties the average wage was 11s. 6d. . . . In eighteen southern counties the average was 8s. 5d'.[1] This would put the national annual average wage at around £25, which meant a novel cost three weeks' full income.

Domestic workers were paid even less in actual cash. The social historian Frank Huggett has recorded a typical household some years later: 'Frances Marlow came as a nurserymaid at £7 a year in 1864 and left in 1876 . . . by which time she had become a £20-a-year lady's maid'.[2] In addition she would have received board and accommodation, but it was still not an income that allowed luxuries such as books, even if Frances Marlow had had time and education to read them.

In the second half of Victoria's reign even some of those employed in the expanding railway business were not prospering. In 1874 it was reported, when they went on strike, that a section of railway workers: 'upon an average, worked 16 and 17 hours per day, while hundreds of them were not receiving higher wages than 15s. or 16s. per week' (*The Times*, 4 April 1874). The newspaper was unlikely to have been biased in the strikers' favour, who on these figures spent most of their lives at work in order to produce an annual income of about £40.

Those workers with a better formal education, still a small minority in the middle of the Victorian period, did not necessarily have a lot of spare income either. Following the 1870 Education Act, for example, a new generation of elementary school teachers were required, and a correspondent in a journal recommended:

what appears to be a field of remunerative labour for gentlewomen ... the calling of National School-mistresses. ... Salaries range from £40 to £70 a year, generally with rooms and other extras besides ... a sum that compares favourably with the remuneration of private governesses.

(*The Monthly Packet*, February 1874)

Clearly the increased provision of State schooling for the lower classes, because of the need it created for additional teachers, gave an impetus to the further education of women from higher social strata. Such women had the time and literacy needed to read three-decker novels, but even with the 'extras' the highest paid of them received less than £2 a week, only slightly more than the cost of a novel. They may have been part of the reading public, but they were not purchasers of literature.

In such economic conditions it was more realistic for the literate to pay a subscription to a private circulating library. It was possible to join Mudie's Select Library for an annual cost of 21 shillings (£1.05p.). The demand for their services made the libraries large purchasers of books, and therefore gave them a good deal of influence, almost a commercial stranglehold, over publishers – which the latter in turn exercised over writers. Selling novels, as either author or publisher, meant in general meeting the requirements of the libraries. Those were, on the whole, commercial and unadventurous. The literary historian Peter Keating has observed of the 1860s in particular: 'The provision of a bland staple diet for Mudie subscribers became a standard criticism of the libraries'.[3] Mudie, of course, was in business for profit, not the benefit of literature, and worked on the premise that the readers knew what they liked, and liked what they knew.

Although they were not immediately a crucial factor for publishers, it was not without significance that the instigation of public libraries too dates from the mid-century. The Public Libraries Act of 1850 enabled boroughs of over 10 000 inhabitants to raise money, through the local rating system, for the purpose of creating free municipal libraries. Subsequent legislation relaxed the constraints of the initial Act, and gradually public libraries did gain in importance – but apart from isolated cases not until later in the century.

Other libraries also existed, often from much earlier times, founded by wealthy local patrons, or emanating from organizations such as the Mechanics Institutes. The latter were a vigorous aspect of mid-nineteenth-century culture, although not generally in the direction of the arts. The historian Pauline Gregg has observed of them: 'The libraries were often – outwardly at least – impressive ... [but] The majority had to rely on gifts, which meant that most of the volumes were unwanted books'.[4] The existence, even proliferation, of such libraries indicates how voracious literate Victorians were as readers, and also the limitations of the services available to them.

Before the widespread availability of libraries such as Mudie's the reader of the long novel – such as Henry Fielding's or Jane Austen's – usually needed three attributes: money, time and education. The development of cheap, or free, libraries obviously curtailed the importance of the first necessity – although the possession of, or access to, some kind of wealth was also relevant to the consideration of time. The typical labourer, railway worker or servant at their job for 70 or 80 hours a week had little leisure, or energy, for reading even if they could get hold of the books. Provision for education was also limited, although it expanded considerably during Eliot's lifetime.

At the time of Eliot's birth a great many people were illiterate. Although subsidiary ones existed, the main avenues of basic education for most people were Church and Sunday schools, and classes run by individuals. Pip attended one of those in Dickens' *Great Expectations*, which was published about the same time as *Silas Marner*, and also set in the early years of the nineteenth century:

> Mr Wopsle's great-aunt kept an evening school in the village; that is to say, she was a ridiculous old woman of limited means and unlimited infirmity, who used to go to sleep from six to seven every evening, in the society of youth who paid twopence per week each, for the improving opportunity of seeing her do it.... Mr Wopsle's great-aunt, besides keeping this Educational Institute, kept – in the same room – a little general shop.[5]

The description is clearly satiric, as the juxtaposition of the capitalized self-important 'Educational Institute' and the 'general shop', 'in the same room', emphasizes. Yet the critic Philip Collins has endorsed the essential accuracy of Dickens' portrait:

> Her school is a splendid example of his ability to epitomise an institution. . . . Dame-schools were faulty in the extreme. Many were something like this one that Pip attended: no type of school was so universally damned by official and unofficial observers . . . one can provide confirming footnotes from Reports on elementary education.[6]

Official concern over the state of education was registered in the number of commissions that conducted enquiries into various aspects of it.

In 1833 the government made its first financial grant to organizations that were involved in providing education. Over subsequent decades government intervention in the formulation of an educational system increased, although the initiative for actually providing it remained with voluntary bodies, such as religious denominations. In 1870 Forster's Education Act introduced the idea of government-provided primary schooling. The historian Sir Llewellyn Woodward has summarized its limitations, but concluded:

> the bill was a great step forward. For the first time it secured local expenditure on education. The 'board schools' had more resources than the voluntary schools; the first step towards compulsion had been taken . . . henceforward there were no areas in England without schools, and no children grew up without elementary education merely because their parents were poor.[7]

Compulsory education was finally achieved in the year Eliot died, 1880, with Mundella's Education Act. Those Acts were, of course, too late to affect Eliot's readership during her own life. In any event the people who were only functionally literate were not her readers. That increasing groundswell of concern about schooling, nevertheless, signifies a general social interest in the subject, and it was one Eliot shared. Education recurs as a central theme in the novels.

A sizeable section of society that possessed the appropriate attributes for reading Eliot were females of the middling classes. Indeed, as the pastime of novel-reading expanded rapidly during the 1840s the cultural phenomenon was registered by a rash of cartoons, in such magazines as *Punch*, in which the readers were almost invariably depicted as middling-class women, a situation that had changed little by the time Eliot began writing fiction. In a direct address to the reader of *Adam Bede* the narrator assumes that to be the case: 'That is a simple scene, reader. But it is almost certain that you, too, have been in love – perhaps, even, more than once, though you may not chose to say so to all your lady friends' (p. 537). In the Victorian context this was unequivocally involving the reader as a female. Those readers were often practising Christians; their families were usually financially comfortable; they had a high standard of literacy, based on Bible reading – even if other aspects of their education were deficient; and they were discouraged from working, except for charitable purposes, so that they had plenty of leisure time. Eliot did not deliberately aim at this element of the reading public, but they occupied a world with which she was familiar from her youth – and it was not unnatural that when Eliot began writing fiction it should be set in that kind of milieu. This possibly contributed to the immediate success of the first stories, and their collected appearance as *Scenes of Clerical Life*. Mudie's Select Library, for example, bought 350 copies, a considerable number for a first volume.

Publication in magazines or journals was crucial, usually preceding the appearance in book form. As Lewes wrote regularly for *Blackwood's Magazine* Eliot's first story was submitted to John Blackwood, as written by a friend of Lewes'. Eliot received £52. 10s. for *Amos Barton* in 1857, more than she had been paid for any other single piece of work, and as much as an assistant school-mistress could expect to earn in a year. Although articles in journals such as the *Westminster Review* carried intellectual prestige payment was poor. Writing almost ceaselessly through 1855, for example, Eliot had earned less than £120: more than a teacher, but she was working continuously at that time. Three short stories a year, Eliot realized, would provide a much better income. Eliot was never mercenary about writing, but she and Lewes were short of money in their early days – largely because Lewes was still partly supporting his wife, their four sons, and her four illegitimate children. Paradoxically much of Eliot's earnings apppeared to go to Lewes' wife. Possibly Eliot's attitudes to feminist issues were affected by what she saw in close detail of the extraordinary marriage of the Lewes'.

As Eliot became increasingly successful as a novelist she did use her position to assert artistic integrity. Her first novel, *Adam*

Bede, sold extraordinarily well; Mudie stocked 1000 copies; Eliot earned considerably more than £1000 from it within a few months. By the time Eliot was working on *Romola* in 1862 – with *The Mill on the Floss* and *Silas Marner* also having been published – she and Lewes were financially well-off, despite Mrs Lewes' extravagances and the fact that Lewes' own income was declining. Lewes noted with pride and pleasure in his journal in February 1862: 'George Smith ... made a proposal to purchase Polly's new work for £10,000. . . . It is the most magnificent offer ever yet made for a novel' (GEL, IV, pp. 17–8). This was for *Romola*, and in terms of the wages and salaries quoted above it was indeed an enormous sum of money. Few writers would have quibbled about it, but Eliot was not happy with the publisher Smith's proposals for serialization in sixteen parts, as she felt it would be better understood if it appeared in twelve longer episodes. Negotiations were resolved with Eliot accepting £7000 – still a very large payment for a writer who had received a little over £50 for a story only five years earlier, but nevertheless illustrating that Eliot was willing to sacrifice £3000 mainly on the grounds of artistic integrity.

Romola appeared, in the event, in fourteen instalments in Smith's *Cornhill* magazine, and came out in three-volume book form in 1863. It was not, however, as successful as Eliot's previous fiction, and Smith, unhappy at the commercial outcome, rejected Eliot's next novel, *Felix Holt*. That action resulted in her former publisher, John Blackwood, offering Eliot £5000 for it. In accepting his terms Eliot wrote to Blackwood in April 1866:

> It is a great pleasure to me to be writing to you again, as in the old days. After your kind letters, I am chiefly anxious that the publication of 'Felix Holt' may be a satisfaction to you from beginning to end.
>
> (GEL, IV, p. 243)

There is a placatory tone here. Eliot appears to be obliquely apologizing to her original publisher for having abandoned him over *Romola*.

Blackwood subsequently serialized, and published in volume form, both *Middlemarch* and *Daniel Deronda*. The former appeared in Britain in eight instalments during 1871–2, and in the New York *Harper's Weekly* from December 1871 to February 1873. It was also, as Eliot's previous books had been, translated into various continental languages. In total Eliot received around £9000 for the novel. *Daniel Deronda* was published in eight monthly instalments in 1876, and although it was followed with interest equivocal public responses to the Jewish elements in the novel prevented it from being as successful in the marketplace as Eliot's most popular work. Nevertheless, Eliot had been established as the leading intellectual writer of her day, and not just amongst a small coterie, for the sales of her books indicate that she had a sizeable public following. Despite the fact that Eliot did not produce another novel in the last four years of life her reputation remained high, and her financial state had been secured.

It was a great age of novel writing and reading, characterized by a degree of homogeneity subsequently lost to other writers. The literary historian G. D. Klingopulos has observed:

> the novel-reading public remained fairly homogeneous in taste and reading-power down to the time of George Eliot and Trollope (say, 1855–75) ... thereafter a split into low, middle, and high-brow publics began to develop and has since widened.[8]

Eliot had always been aware of the nature of the arena into which she had entered. The great names of the day included men, such as Dickens, Thackeray and Trollope – but females such as Braddon, Wood and Yonge were enormously popular, and socially, if not artistically, influential. There were also a plethora of minor novelists, most of whom have justifiably sunk into oblivion. Men were among them, but probably most were women, and in any event Eliot was most interested in the female writers who were writing for female readers, as her 1856 essay 'Silly Novels by Lady Novelists' illustrates.

Such novels were written out of, and reinforced, conventional preconceptions, attitudes and moral values. Eliot's own work can be seen as a challenge to popular literature, and it does so not by ignoring the common forms of the day – but by embracing, and extending, them. Some readers, for example, have taken exception to what they consider Eliot's intrusive narrators. The eminent academic Michael Wheeler, for instance, has written of 'the notoriously intrusive authorial narrator'.[9] Such criticism seems to be based on the notion that stories should, as it were, tell themselves; that the narrator must not intrude between the text and the reader. It is certainly true that Eliot's narrators do not remain detached, that they do intervene, and at times overtly direct the reader's attention. There is, of course, no rule that states all fiction must be constructed in one particular way, and objection to any narrative method is valid only if the style is inappropriate to the overall context of the novel concerned.

Eliot's purpose was undoubtedly didactic. The critic F. R. Leavis confirmed what he saw as an overriding concern: 'her distinctive moral preoccupation ... the moral seriousness of George Eliot's novels'.[10] That didacticism was expressed through a narrative style that had two sources: the literary tradition of which Eliot saw herself part; and a prevalent popular contemporary approach to fiction. Eliot realized that in order to challenge demotic literature she had to some extent to utilize its forms. Later novelists – Henry James, Joseph Conrad, James Joyce, Virginia Woolf, for example – were able to explore more obviously experimental forms, but they were writing for smaller, more discriminating readerships in a different financial publishing framework, after the breakdown, in the 1890s, of the circulating libraries' stranglehold. Eliot was constrained by the demands of her publishers, but also she did not want to divorce herself from a readership by using forms that would have alienated it. There is simply no point in being didactic if no one reads the text.

The main literary reference for the didacticism was provided by Bunyan, an influence which is outlined in chapter 1 above. It can be seen too in the writing of the mid-eighteenth-century novelist Henry Fielding who, more importantly, also created the basic narrative mode in which Eliot worked. A representative example of Fielding's technique, taken from his greatest novel, *The History of Tom Jones*, illustrates just how intrusive his narrator can be. After discussing diverse aspects of love the narrator comments:

> Examine your heart, my good reader, and resolve whether you do believe these matters with me. If you do, you may now proceed to their exemplification in the following pages: if you do not, you have, I assure you, already read more than you have understood; and it would be wise to pursue your business, or your pleasures (such as they are), than to throw away any more of your time in reading what you can neither taste nor comprehend.[11]

Here the narrator not only addresses the reader directly, but familiarly: 'my good reader'. That reader is recommended to agree with the narrator before continuing with the novel, emphasizing the wisdom of the text and the fact that it is written *in order* to exemplify the narrator's general tenets – 'now proceed to their exemplification in the following pages'. The narrator is so intrusive that familiarity turns to contempt for the reader who does not agree with the narrative voice. The poor reader is assured that 'you have . . . already read more than you have understood'. Such a reader is recommended not to waste any more time. It is a case of the novel paradoxically casting aside the reader, rather than the other way round. The tone is satiric, hectoring the reader into being a 'good' one; and indeed few readers would admit to not comprehending the novel, therefore they will probably agree with the narrator in order not to identify themselves with the group earlier categorized as 'readers of the lowest class'.[12] The passage is deliberately humorous, but it serves a serious purpose, for the avowed intent of Fielding's fiction is didactic.

Eliot admired Fielding's work very much. In *Middlemarch* the narrator comments approvingly on his:

> copious remarks and digressions . . . where he seems to bring his arm-chair to the proscenium and chat with us in all the lusty ease of his fine English. . . . We belated historians must not linger after his example; and if we did so, it is probable that our chat would be thin and eager, as if delivered from a camp-stool in a parrot-house.
>
> (p. 170)

The comparison of herself and her contemporaries with Fielding – exemplified in 'his fine English' against the squawks of the 'parrot-house' – displays the admiration of him. The extract also manifests Eliot's own ironic mode, for although her narrator confesses 'We . . . must not linger after his example' that is precisely what is happening. The narrative stops, despite claiming that it must not do so, in order to praise a writer whose narrators often paused. This is not merely an attempt to gratuitously lecture the reader on English literature, but draws attention to literature as an artifact, as something consciously created and controlled. The narrator does not pause whilst pretending not to, does not offer a moral homily while masquerading as a detached and objective reporter. The narrator is part of the narrative, is engaged in the thematic pattern and moral discourses, and the reader cannot expect otherwise.

In Mary Braddon's 1863 novel *Aurora Floyd* the lovesick Talbot Bulstrode falls into a physical fever because his emotions overcome his common sense. The narrator comments:

> I might fill chapters with the foolish sufferings of this young man; but I fear he must have become very wearisome to my afflicted readers. . . . The sharper the disease, the shorter its continuance; so Talbot will be better by-and-by, and will look back at his old self, and laugh at his old agonies. . . . Shall I feel the same contempt ten years hence for myself as I am to-day, as I feel to-day for myself as I was ten years ago?[13]

The narrator's intervention here is directly designed to draw the reader into the novel, to pretend that it is real life, rather than emphasizing its artificiality, its status as art. The reader is not to be 'afflicted' with the sufferings of the character, but is treated to the reflections of the narrator who is presented as a bridge between character and reader: 'Shall I feel . . .?', which implies – will you feel? There is no attempt to enlarge the reader's experience, to present new horizons, only to confirm the validity of existing attitudes. The reader is encouraged to reason in the form: the character changes over time, the narrator changes, I change. There is a common experience to which there is a conventional, universal response.

That conventionality is reinforced by a subsequent appeal to folk wisdom:

> Have you ever visited some still country town after a lapse of years, and wondered . . . to find the people you knew in your last visit alive and thriving, with hair unbleached as yet, although you have lived and suffered whole centuries since then? Surely Providence gives us this sublimely egotistical sense of time as a set-off against the brevity of our lives!
>
> (pp. 94-5)

Ultimately 'Providence' is beneficent, and that fact is proved by our own observations. For all the words involved the reader is

simply being retailed a homily such as: time is the best healer, or
time cures all. Whatever the truth or otherwise of the sentiment it
does confirm and validate a complacent attitude to the nature of
experience, and therefore of a common, shared reality.

Braddon was a very popular writer whose fiction Eliot knew,
and of course coincidentally the emblematic name of Bulstrode
recurs in an entirely different, and much more complex, character
in *Middlemarch*. Eliot's use of the intrusive narrator is also more
complex when dealing with the unhappiness of emotional turmoil, such as the period shortly after the Casaubons' disastrous
honeymoon:

> One morning, some weeks after her arrival at Lowick, Dorothea
> – but why always Dorothea? Was her point of view the only
> possible one with regard to this marriage? I protest against all
> our interest, all our effort at understanding being given to the
> young skins that look blooming in spite of trouble; for these too
> will get faded, and will know the older and more eating griefs
> which we are helping to neglect. In spite of the blinking eyes
> ... Mr Casaubon had an intense consciousness within him, and
> was spiritually a-hungered like the rest of us.
>
> (p. 312)

In this case time does not create healing, but causes ageing;
'blooming' skins become 'faded' – and that is indisputably true to
reality. The main point, however, is that the narrator is used to
counter the demotic novelist's tendency to concentrate on the
young, to channel sympathy and understanding into its most
obvious areas. Everyone, the assumption is, knows that young
people have emotional problems. In the populist novels they are
always the attractive characters too. Talbot Bulstrode in *Aurora
Floyd* has an exemplary personality which is shown in: 'purity,
probity, and truth ... fond of scientific pursuits. He neither
smoked, drank, nor gambled' (p. 27). He clearly embodies all the
conventional virtues, and combines them with an equally unim-
peachable physical appearance: 'Tall and broad-chested, with a
pale whiskerless face, aquiline nose, clear, cold, grey eyes, thick
moustache, and black hair' (p. 28). For the average reader of these
novels, a middling-class female brought up on the conventional
literature of the period, the character is likely to be irresistibly

attractive. That reader is not at all stretched in being asked to extend sympathy.

Casaubon, on the other hand, is an elderly pedantic clergyman – just under fifty years old in fact, but much older in attitudes and behaviour – with 'blinking eyes and white moles' (p. 312), whose smile is 'like pale wintry sunshine' (p. 48); and who is described as 'no better than a mummy' and 'A great bladder for dried peas to rattle in' (pp. 81–2). Attempting to divert a sympathetic attention from the young and unhappy Dorothea to such a character is to challenge normative expectations. Yet Eliot achieves that – extending the reader's easy, and conventional, interest from its obvious focus to a character outside the normal range of emotional experience. This broadens, rather than merely confirms, the reader's moral horizons. Old men with young wives should not be simply condemned, for Casaubon is himself a victim of social attitudes:

> He had done nothing exceptional in marrying – nothing but what society sanctions . . . and he had reflected that in taking a wife, a man of good position should expect and carefully choose a blooming young lady . . . of a rank equal to his own, of religious principles, virtuous disposition, and good understanding. On such a young lady he would make handsome settlements.
>
> (p. 312)

Casaubon 'had done nothing exceptional', he was, in the earlier quotation, 'like the rest of us'. Readers are invited not to condemn Casaubon – for he is not vicious at this stage, but willing to make 'handsome settlements' – but to recognize the similarities between the character and themselves. His expectations and attitudes were normal for the society in which he was placed, which is close to that of most readers. Since society is not an abstraction, but made up of the people in it, everyone contributes to its mores. The reader with conventional attitudes and aspirations is in that respect like Casaubon; but more than that, has actually helped to perpetuate the web of ideas that entrap the character. Casaubon's expectations of marriage are not likely to be entirely different from those of the reader: the reader is also ensnared. The paragraph has moved a long way from that initial narrative intrusion 'I protest'. Eliot uses that traditional and popularly common technique not to tell the reader what to think, or to confirm prejudices – but to provoke the reader into thought. It is truly didactic: educational in the profoundest sense.

Eliot also helped to develop the novel form away from caricature. Because Dickens was such a powerful and popular writer one of his strengths, the ability to focus on physical attributes, or aspects of personality, and expand them into a recurring feature of characterization, became a fundamental technique of novel writing. It had a respectable pedigree, Fielding again providing the historical precedent in the novel; with the earlier sources emanating from Shakespeare in drama and Chaucer in narrative poetry. It is a technique most obviously associated with comic characters, but Dickens presents serious thematic figures through that method too. The aptly-named Josiah Bounderby in *Hard Times*, for instance, is described with typically Dickensian genius:

> He was a rich man: banker, merchant, manufacturer, and what not. A big, loud man, with a stare, and a metallic laugh. A man made out of a coarse material, which seemed to have been stretched to make so much of him. A man with a great puffed head and forehead. . . . A man with a pervading appearance on him of being inflated like a balloon. . . . A man who was always proclaiming, through that brassy speaking-trumpet of a voice of his, his old ignorance and his old poverty. . . . 'I was born in a ditch.'[14]

The comedy contains menace. Words such as 'metallic', 'coarse', 'puffed', 'inflated', 'brassy' indicate that the character is not simply a figure of fun; he is threatening. The element of caricature, though, ensures that the character cannot change or develop; and the reader who understands how Victorian novels are encoded knows that nothing good will come from the character. Additional, and even contrary, details about him may be released, but the core of the character is set. He can be only what the external facts about him reveal.

Casaubon is clearly presented in a more complex way. His moles, weak eyes, thin legs and dry manner can still contain a bewildered man with complicated feelings, and at least some more or less ordinary aspirations. The character is capable of development because the *basic* truth of it is psychological and emotional rather than merely physical. D. H. Lawrence is reported to have told his friend Jessie Chambers: 'it was really George Eliot who started it all. . . . It was she who started putting all the action inside. Before . . . it had been outside'.[15] Although Eliot was not the first novelist to search into character her particular analytical style did help to develop the novel considerably. Whilst retaining links with the novel as a form of entertainment she pushed it on artistically and intellectually. They are qualities Virginia Woolf recognized when she wrote that *Middlemarch*: 'is one of the few English novels written for grown-up people'.[16] These two views of great twentieth-century novelists attest to the seminality and originality of Eliot's fiction. Yet she maintained a base of popularity in the marketplace. Her earned income alone illustrates that, and Eliot – and perhaps even more, Lewes as virtually her business manager (although the term did not then exist) – was aware of the importance of sales; but she also stayed close to popular forms because that was the most effective way of challenging the simplistic assumptions embedded in them.

Because of Eliot's deep concern about morality she is usually aware of its complexity, and of the dangers of drawing simplistic moral conclusions. In *Adam Bede* a hypothetical reader demands of the author: 'Let your most faulty characters always be on the wrong side, and your virtuous ones on the right. Then we shall see at a glance whom we are to condemn, and whom we are to approve' (p. 222). The author refutes this requirement on the grounds that a novel written in such a form would be false to experience, and display moral narrowness, for 'it is needful you should tolerate, pity, and love' (ibid.). There is, however, a moral chain of cause and effect in Eliot's fiction, payment is always exacted for misdemeanour. Hetty in *Adam Bede* and Molly in *Silas Marner* are both punished for their sins. Moreover, it could be argued that the punishment is not for their ostensible transgressions, but for contravening social mores. In such an argument Hetty's legal crime is infanticide, but her real sin is the sexuality she indulged. As an unmarried woman her moral duty was to remain virgin, to repress any sensual desires. The moral scheme of the novel, it might be argued, in effect demands that she suffers for that initial transgression. Molly is literally killed by 'the demon Opium to whom she was enslaved' (p. 164), but again sub-textual reading might conclude that her fundamental transgression is getting into an obviously unworkable marriage –

because it is secret and with a man far above her social class – through an indulgence of their sexuality, 'an ugly story of low passion' (p. 80). This form of argument would partly be based on the fact that the men involved are punished very much less severely. The fiction appears to be reinforcing a double standard of 'gender/sexual behaviour.

In the imperfect world in which Eliot lived, and she was fully aware of its imperfections, women were liable to suffer more than men from sexual indulgence. A man was literally able to walk away from the biological consequences, as Godfrey does deliberately and Arthur through ignorance, while the woman had to live with pregnancy if that occurred, and in a time before reliable contraception it was always likely to, and then face the problem of bringing up a child in an age of no welfare benefits and services and a great deal of prejudice against women in such a position. The moral scheme of the novels, then, is based less on an abstract Nemesis as on purely practical considerations. Although having transgressed the characters have to bear the consequences of their actions, Eliot is not primarily concerned simply with condemning them. Her moral purpose is mainly to gain a deeper, and express a more compassionate, understanding of characters in those circumstances.

Again it is revealing to place Eliot in the context of the demotic literature of her time, for female sexual misdemeanour was a recurring theme. In Mrs Henry Wood's extremely popular novel *East Lynne*, published in 1861, for example, a wife leaves a caring husband for the sexual excitement of an attractive adventurer. Before the momentous decision is made the narrative conveys the dichotomy of Lady Isabel's feelings:

> She was aware that a sensation all too warm, a feeling of attraction towards Francis Levison, was working within her; not a voluntary one; she could no more express it than she could repress her own sense of being; and, mixed with it was the stern voice of conscience, overwhelming her with the most lively terror.[17]

The force impelling Isabel is clearly sensual – 'a sensation all too warm ... not a voluntary one' – and the 'terror' she feels in acknowledgement of its danger. There is no passage in Eliot's work expressing sexual desire so overtly, but the *moralizing* here, 'the stern voice of conscience' , is also stronger.

Isabel and Francis eventually go to France in order to live together, and he, predictably, loses interest in her when she inevitably becomes pregnant. There is no attempt to analyse or explore the character's emotions. The narrative comment is entirely in moralizing terms:

> poor Lady Isabel! She had sacrificed husband, children, reputation, home, all that makes life of value to woman: she had forfeited her duty to God ... and she knew that her whole future existence ... would be one dark course of gnawing, never-ending retribution.
>
> (p. 289)

Not only is there no hope of re-establishing her social status – a quite realistic position Eliot could thematically endorse – there is an assertion that it is 'all that makes life of value to woman', an extremely conservative doctrine. Wood also goes beyond Eliot by introducing God's wrath, and the idea of 'never-ending retribution' evokes for a Bible-reading public an image of eternal hell. The word 'retribution' itself is related to an Old Testament concept of damnation. Dinah does use religious language to Hetty, of course, in *Adam Bede*, but it is important to make a distinction between the diction of a character – and any true characterization of a nineteenth-century Methodist would have to use Biblical language – and that of a narrator. Wood's moralizing is stronger because it does carry narrational authority.

It is demonstrated too in the direct address of the intrusive narrator:

> Oh, reader, believe me! Lady – wife – mother! should you ever be tempted to abandon your home, so will you awaken! Whatever trials may be the lot of your married life ... *resolve* to bear them; fall down on your knees and pray to be enabled to bear them.
>
> (ibid.)

This is an unequivocal affirmation of the place of woman, made more powerful because written to women – the gender of the 'reader' addressed is obvious in the evocation 'Lady – wife –

mother!' – by a female novelist; and an implicit justification of the moral laws of punishment and retribution. The woman who has abandoned virtue – whether from a position of marriage, or before it, for the issue is explicitly the force of sexual desire – deserves to be punished, socially and Divinely, because she has refused to ask for and accept God's help. The moralizing tone is reinforced by the narrative action when later the child of the union is killed in a railway accident. 'A Sister of Charity' consoles Isabel with the message that it is, 'a just recompense for your sins' (pp. 327–8).

In *Daniel Deronda* Lydia Glasher also abandons a son and husband in order to live with another man, Grandcourt. She too suffers terribly as a consequence, but there is no Divine nemesis, the suffering is emotional and social in basis. Indeed, she, unlike Lady Isabel, is allowed several years of happiness; and the 'four beautiful children' (p. 385) who are the physical result of the union are metaphors for its fruitfulness too, and are not taken away by God's retribution. In fact Lydia 'had no repentance except' that the children were illegitimate and would be at a 'disadvantage with the world' (p. 387). Eliot is fully aware of Lydia's torment when Grandcourt decides to marry Gwendolen, but it is presented not so much as an inevitable punishment for adultery as an illustration of the vulnerability of a woman's position in such a situation. Where Mrs Wood simply condemns the woman Eliot shows an understanding of, and compassion for, 'her helplessness' (p. 392). In working away from the crude, but dominant, ethical position represented by Wood to something more humane, complex – and realistic – Eliot contributed to the development of both the Victorian novel as an artistic form and the period's morality.

In accomplishing these major achievements Eliot, like most novelists, was influenced by many other writers. Bunyan and Fielding have already been touched on, and the great breadth of her reading outlined in chapter 1. Although her own fiction went far beyond his artistically and intellectually Eliot was indebted to the novels of Sir Walter Scott for firing her young imagination. Edith Simcox, for instance, recalled an anecdote about one of Scott's novels:

Somewhere about 1827 a friendly neighbour lent 'Waverley'. . . . It was returned before the child had read to the end, and in her distress at the loss of the fascinating volume, she began to write out the story ... continuing until the surprised elders were moved to get her the book again.

(LIFE, p. 11)

This was quite a feat for a child of seven or eight years of age. The incident was not forgotten by the older Eliot, and forms the basis for the epigraph to chapter 57 of *Middlemarch* (p. 616).

The slightly older Eliot was much impressed by the female French novelist George Sand. In 1849 she wrote to Sara Hennell:

I should never dream of going to her writings as a moral code ... [but] I cannot read six pages of hers without feeling that it is given to her to delineate human passion and its results ... with such truthfulness such nicety of discrimination such tragic power and withal such loving gentle humour that one might live a century ... and not know so much as those six pages will suggest.

(SL, pp. 52–3)

These were the kind of qualities, apart from the lack of a moral code, Eliot eventually incorporated into her own fiction. During their early days together Lewes wrote a book on the German poet and philosopher Goethe, for which Eliot did a great deal of translation, and as she had already translated Strauss and Feuerbach German metaphysics clearly had some influence on her thinking. Given her prodigious facility with languages it is not surprising that Eliot was influenced by non-English writers, and it is a feature of some of her novels, *Romola*, *Middlemarch* and *Daniel Deronda* in particular, that they show a greater awareness of European culture than was customary for most English fiction of the time. Broadening the intellectual and cultural horizons of the English novel was another of Eliot's important achievements. It is also typical of Eliot's eclectic interests that she was influenced by writers who were not novelists or poets. In the letter quoted above, referring to another French writer, she acknowledged that his: 'genius has sent that electric thrill through my intellectual and moral frame which has awakened me to new perceptions, which has made man and nature a fresh world of thought and feeling to me' (ibid.). This was the philosopher Rousseau, one of the leading figures of the eighteenth-century enlightenment. Ten years after that letter was written Eliot could write of someone else who was not a creative writer in the narrow sense, the art critic John Ruskin, 'I think he is the finest writer living' (SL, p. 158). Eliot's appreciative intellect was not closed to any beneficial influence.

Another vital influence, again not a novelist, was the poet William Wordsworth. An 1839 journal entry reads:

> I have been so self-indulgent as to possess myself of Words-worth at full length. . . . I never before met with so many of my own feelings expressed just as I could like them. . . . To-day is my 20th birthday.
>
> (LIFE, p. 30)

Her eventual husband confirmed that appreciation of Wordsworth's poetry lasted throughout Eliot's life: 'This allusion to Wordsworth is interesting, as it entirely expresses the feeling she had to him up to the day of her death' (ibid.). All her most pastoral fiction is suffused with a Wordsworthian tone, and the epigraph to *Adam Bede*, for instance, a quotation from Wordsworth's long philosophical work *The Excursion*, which was published in 1814, is a clear advertisement of that. Wordsworth's influence can perhaps be seen most overtly in *Silas Marner*, for which the epigraph is a quotation from his 1800 narrative poem *Michael*. Eliot wrote of her novel to its publisher, Blackwood: 'I should not have believed that any one would have been interested in it but myself (since William Wordsworth is dead)' (SL, p. 258). Wordsworth had died eleven years earlier, in 1850, and clearly the novel is an attestation of – if not an actual tribute to – his influence.

The misanthropic Silas is rehabilitated and redeemed by Eppie, a child of nature:

> the child created fresh and fresh links between his life and the lives from which he had hitherto shrunk continually into narrower isolation. . . . seeking and loving sunshine, and living sounds, and living movements . . . with trust in new joy, and stirring the human kindness in all eyes that looked on her.
>
> (p. 184)

The diction here stresses movement, the active processes at work between nature and humanity, that create joy. Wordsworth too, in his 1798 poem *Lines Composed A Few Miles Above Tintern Abbey* . . ., found 'harmony, and the deep power of joy' through a sense of a similar natural activity:

> A motion and a spirit, that impels
> All thinking things, all objects of all thought
> And rolls through all things.[18]

The repetitions of 'all' strongly emphasize the unity not only between humanity and animate nature but the inanimate too. The words of movement – 'motion', 'impels', 'rolls' – stress the importance of process. In Silas Marner's case his life had become static, a stagnating obsession with the accumulation of wealth. Eppie provides 'A motion and a spirit, that impels' him towards natural things and a 'new joy'. The influence of Wordsworth can be seen in the description of the change wrought in Silas by Eppie:

> It is as if a new fineness of ear for all spiritual voices had sent wonder-working vibrations through the heavy mortal frame – as if 'beauty born of murmuring sound' had passed into the face of the listener.
>
> (pp. 225–6)

The fusion of 'spiritual' and material, or 'mortal', is again emphasized. The presence of Wordsworthian thought is confirmed by the quotation, from one of his Lucy poems, 'Three years she grew', in which 'Nature said . . . This Child I to myself will take' (p. 148). The declaration could certainly fit the nature-child Eppie.

It was Wordsworth who most popularly expressed an issue that was to become a central concern of the nineteenth century – the dynamic of the change from rural to urban living. The eponymous Michael's life stagnates into despair because he loses his only son, who had been dutiful and loving whilst in the country, but:

> in the dissolute city gave himself
> To evil courses: ignominy and shame
> Fell on him.
>
> (p. 109)

The poem *Michael* makes a direct correlation between honourable actions in the countryside, and dishonourable behaviour in the city. Michael's son would not have lost his moral way had he remained a rural-dweller.

Although Silas is betrayed in the town – which significantly has such area-names as 'Prison Street' (p. 239) – Eliot was aware that by the 1860s the rural/urban dynamic could not be reversed, and that society had to come to terms with it. When Silas returns to the town of his birth he finds it 'a great manufacturing town' and is: 'bewildered by the changes thirty years had brought over his native place' (p. 238). The transformation is crystallized in the replacement of the chapel by 'a large factory' (p. 240). The differences between urban and rural surroundings are remarked on by Eppie, seeing them for the first time:

> O, what a dark ugly place! . . . How it hides the sky! It's worse than the Workhouse. I'm glad you don't live in the town now, father. . . . I couldn't ha' thought as any folks lived i' this way, so close together. How pretty the Stone-pits 'ull look when we get back!
>
> (pp. 239–40)

By the time *Silas Marner* was written many people were living in similar conditions, and although they could not be rehabilitated to rural life some contact with natural life had to be found. Urbanization had broken, as Wordsworth had predicted, the continuity Eliot so ardently desired in her essay 'The Natural History of German Life' (cf. chapter 2 above). Whereas much of the popular fiction of the period 1850s–70s tended to present a relatively static and narrow social perspective, eschewing problematic areas, Eliot showed an awareness of them and continued to explore that dynamic. *Felix Holt* and her last two novels in particular deal with a very broad, and changing, class range.

One of Eliot's overall achievements was to link the demotic forms of her day, methods of story-telling and characterization, didacticism – exemplified by Braddon, Wood and Dickens – with older emblematic and narrational traditions, and by doing so expanding her, mainly female, readers' cultural and moral horizons. She also extended those readers intellectually by exploring some of the major social issues of the time. Eliot's purpose went beyond mere moral instruction, the inculcation of conventional female virtues: it was to educate her readership in the profoundest sense. That Eliot achieved her purpose, and advanced the novel artistically whilst retaining a place in the popular marketplace, is a testimony to her subtlety and intelligence.

4

Towards a Godless Society

In a century of conflicts one of the most urgent was that which appeared to be between religion and science. It was crystallized by the publication of Charles Darwin's *The Origin of Species* in November 1859, but had in fact been mounting in intensity over several decades, and was a great deal more complex than is suggested by the terms of the dichotomy in which it is most usually expressed.

There had been a growing body of rationalist thought since the Enlightenment of the late eighteenth century, and in the nineteenth that was seen as manifest in the advancement of scientific ideas. The application of those in such practical every-day fields as medicine and technology, affecting the lives of virtually everyone, gave rationalism an additional impetus. Lydgate the doctor was a character who 'felt the growth of an intellectual passion' (p. 173), and who: 'longed to demonstrate the more intimate relations of living structure and help to define men's thought more accurately after the true order. . . . to do good small work for Middlemarch, and great work for the world' (p. 178). The doctor in him was ultimately rather let down by the man, but he represents a not uncommon type of the period, intending to achieve good work by the application of rational, intellectual activity in practical ways. In the same novel Vincy, as a manufacturer, is affected by the technological advances in dyes; and being a little old-fashioned gets into difficulties. Progress required flexible minds.

Society as a whole felt it had the flexibility to meet the challenge of the new. The mathematician and philosopher A. N. Whitehead, expressing an earlier twentieth-century view of the preceding century, concluded:

What is peculiar and new to the century, differentiating it from all its predecessors, is its technology. It was not merely the introduction of some great isolated inventions. . . . the process became quick, conscious, and expected. . . . It was a peculiar period of hope. . . . The greatest invention of the nineteenth century was the invention of the method of invention.[1]

Technology, which provided evidence of the usefulness of scientific ideas, became not a mysterious phenomenon engaged in by isolated genius, but an 'expected' and 'conscious' one. It was taken by some people as a form of proof that humanity could master its own destiny, that the human mind was capable of limitless knowledge and understanding. Rational thought was neither merely a theoretical nor a sterile avenue of cold intellectualism – it created 'hope', which was fundamentally a hope that rationalism, the application of scientific method, 'the invention of the method of invention', could and would solve the difficulties and problems of the times.

Many of those problems had, paradoxically, been caused by technological innovation – as, for example, the expansion of factory methods of production in order to gain maximum economic benefit from the invention of new machinery, and the consequent rapid growth of urban living. As industrialism increased the demand for mineral deposits – especially coal, since most of the initial power was steam generated – a further paradox occurred. An impetus was given to the branch of science that was itself to provide a seismic philosophic shock to the basis of society's formal beliefs. The historian Asa Briggs has written of scientific advances in the period:

> they had a special appeal for the middle classes who found in geology in particular a science which could account for their wealth – thick coal seams – and could enliven their leisure hours through the favourite Victorian pursuit of collecting fossils and shells. The British Association for the Advancement of Science was founded in 1831, largely as a result of the activities of geologists, with the twofold purpose of increasing public interest in useful knowledge and of inspiring scientific discovery.[2]

At that time, between 1830 and 1833, Sir Charles Lyell brought out his seminal three-volume scholarly study *Principles of Geology*. One of the conclusions was that the Earth was very much older than the age given it in *The Bible*, a hypothesis Lyell had held for some time. Referring in an 1827 letter to the influential French scientist, Lamarck, Lyell claimed: 'His theories delighted me. . . . That the Earth is quite as old as he supposes, has long been my creed'.[3] Lyell was not necessarily against religion in general or Christianity in particular, but he recognized as early as 1831 that dogmatic literal application of *The Bible* could retard scientific investigation. Writing to Dr Fleming, a fellow scientist, of a specific instance Lyell observed: 'it is one of ten thousand proofs of the incubus that the Mosaic deluge has been, and is I fear long destined to be on our science'.[4] The conflict quickly became, indeed, one between the literal truth of *The Bible* and scientific evidence. It was possible, eventually, to believe in *The Bible's* metaphoric truth and the theories of science, but that was not an easy position to achieve immediately. Many people could not accept a resolution, conservative defenders of Christian teaching continued to attack scientists throughout Eliot's lifetime; and many rationalists, such as Eliot herself, were not able to hold onto their religious faith.

In 1844 the conflict was intensified by the appearance of a popularly influential, if unscholarly, book, *Vestiges of Creation* by Robert Chambers. Its popularity may be gauged from the fact that eleven editions were published between its first appearance and the publication of *The Mill on the Floss* in 1860, illustrating the enormous interest that was shown in the subject. Chambers' book was also important in linking theories of geology, biology, botany and natural history. Although the latter were crystallized in the 1859 *The Origin of Species* they were by no means unknown earlier. Darwin began the 1860 third edition of his book with 'An Historical Sketch' of the subject, which even as an outline consists of about 3000 words. Echoing Lyell over 30 years earlier, although in relation to biology rather than geology, he acknowledged that: 'Lamarck was the first man whose conclusions on the subject excited much attention. This justly-celebrated naturalist first published his views in 1801'.[5] Darwin's own book was the result of a long gestation, as his Introduction reveals:

> When on board H.M.S. *Beagle*, as naturalist, I was much struck with certain facts in the distribution of the inhabitants of South America. . . . These facts . . . seemed to me to throw some light on the origin of species – that mystery of mysteries, as it has been called by one of our greatest philosophers.
>
> (p. 65)

Darwin was on the *Beagle* from 1831 to 1836, indicating just how early his own ideas had begun to form. It is also clear that he saw they had philosophic implications. He published 'a sketch of the conclusions, which then seemed to me probable' (ibid.) in 1844. The eventual book endorsed those initial ideas with very substantial evidence, gathered during the intervening years. The motivation for its publication was Darwin's discovery that another scientist, A. R. Wallace, had reached the same conclusions and might soon publish his, illustrating that Darwin was working in the intellectual mainstream of the time, not as an eccentric individual.

In addition to being aware of the general interest in the field Eliot had some personal involvement in the issues, in 1856, for example, she had helped Lewes begin his seaside studies. In that year she also wrote a book review on Bohlen's *Introduction to the Book of Genesis*, in *The Leader* – reprinted in SEP, pp. 358–62 – that explored the relation between the Biblical version of Creation and that of development theory – the conceptual precursor of the idea Darwin termed Natural Selection, and which later became commonly known as Evolution. Lewes' *Physiology of Common Life* appeared earlier in the same year as *The Origin of Species*, and Eliot had read the latter within weeks of its appearance.

Darwin's book, catching a rising tide of scientific rationalism, religious doubt and Church defensiveness, caused immediate controversy. At the first meeting of the British Association for the Advancement of Science to take place after the book's appearance, the Bishop of Oxford publicly asked of Darwin which of his grandparents were monkeys. In an unsigned review of *The Origin of Species* the bishop attacked the book on more nominally intellectual grounds, concluding:

> On what then is the new theory based? ... on the merest hypothesis, supported by the most unbounded assumptions ... extravagant liberty of speculation ... wantonness of conjecture ... utterly dishonourable to all natural science.
>
> (*The Quarterly Review*, July 1860)

The bishop's own evidence was substantially less than that provided by Darwin, and the reason for his invective revealed in subsequent comments: 'Few things have more deeply injured the cause of religion than the busy fussy energy with which men, narrow and feeble alike in Faith and in science, have bustled forth' (ibid.). The suggestion is clearly that a man of strong scientific mind must also be one of strong religious 'Faith'. There is also a sense, which harks back to Lyell's fears, that if religion and science were thought to be in conflict the latter should withdraw.

The profundity that the shock of development theory could have, years before *The Origin of Species* was published, is seen in the work of Alfred, Lord Tennyson, the most intellectually important Victorian poet. In the year, 1850, in which Tennyson was appointed Poet Laureate his long meditative poem *In Memoriam A.H.H.* appeared. He had worked on it since the death of his friend A.H.H., Arthur Henry Hallam, at the age of 22 in 1833, and the poem wrestles with the problems of mortality and belief in an age of scientific rationalism:

> Who trusted God was love indeed
> > And love creation's final law –
> > Though Nature, red in tooth and claw
> With ravine, shrieked against his creed . . .
>
> O life as futile, then, as frail!
> > O for thy voice to soothe and bless!
> > What hope of answer, or redress?[6]

The juxtaposition of the old idea of God and nature representing love with the new notion of violent destruction – which became associated with the concept of the survival of the fittest – crystallizes the early Victorian conflict. The argument that is here presented in Darwinian terms has also been viewed in the light of Lyell's geological theories, which coalesce within the ambit of Natural History:

> Are God and Nature then at strife,
> > That Nature lends such evil dreams?
> > So careful of the type she seems,
> So careless of the single life . . .
>
> 'So careful of the type?' but no.
> > From scarped cliff and quarried stone

> She cries, 'A thousand types are gone:
> I care for nothing, all shall go.'
>
> (pp. 910–11)

If fossils show that species of the past have disappeared from the Earth, the argument goes, is there an infinite future for humanity? The traditional consolation that the death of one human being – even someone lost before their prime as Hallam was – does not diminish the eternal value to God of humanity as a whole is denied. The evidence of science suggests that the processes of nature may eradicate any, or all, species.

Despite that awful dilemma scientific thought and religious belief were not necessarily inimical. Although the development theory explicated a process of events that was contrary to a literal reading of *The Holy Bible*, the idea of an omniscient initial prime mover, the creating God, could be subscribed to; and belief in the fundamental, if not actual, truth of *The Bible* could be held. An author Eliot read, John Lubbock, wrote in 1870 that: 'Science is still regarded by many excellent, but narrow-minded, persons as hostile to religious truth, while in fact she is only opposed to religious error ... true religion is, without science, impossible'.[7] Eliot shows a reconciliation of faith and science in the character of the Reverend Farebrother, whom Mary Garth thinks 'the cleverest man in her narrow circle' (p. 561), and who followed his profession, as Vicar of St Botolph's in Middlemarch, and his vocation of entymology without serious intellectual or theological conflict.

Some Christians perceived science as actually revealing God's pattern, an idea Tennyson records only to reject:

> I found Him not in world or sun,
>   Or eagle's wing, or insect's eye
>   Nor through the questions men may try ...
>
> (p. 974)

There was also the possibility that development theory itself pointed to the spiritual, higher state that humanity was moving towards, which proved God's grand design. Tennyson expressed that too:

> Arise and fly
> The reeling Faun, the sensual feast;

> Move upward, working out the beast,
> And let the ape and tiger die.
>
> (p. 970)

The irrational, bestial aspects of humanity were, in this theory, seen as inheritance from a past that was being left behind. Drunkenness, lechery and viciousness – and they existed plentifully in Victorian reality – would eventually be developed out of, removed from, human character as it evolved towards the perfection of its creator. Ultimately Tennyson, like many of his fellow-believers, falls back on pure intuitive faith:

> all is well, though faith and form
> Be sundered in the night of fear . . .
>
> That God, which ever lives and loves,
> One God, one law, one element,
> And one far-off divine event,
> To which the whole creation moves.
>
> (pp. 976–88)

The long, extensive debate culminates in a simple assertion, recognizing the existence of the 'night of fear' of unbelief but able to affirm the 'One God' despite all doubt. Eliot could not subscribe to such an affirmation, but remained interested in the issues raised, and evaded, by it.

Though science was often seen to challenge theology it was by no means the only threat to religion. Rationalism in its wider manifestations was a powerful intellectual force. There was, for instance, a good deal of Biblical scholarship that took the direction of interpreting *The Bible* metaphorically and humanistically, much of it initially coming from Germany. Darwin's work was quickly appreciated in Germany after its translation in 1860. Darwin's son, Francis, later commented: 'the voice of German science was to become one of the strongest of the advocates of evolution'.[8] It is a scholary failing of the pedantic Casaubon in *Middlemarch* that he is unaware much of his work for *The Key to All Mythologies* has been anticipated:

If Mr Casaubon read German he would save himself a great deal of trouble. . . . the Germans have taken the lead in historical inquiries, and they laugh at results which are got by groping about in the woods with a pocket-compass while they have made good roads.

(p. 240)

It is significant that the observation comes from the cosmopolitan Ladislaw, with his partly Polish ancestry. Eliot was herself again in the intellectual centre of the ideas with her translations of Strauss and Feuerbach. In 1855 Eliot wrote an article, 'Evangelical Teaching: Dr. Cumming', in the *Westminster Review*, in which she criticized the demotic theologian for postulating: 'a God who instead of sharing and aiding our human sympathies, is directly in collision with them' (SEP, p. 67). Eliot's own notion of a religious sense is the opposite of Cumming's:

> The idea of God is really moral in its influence – it really cherishes all that is best and loveliest in man – only when God is contemplated as sympathizing with the pure elements of human feeling, as possessing infinitely all those attributes which we recognize to be moral in humanity.

(p. 66)

This is a humanist God, a fusion of physical humanity and 'all that is best and loveliest in man'. The human spirit that is celebrated here also emanates from Romanticism. Wordsworth wrote in *Intimations of Immortality*:

> Thanks to the human heart by which we live,
> Thanks to its tenderness, its joys, and fears[9]

arguing that only by living through 'human' emotion, in harmony with natural life, is it possible to achieve full moral and spiritual existence. Eliot's repetition of 'really' in her essay indicates how much she wishes to discriminate between theoretical concepts of morality, those imposed by religious systems of 'dogmatic beliefs' (p. 67), and the realities 'of human feeling' and experience.

This was certainly an important issue at a time when Christians felt they were losing their traditional influence over morality and behaviour; and for humanists, such as Eliot, who could not subscribe to religious systems and doctrines, but were concerned with moral questions and what they perceived as a general decline in private and public morals. Those concerns were created partly by the dynamic of the age: the rapid increase in population, and the even greater expansion of urban living with its concomitant squalor, disease, poverty, prostitution and crime; and in contrast, the opportunity for a relative few to make a lot of money quickly.

In 1851 a nationwide census of attendance at places of religious worship was undertaken, the statistics arising from which highlighted the problem of churches. Asa Briggs has written of its results: 'In the words of Horace Mann, the chief statistician, the "labouring myriads, the masses of our working population . . . are never or but seldom seen in our religious congregations."'[10] The drift away from church attendance had been going on for many years, and within the overall Christian community of belief there were two major, and opposing, responses: that known as the Oxford Movement, which drifted with John Henry Newman – later Cardinal Newman – towards, or into, Roman Catholicism; and the broader one of Nonconformity, or Dissent. Both were complex, and to some extent characterized by internal schisms. The processes which began in earnest in the 1830s, and reached critical stages in the two subsequent decades, continued not only throughout Eliot's lifetime, but well beyond.

Darwin went on to publish several important books after *The Origin of Species*, among which were *The Descent of Man* and *The Expression of Emotions in Man and Animals* in 1871 and 1872 respectively. Since in the intervening decade he and Eliot were members of the same intellectual circles she was aware of the conceptual developments, and their continued implications. Of *Romola* the critic Joan Bennett has validly argued:

> When George Eliot chose the place and the time for the setting of her 'historical romance', she was doubtless attracted by the apparent similiarities between the Florence of Savonarola and the England of Cardinal Newman. There was a similar cleavage of thought between the Renaissance humanists and the religious reformers as there was in the nineteenth century between the rationalists and the religious revivalists. . . . In both periods there was strong hope and belief in the expansion of human knowledge and power; there was also, among Christian believers in both periods, the recognition of a relaxation and even corruption in Church teaching and of a consequent deteriora-

tion in human conduct, resulting in a zealous desire to reform
the Church.[11]

Catholics and Nonconformists were not so much concerned with
reforming the Church of England as with transforming it, into
either the Roman or the Chapel model. Nevertheless Bennett's
point is perceptive, and succinctly illustrates that Eliot's fiction
refracted the central concerns of her time, although all of it was
set specifically at some distance.

The Oxford Movement started in 1833, the year of publication
of the final volume of Lyell's *Principles of Geology*. The movement's
initial object was the transformation, from within, of the Anglican
Church's lack of rigour in theology, moral teaching and ritual.
The debate became public in a series of *Tracts for the Times*, which
Eliot read in her teens, during her Evangelical, reforming period
of religious enthusiasm. Newman became a leading figure partly
due to the vigour of his opposition to Church of England practices, and in 1845 he converted to Catholicism and was followed
by a number of his supporters.

This was not a purely theological matter, for it gave rise to a
good number of novels, many written by female authors, which
despite their being largely now forgotten, were widely read
throughout the period of Eliot's life. A fairly typical example is
Elizabeth Harris' 1847 *From Oxford to Rome*. It begins literally in
'the High Street of Oxford',[12] but the title unequivocally signified
to its original readers a theological journey of disillusionment and
conversion: from Anglicanism to Catholicism. In this case, however, the novel warns against following the precept of the Oxford
Movement's leading light. After detailing the achievements of the
reformed Church of England the narrator, who claims to have
been 'a Companion Traveller' (title page) and therefore know the
issues from both sides, asserts:

> Who then can look over the facts of the Anglican Church in
> these years of its revival, and not piously exclaim, 'What hath
> GOD wrought!' True, there are hours when circumstances or
> events are adverse or unexplained; hours when the heart of the
> most devoted Anglican will almost fail within him. Hours when
> it seems to him that his Chruch assumes too low a place, too
> low a tone.

(p. 239)

At those times the faithful must not lose heart and turn to Rome, but think of the achievements and remember the mystery of the Divine pattern: 'who shall call in question His inscrutable purposes? Who shall fathom His designs?' (p. 240). Harris here takes consolation in terms of a favourite Victorian hymn, although written in the late eighteenth century, William Cowper's 'Light Shining out of Darkness':

> God moves in a mysterious way
> His wonders to perform.[13]

These are both simple injunctions to submit to the will of the established Church, or to that of God. Newman felt sufficiently incited by Harris' novel to write a riposte which was published in the following year, 1848. Its polemical nature is again signalled by the title, *Loss and Gain*, and the novel is a didactic defence of conversion to Rome. It concludes with the main character, Charles Reding, on his knees:

> Charles had been admitted into the communion of the Catholic Church about an hour since. He was ... in the possession of a deep serenity of mind ... like the stillness ... when a vessel, after much tossing at sea, finds itself in harbour.[14]

The tone here is intended to be reverential, but the need to convince, to draw the reader in, leads Newman into clichéd simile in his desire not to write above the reader's head. Eliot is difficult and challenging to read partly because she never condescends to readers in this way. There is no fundamental exploration of the problems caused by the philosophic and moral complexities of the age's dilemmas in most of the novels of this type. Those were left to less narrowly didactic novelists.

James Froude's *The Nemesis of Faith*, published in 1849, the year following Newman's novel, is an example of a serious, although artistically flawed, attempt to address loss of faith. Froude was an ordained deacon, the son of an archdeacon, who lost his religious belief, amidst great spirtual torment, in the 1840s. Despite the novel's artistic limitations it is an honest exposure of increasing doubt, which does not seek to persuade the reader, as both Harris and Newman do, to adopt a particular form of action or attitude. The fact that it was ceremoniously burnt in Oxford perhaps registers something of its quality. Its main protagonist, Markham Sutherland, ends the novel very differently from either Harris' or Newman's heroes. Sutherland dies:

> amidst the wasted ruins of his life, where the bare bleak soil was strewed with wrecked purposes and shattered creeds; with no hope to stay him, with no fear to raise the most dreary phantom beyond the grave, he sunk down into the barren waste, and the dry sands rolled over him where he lay.[15]

There is no sustaining image at all here: it is impossible to live without faith, but not possible to have it. The only strength is recognizing and accepting that emptiness. Although Eliot never touched such depths of philosophic nihilism her review of the novel, in the *Coventry Herald and Observer*, shortly after its publication was appreciative. She criticized its artistic inadequacies, such as its excessively melodramatic plot, and praised what she saw as its truthfulness and relevance to the times:

> Much there is in the work of a questionable character: yet . . . its suggestive hints as to the necessity of recasting the currency of our religion and virtue, that it may carry fresh and bright the stamp of the age's highest and best idea – these have a practical bearing.
>
> (SEP, p. 265)

Eliot understood loss of faith, and realized that under the glow of Victorian confidence it was one of the aspects of life that could cause individuals pain.

Her own handling of religious belief in fiction was scrupulous. Adam Bede balances between proper reverence and mild scepticism:

> I'm not for laughing at no man's religion. Let 'em follow their consciences, that's all. Only I think it 'ud be better if their consciences 'ud let 'em stay quiet i' the church – there's a deal to be learnt there. And there's such a thing as being over-speritial; we must have something beside Gospel i' this world. Look at the canals, an' th' aqueducs, an' th' coal-pit engines . . . a man must learn summat beside Gospel to make them things . . . and if a man . . . scrats at his bit o' garden and makes two

potatoes grow istead o' one, he's doing more good, and he's just as near to God.

(p. 53)

In the context Adam is offering a partial defence of the estab-lished Church – 'there's a deal to be learnt there', if only the Dissenters would listen; and he is berating Nonconformist preachers in general, and Methodists in particular, people who insist on 'being over-speritial'. Yet he eventually marries a Methodist preacher (although she has been forced to relinquish the practice by the time of their marriage). The paradox of that aspect of the plot emphasizes Eliot's deliberate avoidance of prejudice. The terms of Adam's juxtaposition, over-insistence on Gospel against material progress and productivity, might appear to be very secular and unreligious, but he sees it not as one or the other but as a balance, 'something beside'. Also, canals and so on are wonders of achievement, a kind of celebration of spirit; and doubling the food supply is 'doing more good' than mere Bible reading, a sentiment with which the poor would certainly agree. God is near to those who work hard and honestly. It is essentially a practical religion based on tolerance, 'Let 'em follow their consciences' providing all manner of believers live good useful lives. Nevertheless, Adam is also a Bible-reader:

> The book Adam most often read on a Sunday morning was his large pictured Bible ... he never opened it on a weekday, and so he came to it as a holiday book, serving him for a history, biography, and poetry.

(pp. 541-2)

Although Adam has some religious feeling he is not a theologian, and uses the book in virtually a secular, humanist manner. His use of dialect speech, and the description of his 'large pictured Bible', signify lack of sophistication, perhaps even a child-like – certainly innocent – approach to life. Adam's attitudes synthesize the period's problematic contraries: eternal/temporal, spiritual/ material and intuitive/intellectual – by accepting their respective demands.

The other main response to the crises of an ineffectual Anglican Church, and a moving away from faith, was into Nonconformity, or Dissent – the two concepts are not strictly synonymous, but have become almost so in usage. The terms generally mean those Protestants who are outside, and even against, the Church of England, and without question in complete opposition to the Church of Rome. Nonconformity emerged from the 1851 religious census comparatively well, as Briggs observed:

> Nonconformists knew that they had considerable strength in the great provincial cities. ... They were far more important, however, than even their numbers suggested in leading the local politics of cities and in presenting the 'urban case' to their contemporaries.[16]

A more satirical view of Dissent, suggesting stolidity rather than 'strength' and self-important rather than 'important', is provided by Margaret Oliphant in her series of novels *Chronicles of Carlingford*. In that fictitious, but representative, town of her 1863 novel *Salem Chapel* Oliphant details how Anglican Church and Nonconformist/Dissenting Chapel strictly differentiated themselves from one another: 'To name the two communities, however, in the same breath, would have been accounted little short of sacrilege'.[17] This is, however, not the unprejudicial approach of Eliot, criticizing – or accepting – both sides more or less evenly. The narrative tone is quickly established as being critical of Dissenters. The chapel itself is described as a 'little tabernacle', 'on the shabby side of the street' its environs 'flowerless and sombre', and its architecture both mean and ludicrous: 'a red brick building, presenting a pinched gable terminated by a curious little belfry, not intended for any bell' (p. 1). Oliphant's satire is clear enough not to be misinterpreted, but it is a view of a writer outside of, and simply hostile to, the culture. It lacks the finesse of Eliot's critical understanding. When the Congregationalists are introduced in *Felix Holt*, for example, the minister's circumstances are described:

> Mr Lyon lived in a small house, not quite so good as the parish clerk's. ... The new prosperity of Dissent at Treby had led to an enlargement of the chapel, which absorbed all extra funds and left none for the enlargement of the minister's income.
>
> (p. 131)

Rufus Lyon's social position as a Dissenting minister is nicely delineated in relation to the parish clerk, who has more status within the town's establishment. His congregation's material priorities are satirized in the fact that the size of the place of worship is considered more important than the comfort, or just reward, of their spiritual leader. Oliphant outlines the worshippers at Salem Chapel in terms of sources of income:

> Green-grocers, dealers in cheese and bacon, milkmen, with some dress-makers of inferior pretensions, and teachers of day-schools of similar humble character, formed the *élite* of the congregation. ... Tozer, the butterman, who was senior deacon, found it difficult to refrain from an audible expression of pity for the 'Church folks' who knew no better.
>
> (pp. 2–3)

The juxtaposition of 'inferior', 'humble' and '*élite*', in addition to the actual occupations of the characters, indicates narrational disapproval. Chapels are frequented by tradespeople, therefore by implication churches are for the better classes – and perhaps any of the lower classes who are willing to recognize their natural, as well as social, superiors. The character who criticizes the 'Church folks', and has the audacity to feel 'pity' for them, is merely a 'butterman', and just to enforce the point is given a silly name of canine associations. Such simplistic views are criticized in *Adam Bede*:

> to some of my readers Methodism may mean nothing more than low-pitched gables up dingy streets, sleek grocers, sponging preachers and hypocritical jargon – elements which are regarded as an exhaustive analysis of Methodism in many fashionable quarters.
>
> (p. 82)

Margaret Oliphant's *Salem Chapel* appeared after Eliot had written this, and clearly falls into the stereotypes of architecture, environs and character outlined and warned against here. The Chapel is not only seen and presented from the outside, but from a lofty religious height. From such a perspective it is not possible to distinguish, as Eliot could, fine details of distinction.

In Victorian reality such discriminations were imperative. The term, whether Nonconformist or Dissent, is a portmanteau one, and the immense diversity of sects has to be appreciated: Baptists, Congregationalists, Methodists, Moravians, Quakers, Plymouth Brethren, Unitarians were simply some of the main groups; but they were often sub-divided, as between the General Baptists, who helped to educate the young Eliot, and the Particular Baptists; and the Primitive and Wesleyan Methodists, for example. In a period before instant mass communications there were often very vigorous local or regional versions and variations of all sects too. The critic Valentine Cunningham, noting the sectarian proliferation from the 1830s, has commented: 'varieties of sects continued to multiply, markedly. ... According to lists *Whitaker's Almanac*, 101 different names of places of worship were lodged with the Registrar-General in 1869; in 1890 there were 244'.[18] This frenzy of activity reflected the zeal of people who were determined to get belief right, even to the fine details, on which they were likely to argue with their neighbours. It was in part an urgency created by a world in which faith was becoming ever-increasingly difficult. The more tenuous the hold on an idea of divinity became, the closer it was clutched – and the interpretation of a verse of scripture could become a point of everlasting schism, as Cunningham remarks in a nice paradox, 'the life-blood of Dissent is dissent',[19] and they often did disagree with one another.

Eliot shows an awareness of the complexity in *Silas Marner*, where without specifying a particular sect she illustrates the peculiarities of: 'that little hidden world known to itself as the church assembling in Lantern Yard' (p. 56). It was indeed a 'little hidden world' known, and important, only 'to itself'. The members have a belief that 'Silas's cataleptic fit' must be either 'a visitation of Satan' or 'a proof of divine favour' (p. 58). They also have faith in revelation, for Wiliam Dane has possessed: 'Assurance of salvation ... ever since, in the period of his conversion, he had dreamed that he saw the words "calling and election sure" standing by themselves on a white page in the open Bible' (pp. 57–8). This was not an uncommon hope, or even occurrence, in the novel and in reality. In an age when rational hope in the possibility of divine salvation became increasingly difficult to embrace, assurance through revelation was a main source of spiritual consolation. Its limitations are shown in the novel by the hypocritical behaviour of the divinely elected William; and the faith's degeneration into superstition, illustrated by Silas' trial by the 'drawing of lots' (p. 61). These were features of Dissent severely criticized in the moral structure of *Silas Marner*.

Earlier Eliot had acknowledged the value of some aspects of Nonconformity. If Dinah is something of a paragon of virtue, in *Adam Bede*, she may be seen as a stereotype to counter the epitomes of Dissenting hypocrites presented in the popular fiction exemplified, for example, by Oliphant's work. The presentation of Rufus Lyon in *Felix Holt* is more complex, a physically ludicrous figure who nevertheless has moral worth:

> every one thought him a very odd-looking rusty old man; the free-school boys often hooted after him and called him 'Revelations'; and to many respectable church people, old Lyon's little legs and large head seemed to make Dissent additionally preposterous. But he was too shortsighted to notice.
>
> (p. 131)

Here Eliot links the common social assumptions that equate physical unattractiveness with disreputableness and popular, simplistic, literary traditions that trade on such appearances. It is the 'respectable church people' who judge the whole of religious Dissent/Nonconformity on the basis of the mere physical appearance of one of its members who are truly 'preposterous'. The value Dissent put on personal revelation, as in *Silas Marner*, and the apocalyptic visions taken from the *Book of Revelation* beloved by many Dissenting preachers, partly explains his nickname – although it also refers to the monstrous quality of his appearance. Eliot fuses many aspects of, and attitudes to, Dissent in this concise portrait – in which Rufus bears some physical resemblance to Silas Marner, who was also bent and had large shortsighted eyes, that caused him to be a wonder to the local children. Large myopic eyes are, incidentally, a characteristic also shared by Dorothea Brooke. To some extent the physical detail always has a metaphoric extension: they are all essentially altruistic characters who fail to see reality in its entirety at crucial moments.

Eliot certainly does criticize Dissent, but not in the supercilious terms of Oliphant, and many other popular writers. Seeing the virtues and strengths Eliot also depicts the limitations and weaknesses of Nonconformity. Rufus has 'looked into' Shakespeare, for instance, but tells Felix: 'the fantasies therein were so little to be reconciled with a steady contemplation of that divine economy which is hidden from sense and revealed to faith, that I forbore the reading' (p. 369). Again the important concept is 'faith', for that is the quality susceptible to revelation of divine truth. Imagination, 'fantasies', is inimical to divine revelation. There is a Dissenting fear that imagination, by creating alternative realities, or unrealities, distracts attention from the one true reality that is 'revealed to faith'. Nonconformity was not new in the Victorian period, but it did expand enormously then, and particularly in an age of scientific and rational doubt 'faith' had to be maintained as a pure, uncontaminated experience. It alone was not vulnerable to argument. Nevertheless there is a complicating irony in the discussion between Felix and Rufus, for the latter quotes John Milton approvingly, the writer who perhaps above all others epitomizes the fusion of Dissent and the poetic imagination.

In *Felix Holt* it is the Dissenting narrowness of spirit as a whole, as opposed to individual traits, that is castigated. Rufus finds his congregation turning against Felix, whose attitudes and behaviour they do not understand or like:

> the state of feeling in Treby among the Liberal dissenting flock was unfavourable to Felix. . . . [he] had spoken ill of respectable tradespeople. He had put a stop to the making of saleable drugs, contrary to the nature of buying and selling. . . . He had done no good to 'the cause'; if he had fought about church-rates, or had been worsted in some struggle in which he was distinctly the champion of Dissent and Liberalism . . . sermons might have been preached on him.
>
> (p. 465)

The yoking of 'Liberal' and 'dissenting', 'Dissent' and 'Liberalism', reveals the Nonconformist mind in the mass identifying religious and political interests as standing together. The 'respectable tradespeople' are not criticized here solely for being vendors of cheese, milk, etc., as in *Salem Chapel* and many novels of similar ilk, but because they do identify economic and political interests with theological ones. There is a certain convenience in being allied against church-rates, just as it is comfortable to have a religion that reconciles spiritual well-being and rousing sermons with 'the nature of buying and selling'.

One of the moral problems of religious zealots is that they could, or do, become hypocrites – not merely reconciling private interests with religious convictions, but actually pursuing personal advantages whilst pretending to follow communal ones; or even exhorting public virtues in order to more effectively gain personal power and wealth. Nonconformity did not have a monopoly, even in the demotic imagination, on hypocrisy – which became a major Victorian theme as the pressure on religious belief intensified, and to many non-believers the subscribers to Christianity appeared by definition of subscribing to something that seemed irrational to have corrupt reasons for doing so.

The Rev. Walter Tyke in *Middlemarch* is one of Eliot's most stereotyped characters: 'Nobody had anything to say against Mr Tyke, except that they could not bear him, and suspected him of cant' (p. 210). Even the emblematically demeaning name springs from demotic fiction, and his predilection for 'Dissenting hymnbooks and that low kind of religion' (p. 800) places him firmly in a popular tradition. Tyke, however, is a very minor character whose structural function in the novel is to help expand the role and analysis of Bulstrode. This latter is a far more complex figure, a man of humble and obscure origins who gains wealth illegally, and dispenses power from his position as a banker. Nicholas Bulstrode's rise is left deliberately ambiguous for much of the narrative, even Harriet knows little about it:

> That her husband had at first been employed in a bank, that he had afterwards entered into what he called city business and gained a fortune before he was three-and-thirty, that he had married a widow who was much older than himself – a Dissenter ... was almost as much as she had cared to learn.
>
> (p. 661)

That calculated ignorance is in fact a form of self-deception, for marriage to Bulstrode: 'had been the means of raising her own position' (ibid.). Self-deception, or a blinding of oneself to possible unpalatable truths, is a characteristic of particular kinds of theological positions.

Early in the novel Farebrother expresses a view of the Bulstrode-type that was not at all uncommon at the time:

> I don't translate my own convenience into other people's duties. I am opposed to Bulstrode in many ways. I don't like the set he belongs to: they are a narrow ignorant set, and do

more to make their neighbours uncomfortable than to make them better. Their system is a sort of worldly-spiritual cliqueism.

(p. 206)

This might well be a critical description of the Nonconformists of Treby who take against Felix Holt. Yet even so Farebrother has to admit 'that Bulstrode's new hospital' will benefit the community at large, so that the condemnation is ameliorated.

When Bulstrode's illicit dealings catch up with him the narrative emphasizes the complexity of his motives:

Bulstrode's course up to that time had, he thought, been sanctioned by remarkable providences, appearing to point the way for him to be the agent in making best use of a large property ... for God's service.... There may be coarse hypocrites, who consciously affect beliefs and emotions for the sake of gulling the world, but Bulstrode was not one of them. He was simply a man whose desires had been stronger than his theoretic beliefs, and who had gradually explained the gratification of his desires into satisfactory agreement with those beliefs. If this be hypocrisy, it is a process which shows itself occasionally in us all.

(pp. 666–7)

Bulstrode had not set out on a premeditated course of deception and self-aggrandisement, but his religious leanings towards Dissent – which implicitly included faith in divine revelation as opposed to rational thought or scientific analysis – encouraged him to perceive reality, even down to his own circumstances, as emanating directly from God. Therefore he had divine endorsement – 'sanctioned by remarkable providences' – for socially illicit actions. By chance they simultaneously furthered God's cause and Bulstrode's career. The narrative makes it clear that Bulstrode is not part of the popular literary tradition of 'coarse hypocrites'; the character is written against that kind of simplification. The reader is not put into an easily superior position from which to judge the sinner, but rather is discomfortingly included in 'a process which shows itself occasionally in us all'. No Dissenter is allowed to take comfort in his/her own righteousness, and no non-Dissenter – whether Anglican, Catholic, atheist or agnostic –

can gain pleasure from the fall of a character with whom they hold more in common, through a mutual human nature, than they can claim in theological dissimilarity.

The problem with religion for Eliot, in addition to her personal inability to believe, was that it could lead people to self-deception in the way it did for Bulstrode. She agreed with the moral tenets, but thought their application was not sufficiently grounded in ordinary reality, the 'theoretic beliefs' were not necessarily strong enough to overcome the need for 'the gratification of . . . desires'. Yet Eliot also realized the need for something like spiritual values, a transcendental aspiration through which the individual could feel contact with larger, and perhaps materially nebulous, areas of experience.

It is typical of Eliot's eclectic broad-mindedness that she could reject Catholic theology but rejoice in its spirituality. At the time she was writing *Silas Marner* Eliot wrote to her friend Barbara Bodichon:

> I have faith in the working-out of higher possibilities than the Catholic or any other church has presented, and those who have strength to wait and endure, are bound to accept no formula which their whole souls – their intellect as well as their emotions – do not embrace with entire reverence. The highest 'calling and election' is to *do without opium* and live through all our pain with conscious, clear-eyed endurance.
>
> (SL, p. 254)

It is interesting that Eliot here uses the very phrase, 'calling and election', with which William Dane the Dissenter justifies his disreputable actions in *Silas Marner*, but in the context of discussing the Catholic church. For Eliot all theologies held the possibilities and dangers of self-justification. It was too comfortable to feel one was close to God, tempting the weak not 'to wait and endure', not to live with 'clear-eyed endurance'. But when Eliot read the Catholic Newman's *Apologia pro Vita Sua* four years later she wrote to Sara Hennell of how it: 'affects me as the revelation of a life - how different in form from one's own, yet with how close a fellowship in its needs and burthens – I mean spiritual needs and burthens' (SL, p. 297). Eliot was not the only person in her time to feel that dichotomous urge to reject the comforts offered by orthodox religion, yet accept a concept of 'soul' and embrace a transcendental need.

The Metaphysical Society was formed in 1869, and Eliot knew many of its founders. The scientist Thomas Huxley was one of them, and later recalled that at that time he had created the word agnostic:

> I took thought, and invented what I conceived to be the appropriate title of 'agnostic'. It came into my head as suggestively antithetic to the 'gnostic' of Church history, who professed to know so much about the very things of which I was ignorant.[20]

It was obviously a useful concept to complicate the simple bifurcation Christian/atheist. Agnostics merely admitted not having knowledge, although they may adhere to a metaphoric, as opposed to literal, belief in such notions as soul. Eliot clearly came into this category, and also its slightly more militant form: 'Agnostics deny and repudiate, as immoral ... that there are propositions which men ought to believe, without logically satisfactory evidence'.[21] The need for evidence specifically reveals a scientific method of thinking: an hypothesis is set up, experiments conducted, or information collected and analysed, and the hypothesis confirmed, amended or rejected. Although scientists may have shafts of illumination and inspiration those nevertheless have to be tested, and the whole procedure is inimical to simple faith and revelation.

An earlier form of metaphysical inquiry, an attempt to create a religion of humanity, was that known as Positivism which sprang from the theories of Comte. The relationship between Eliot and Comte's work has been touched on in chapter 2 above, and the point made that although Eliot was not a Positivist as such she was certainly attracted to that form of humanism. Frederic Harrison, the leading contemporary English figure of Positivism, wrote of Eliot's attitudes to Comte:

> Much of his system she wholly refused to accept [but] ... With the cardinal ideas of Positivism – the cherishing and extension of all true religious sentiment, and the direction of that sentiment towards the well-being of mankind – not only was George

Eliot in profound sympathy, but no one else in our time has expressed those ideas with such power.

(*The Fortnightly Review*, March 1885)

These ideas can be found to some extent in many of the novels. The critic Terence Wright has argued, for example, that *Romola* can be seen:

> as a Positivist allegory in which the heroine passes through all three of Comte's stages, thereby tracing in her own life the history of Humanity. ... She represents all that is admirable in the moral development of mankind.[22]

Those three basic Comtean stages are: classical intellectual, medieval belief and the modern Religion of Humanity. Wright's fundamental thesis, however, is that Positivist ideas are most thoroughly embedded in the last novel, *Daniel Deronda*. One of the aspects of *Daniel Deronda* generations of readers have found hardest to grasp are the Hebraic elements. Wright argues these are not mere exemplifications of Judaism, but rather, they can be seen as transformed facets of Positivism.

In relation to the three stages of history Comte had written that: 'the whole course of Jewish history was a preparation for the monotheistic separation between the spiritual and temporal powers'.[23] The Christian era had developed from the polytheistic beliefs of the ancient Greek civilization, from which so much of modern art, literature and philosophy had evolved. Eliot, with her passion for Greek tragedy, was certainly not oblivious to that influence. On the novel's publication she wrote to Harriet Beecher Stowe: 'towards the Hebrews we western people who have been reared in Christianity, have a peculiar debt' (SL, p. 476). This echoes Comte's observation, made specifically from the perspective of Catholic France: 'Catholicism owes a debt of gratitude to Judaism which it has never paid; Positivism alone can discharge it'.[24] Eliot defined the debt, in her letter to Stowe, as: 'a peculiar thoroughness of fellowship in religious and moral sentiment. ... Christ was a Jew' (SL, p. 476). In the novel specifically Zionist concepts are presented in a Positivist context, partly by having Mordecai argue from genuine Rabbiac sources but with slight, very significant, variations. William Baker has observed:

> Mordecai's speeches at the 'Hand and Banner' contain many
> historical references which are to be found in the *Kuzari* ...
> [but] Mordecai and Halevi differ in their presentation of similar
> arguments. The Rabbi constantly refers to God and the Divine
> as the final arbiter. George Eliot's emphasis with Mordecai is
> more naturalistic and empirical than Halevi's.[25]

Baker argues a convincing case in some detail, illustrating how
the supernatural elements of Jewish theology in the twelfth-
century text referred to are converted in the novel into more
humanist ideas.

Comte had attempted a resolution of the apparent dichotomy
between intellect and feeling, or reason and emotion, which was a
central nineteenth-century concern. It required a paradoxical kind
of scientific intuition. Deronda, at Cambridge University, 'applied
himself vigorously to mathematics' (p. 219), the epitome of intellectual disciplines; but felt a 'wearing futility' because he was not
gaining: 'any insight into the principles which form the vital
connections of knowledge' (p. 220). The 'insight' comes from
intuition, and the 'vital connections' are those between intellect
and emotions. Deronda's dissatisfaction with his studies reflects
Comtean attitudes: 'even in Mathematics, the scientific character
is but too often purely superficial ... [because] of the tendency to
substitute the combination of signs for the higher processes of
thought'.[26] By 'knowledge' Comte, and in this instance Eliot, did
not mean the simple accumulation of facts, but a deep understanding into a subject, based on, but transcending, empirical
scientific method.

Klesmer is described as 'a felicitous combination of German ...
Semite ... artistic' (p. 77). Being German he is associated with
intellectual scholarship and the scientific method – cf. Casaubon's
inadequacy, and Eliot's work on Strauss and Feuerbach – and
Klesmer is also artistic. Music is, of course, the form of art closest
to science, fusing imagination and precision. When Klesmer criticizes Gwendolen it is for her inexactitude: 'you have not said to
yourself, "I must know this exactly," "I must understand this
exactly," "I must do this exactly"' (p. 297). The reiterated 'exactly'
is not intended pedantically, but scientifically: science is an exact
art for the Comtean. Deronda later points out that Gwendolen is
self-obsessed, and that: 'some real knowledge would give you an
interest in the world beyond the small drama of personal desires'

(p. 507). The 'real knowledge' here links with his own earlier desire for the 'vital connections of knowledge'. Deronda ultimately achieves the fusion in his own life when he is able to link his personal destiny with a racial one – which is also a human one, a bonding of the individual into the communal.

Although Deronda's own vital connections are with Judaism that is to some extent a dramatic exemplification of a wider truth. It is a Positivist belief that the fusing of reason and emotion, objective and subjective experience, will lead individuals towards real knowledge, a full understanding of life, that will reveal the vital connections between the apparent dichotomies and result in the achievement of that state Harrison termed (above) as 'the collective well-being of mankind'. Indeed, Deronda becomes interested in Judaism long before his own Jewishness is known to him. Mirah's experiences: 'had flashed on him the hitherto neglected reality that Judaism was something still throbbing in human lives' (p. 411). He acknowledges that those 'human lives' are like his, they are all part of the Positivist collective well-being of mankind. This is eventually expressed by Mordecai:

> what is it to be rational – what is it to feel the light of divine reason growing stronger? ... It is to see more and more of the hidden bonds that bind and consecrate change ... the past becomes my parent, and the future stretches towards me the appealing arms of children.
>
> (pp. 587–8)

The humanly 'rational' is synthesized here with 'divine reason' to illuminate the 'hidden bonds' that exist across and through time. Despite its being expressed in a Jewish context in the novel this is a Comtean concept: 'The Great Being is the whole constituted by the beings, past, future, and present, which co-operate willingly in perfecting the order of the world'.[27] It is also an idea Eliot had held for a long time, and had explicated twenty years earlier in her essay 'The Natural History of German Life' (cf. chapter 1 above). It is impossible to determine precisely whether she came to the idea directly from Comte, who had published it in French in 1854, or Riehl, or had formulated it herself and merely found it confirmed in other sources. To some degree it may be linked to the Wordsworthian influence discussed in chapter 3 above. At his spiritual nadir Silas Marner 'hated the thought of his past' (p. 65), and had no sense of future, and even very little of the present. His rehabilitation occurs when these factors are united in his perception. In any event, wherever the original source lies, the idea of commonality embracing different times and places cannot be extricated from the novel and simply be categorized as Zionist.

Mordecai, although Jewish, does also appear to be a visionary in a Positivist manner. On meeting Deronda his response is: 'the long-contemplated figure had come as an emotional sequence of Mordecai's firmest theoretic convictions; it had been wrought from the imagery of his most passionate life; and it inevitably reappeared' (p. 536). His 'most passionate life' is spiritual, but materially so – bound into the actual destiny of the race. The synthesis of 'emotional' and 'theoretic' is again a resolution of the dialectic of intuition/feeling/emotion and intellect/scientific/reasoning. Mordecai's hypothesis that an emissary will appear is 'inevitably' confirmed by the arrival of Deronda. The narrative voice itself argues:

> even strictly-measuring science could hardly have got on without that forecasting ardour which feels the agitations of discovery beforehand, and has a faith in its preconception that surmounts many failures of experiment.
>
> (p. 572)

There has to be a reconciliation between the apparent opposites of 'strictly-measuring science' and 'faith' – a synthesis that makes Huxley's agnosticism positive and creative rather than merely sterile. It is achieved by an 'ardour' that is intellectual and emotionally spiritual.

This form of humanism, the religion of humanity, was one of the ways in which Victorians like Eliot came to terms with loss of conventional religious faith. Not being able to embrace either the bleak despair of Froude's philosophic nihilism or the complacent certainties of Oliphant and Wood, Eliot searched for some kind of purpose and found it in the linking of all humanity. Mordecai's teaching of Deronda reverberates with that idea: 'Revive the organic centre' (p. 592), 'the divine Unity embraced . . . the ultimate unity of mankind' (p. 802). It is significant that 'Unity' rather than 'divine' is capitalized. A more conventionally Judaic text might have reversed that, and the orthography is another way in which Eliot as the writer emphasizes the humanism against the theological.

Eliot's first contribution to the *Westminster Review*, in 1851, had been a review of Robert Mackay's book *The Progress of the Intellect*. In it she had quoted with approval Mackay's assertion 'Religion and science are inseparable' (SEP, p. 272), whilst 'The Positivist Creed' also began with the affirmation: 'I believe in the unity of science and religion'.[28] In her fiction Eliot worked with increasing intensity towards illustrating not only the possibility, but the actual necessity of synthesizing the great dialectical dichotomies of her time. She fused diverse forces – French Enlightenment, German Metaphysics, Romanticism, Positivism, and a good deal of actual scientific understanding – to forge her own belief in the unity and value of human experience. That faith can be seen in the celebration in *Adam Bede* of 'the secret of deep human sympathy' (p. 224); Silas Marner's rescue from spiritual nihilism when his compassion is roused by the vulnerable Eppie; whilst in *Felix Holt* Esther makes the decision in favour of emotional fulfilment in the light of 'the largeness of the world' (p. 590), prefiguring Dorothea's similar choice in *Middlemarch* just as: 'she felt the largeness of the world and the manifold wakings of men to labour and endurance' (p. 846). In *Daniel Deronda*, on the other hand, Gwendolen is trapped by her egoism into isolation: 'I have been a cruel woman. And I am forsaken' (p. 877). It is Deronda and Mirah, who have 'awakened' to 'duty' (p. 875), who find the mutual 'blessings of love' (p. 879). Characters become aware of their own profound desires at moments of crisis, and those needs are always perceived in terms of the unity of human experience.

Almost at the end of her life the reviewer W. H. Mallock wrote of Eliot's philosophic adventurousness: 'She is the first great *godless* writer of fiction that has appeared in England ... the first that has appeared in Europe' (*The Edinburgh Review*, October 1879). This would have read shockingly to many of those readers who enjoyed Eliot's novels, and later in the article Mallock qualifies his statement: 'without God, not against Him. ... The glory and the devotion that was once given to God is transferred silently to man' (ibid.). It is a measure of Eliot's greatness as a novelist, in addition to her stature as a thinker, that for many of her contemporaries she embodied that spirit which, seeing the effective death of God, was nevertheless able to affirm the reality of humanity's moral being and celebrate a purposive life.

5

Education and Women's Roles

Mr Tulliver, in *The Mill on the Floss*, decides 'to give Tom a good eddication: an eddication as'll be a bread to him' (p. 56). As a consequence Tom, his son, is sent away to live in the house of the Reverend Stelling who boarded and taught two pupils in order to supplement his income. Maggie, Tulliver's daughter, however, has to make do with a local education. It is important that Tulliver does not look upon this as a deprivation of the girl, and he certainly does not act from any malevolence towards his daughter. He explains that Maggie is: 'allays at her book! But it's bad – it's bad . . . a woman's no business wi' being so clever; it'll turn to trouble . . . she'll read the books and understand 'em, better nor half the folks as are growed up' (p. 66). Tulliver oscillates between concern at Maggie's propensity for reading, and admiration for it: 'being so clever' is a great talent, but it is unnatural in a female and will lead 'to trouble' for 'a woman'. It is for this reason Tulliver's attitudes towards his daughter's education are not deliberately repressive, but protective – he is both admiring and regretful of Maggie's intelligence. His comment on the gender difference between Maggie and Tom is: 'It's a pity but what she'd been the lad' (p. 68). This is a recognition that Maggie is more scholarly than Tom, and not only acknowledges by implication - although Tulliver himself cannot quite comprehend it – that Maggie is being deprived, but that Tom too will be subjected to the kind of education that is not in his best interests. For Tom has 'a sort o' commonsense' but: 'he reads but poorly, and can't abide the books, and spells all wrong' (p. 69). Nevertheless Tulliver goes ahead with his plans, and predictably Tom's education is a burden and a failure. Tulliver is not presented as particularly stupid or oppressive, but a man holding typical attitudes of his day – and although the novel is set thirty years or so earlier, the beliefs prevalent in the initial reader's society too. Indeed, Tulliver is supported by Riley, a man who was himself 'rather highly educated for an auctioneer and appraiser' (p. 63).

This discussion of education illustrates Eliot's concern with an issue of immense contemporary interest, whilst the juxtaposition of son and daughter in relation to the theme reveals her awareness of the gender discourse underlying – or being excluded from – that social development. Her relatively complex presentation of the issues, however, the way in which Tulliver is well-meaning, although in practice harmful, and the fact that the male Tom is as much victim as the female Maggie, again demonstrate that it is never easy to categorize Eliot's position. She clearly believed in the benefits of real female learning, but also the necessity for the right education for everyone.

Eliot realized that education was both formal and informal, scholarly and cultural – in the broadest, social sense. Also, that it was not merely a matter of knowledge or accomplishment, but more profoundly, a force with truly moral – not narrowly moralistic – dimensions, concerned with self-understanding as well as comprehension of the external world. All these aspects of the subject are explored in the novels.

At the beginning of the nineteenth century there was no national system of education in Britain. The sons of the wealthy attended public schools, epitomized by Eton and Harrow, then went up to university at Oxford or Cambridge. The daughters of such families were educated at home by governesses, and perhaps specialist private tutors. The sons of middling-class families went to private schools, which were smaller, newer and less expensive than public schools, and whose curricula tended toward subjects of value in trade and commerce rather than the traditional university tripos. Increasingly throughout the nineteenth century grammar schools also became an important channel for the education of the sons of fee-paying bourgeois families. Middling-class daughters were taught in small private schools or by tutors visiting the home. The mass of the people either gained a rudimentary learning in one or more of the diverse establishments available – local dame, Free, Radical, Sunday, schools – or remained illiterate. There were, of course, many specific exceptions to this overall pattern, but they do not negate its general truth.

A social pyramid existed, with the great majority of the people forming the unlettered base. Even within that picture of privilege and discrimination there were further issues: such as the concern that at all levels the standard of education was relatively poor; and females, on the whole, fared less well than males.

Two organizations were set up just before Eliot's birth with hopes of remedying the situation. In 1811 Andrew Bell created the National Society for Promoting the Education of the Poor; and three years later Joseph Lancaster's British and Foreign School Society came into being. These were both organized around religious beliefs: the former, Anglicanism; and the latter, Nonconformity – and to some extent both systems were motivated by a moral missionary zeal, the concept that a better educated populace would embrace a stricter idea of morality. The perceived need for this arose from the pressures caused by an expanding population that was also becoming increasingly urban. In earlier small rural communities people did commit sins and crimes, but they were generally contained by, and within, the community. The village parson's control or influence, with the squire's support, however, was not replicated in the rapidly expanding industrial areas, in which crime and immorality were often seen as endemic.

Eliot's three great novels that are set in the period of the late 1820s/early 1830s are not mere attempts to recapture the nostalgia of her girlhood. It is not coincidental that in all of them both education and the theme of the relationship between urban and rural are central. In the first of them the mill that is on the Floss is in the country, but the characters become increasingly reliant on the town of St Ogg's. In the middle book, *Felix Holt*, the town of Treby is dominant in some respects, but in others subordinate to Transome Court, the equivalent of the manor house. In *Middlemarch* action and power is divided between the manufacturing town and the landed gentry, with the metropolis ultimately triumphing over both.

The immorality of urban life was not simply theologically or theoretically offensive, it was perceived as giving rise to a general lawlessness that threatened public order, and even the political fabric. As early as 1806 Patrick Colquhoun argued that a system of universal education would have the:

> noble aim of preventing those calamities which lead to idleness and crimes. ... By shielding the minds of youth against the vices that are most likely to beset them ... sufficient education to enable them to preserve ... the religious and moral instruc-

tion they receive, is all that is, or ought ever to be, in contemplation.[1]

The purpose of education is stated unequivocally in terms of its parameters, 'religious and moral instruction'; and very concept of instruction, the learning and assimilation of definite rules, rather than an educational discovery of ideas, signifies how strictly utilitarian is Colquhoun's approach. Although the individual will benefit, by being shielded from 'vices', the main 'noble aim' of the process is to protect society at large from the 'calamities' of 'idleness and crimes'. It is probably significant that Colquhoun was writing shortly after the death of the Prime Minister, William Pitt, at a time when the French were dominating western Europe in the Napoleonic Wars. There was a widespread sense of despondency, a double fear of the possibility of invasion by the rampant French army, and that of internal insurrection inspired by the French Revolution of the previous decade. Certainly Colquhoun was not alone in looking to education, or instruction, to bolster the security of the classes with most to lose. In the following year Richard Sharpe spoke in parliament of the need for formal education, which:

> would give habits of industry and attention ... though they [children] should forget all their learning, [they] would have collected many beneficial habits of an indelible nature; habits of submission and respect for their superiors ... and the fear of punishment.
>
> (*Hansard*, 24 April 1807)

This is putting the case very bluntly, but even so Sharpe was ahead of his time. As Napoleon's army and navy gradually began to be overcome, the fear of taking a step into a system of national education for the very first time, and the foment that might follow, became greater than that of invasion or insurrection. In his 1814 poem *The Excursion* Wordsworth, the poet who most influenced Eliot, nevertheless recorded the need for a universal system of education:

> O for the coming of that glorious time
> When, prizing knowledge as her noblest wealth

> And best protection, this imperial Realm,
> While she exacts allegiance, shall admit
> An obligation, on her part, to *teach*
> Them who are born to serve her and obey;
> Binding herself by statute to secure
> For all the children whom her soil maintains
> The rudiments of letters, and inform
> The mind with moral and religious truth.[2]

Wordsworth is clear that the purpose of education is, at least partially, the maintenance of social order. Those who 'are born to serve ... and obey' will not be made discontent by their new 'knowledge', but because it consists of 'moral and religious truth' will presumably become more socially and politically acquiescent. In such a case education is seen as an investment for the State as well as 'An obligation', for a knowledgeable populous is a government's 'noblest wealth', to be secured by parliamentary 'statute'. The 'her' and reiterated 'she' genders the nation as matriarchal, as caring and protective of its 'children', a term used literally of the prospective pupils, and also metaphorically of all the population who serve and obey. Wordsworth's own note to these lines draws attention to the fact that he sees Bell's work as providing an embryonic State and national education system: 'it is impossible to overrate the benefit which might accrue to humanity from [its] universal application ... under an enlightened and conscientious government'.[3] The idea that education had a primarily moral value – though in a much narrower sense than Eliot conceived it – recurred throughout the century. Despite the support from such diverse people as politicians and poets, however, the religious societies organizing a more or less nationwide scheme of education were left without formal government support until the year after the Franchise Reform Act of 1832.

The financial grant made in 1833 to the voluntary agencies began a process of government involvement that accelerated through the period in which Eliot was writing the novels, and led to the completion of a system of compulsory schooling very shortly after her death. The claims and needs of industrialists were an important feature of the development of national education. Only two years after the government had begun to give the voluntary educational organizations grants Andrew Ure wrote from an economist's perspective of the necessity for industrial and economic expansion, and the need for education in order to achieve that:

> since for the physical well-being of men a sound mind must actuate a sound body ... the uneducated state of the 'lower orders' ... is the dark den of incendiarism and misrule ... which, if not cleared out, will give birth ere long to disastrous eruptions in every other province.[4]

Clearly Ure, on behalf of employers, had come to Sharpe's earlier conclusion that education would teach the 'lower orders', the employees at large, due 'respect and submission'. The conflicts of the intervening period had led to a pragmatism – revealed by the uncompromising language, 'if not cleared out', 'disastrous eruptions' – in which Wordsworth's earlier sentiments of noblest wealth and obligation had little place. It was that pragmatic world, orientated towards the economics of capitalism, in which Eliot addressed the issues.

That the government took the capitalist argument seriously is illustrated by the appointment of a Royal Commission, under the Chairmanship of the Duke of Newcastle, into the State of Popular Education in England. It reported in 1861 – a year in which Ure's book, significantly, was reprinted – and the most immediate result was the instigation of a system of payment by results, whereby teachers were paid according to the attendance records of their pupils, and the success those children had in passing examinations in the three R's (reading, writing and arithmetic). It was an attempt to improve educational productivity by applying the theories of manufacturing economics to the problem. Robert Lowe, supervising the legislation through parliament, displayed an awareness of this:

> I cannot promise the House that this system will be an economical one, and I cannot promise that it will be an efficient one, but I can promise that it shall be one or the other. If it is not cheap, it shall be efficient; if it is not efficient it shall be cheap.
>
> (*Hansard*, 13 February 1862)

The fact that it failed abysmally to be efficient does not detract from the intent, and the deep concern that intention manifests, to create an educated populace. The terms in which it was attempted were pedagogically absurd, and Lowe's attitude later in the speech rather defensive:

> Now, it is said, that by this plan we are degrading education. . . . The truth is, what we fix is a *minimum* of education, not a *maximum*. We propose to give no grant for the attendance of children at school unless they can read, write, and cipher; but we do not say they shall learn no more.
>
> (ibid.)

Despite this theory payment by results led, inevitably, to the cramming of superficial knowledge that was soon forgotten, and the simple training of pupils to pass examinations. Paradoxically, *education* in its truest sense was the first casualty – teaching the ability to think and perceive, encouraging intellectual curiosity, the exploration of connections between diverse phenomena and subjects, were all activities for which there was no payment, and were therefore not performed by teachers.

Eliot's insistence that learning must not be equated with instruction, a mere recital of unrelated, and uncomprehended, facts is part of the crucial contemporary debate. Almost the first thing Tom tells Maggie about his initial schooling at the Academy is of another pupil: 'I gave Spouncer a black eye, I know – that's what he got by wanting to leather *me*' (p. 86). This is, in effect, a pupil's view of schooling, and refracts the arguments about educational methods current at the time by showing that children are not models that can be made to behave in accordance with theoretical values. The episode reflects Eliot's own life-long distrust of the imposition of theory onto any kind of reality. As it was published in 1860, whilst the Newcastle Commission was sitting, it also shows the degree to which Eliot was exploring the very central issues of her day.

For Eliot true education had to be appropriate to the interests and abilities of the pupil. Teaching an inappropriate curriculum, as many of the schools were, gave no benefits to the pupils - who neither learnt what they were nominally taught, nor those subjects that would have been of use and interest to them, because they were absent from the classroom. Under Stelling's private teaching Tom is subjected to Latin grammar and Euclid, despite his predilections being quite different:

Tom could predict with accuracy what number of horses were cantering behind him, he could throw a stone right into the centre of a given ripple, he could guess to a fraction how many lengths of his stick it would take to reach across the playground, and could draw almost perfect squares on his slate without any measurement.

(p. 208)

Tom's accomplishments are not negligible, they show some mental dexterity, as well as physical skill, and could be of considerable practical value to a countryman. Because Tom is unable to learn the syllabus Stelling:

very soon set down poor Tom as a thoroughly stupid lad; for though by hard labour he could get particular declensions into his brain, anything so abstract as the relation between cases and terminations could by no means get such a lodgement there as to enable him to recognise a chance genitive or dative. This struck Mr Stelling as something more than natural stupidity: he suspected obstinacy.

(pp. 207–8)

The problem is that no one is entirely to blame for the impasse. Tom is being taught the wrong subjects, Stelling as a graduate of Oxford University is unable to appreciate the value of any other type of education, and is simply carrying out – as he understands them – the wishes of Mr Tulliver, who wants Tom to have a better education than he had, a not unlaudable objective in itself, although his motivation is not altogether disinterested. The nature of the education is tested when Tom is pitched into the real world of earning a living. Mr Deane explains:

Your poor father went the wrong way to work in giving you an education. ... you've had a sort of learning that's all very well for a young fellow like our Mr Stephen Guest, who'll have nothing to do but sign cheques all his life; and may as well have Latin inside his head as any other sort of stuffing.

(p. 314)

Deane is not criticizing the idea of education but rather that of 'learning', of the gaining of essentially esoteric knowledge such as

'Latin', which is a 'sort of stuffing'. It has no practical value in the day-to-day business world, and may even get in the way of useful understanding. Tom defends himself, and also condemns his schooling, in more ironic terms: 'I don't see why the Latin need hinder me from getting on in business: I shall soon forget it all . . . I had to do my lessons at school; but I always thought they'd never be of any use to me afterwards' (ibid.). The notion that 'lessons at school' have no connection with life 'afterwards' is one that has bedevilled educationists for a long time, and Tom is echoing the implication in Sharpe's view, quoted above, that learning may be forgottten without concern. Here Tom's naive honesty highlights a fundamental problem for the period in which, in all essentials, our own educational system was being created.

The novel deals with private schooling rather than the Royal Commission's 'Popular Education' – but the principles remain the same, energy is misdirected because of theoretical considerations that are out of touch with the requirements of reality. These issues continued to be central as the age continued its pursuit of widening education. Almost within Eliot's lifetime the cumulative effect of Forster's 1870 Education Act, with Sandon's of 1876 and Mundella's in 1880 was to create a State system of compulsory elementary education for all children in England. The debate about the nature and purpose of education, of course, continues.

Eliot's concern with education went beyond basic issues into wider areas of experience. Although the rudiments of literacy and numeracy were obviously important, for Eliot those were the beginning of a long process. No one was more deeply interested in moral considerations, yet she did not see learning as performing a simple, morally didactic purpose. There were two main functions of education: full development of personal potential, of which the moral sense was a central factor, but that also encompassed emotional and intellectual maturity, and an aesthetic sense; and, when it was appropriate for them, to enable individuals to perform wider social roles than would otherwise be possible. Given the nature of her own education, and gender, and the circumstances of Victorian life, it is not surprising that she explored these facets with particular, although not exclusive, reference to female experience. In 1868, for instance, she wrote to her friend, the feminist Clementia Taylor: 'I do sympathise with you most emphatically in the desire to see women socially elevated – educated equally with men' (SL, p. 333). Most of the women holding Taylor's ideological position saw education solely as a means to a career, but for Eliot equality of education meant having opportunity, choice – which may involve employment, but did not necessarily lead to that end. She was always aware of the diverse needs of different individuals.

Education in its broadest sense is cultural as well as formal. When, in *Adam Bede*, Hetty is infatuated with the upper-class Arthur Donnithorne at the expense of the artisan Adam the narrator comments that it had: 'nothing to do with the love felt by sweet girls of eighteen in our days; but all this happened, you must remember, nearly sixty years ago, and Hetty was quite uneducated – a simple farmer's girl' (p. 145). There is both truth and irony in this laconic commentary. Formal education had changed during the 'nearly sixty years' between the novel's setting and its being written, but the propensity of 'sweet girls of eighteen' to become emotionally involved with young gentlemen had not. That was partly a matter of romantic immaturity, but also because marriage was still the main form of female social mobility. Young women like Hetty could convince themselves a mutual love existed when they thought of their possible futures: either as a hard-working housewife, or as a lady with servants. Hetty's 'little dream-world' of being the squire's wife is shattered by Arthur's letter explaining why, for reasons of social class, they cannot marry: 'the crushing blow ... afflicted her pleasure-craving nature with an overpowering pain' (p. 379). The idea of love has been connected in Hetty's mind with: 'the prospect of the wedding that was to come at last when she would have a silk gown and a great many clothes all at once' (p. 381). This is hardly the kind of wedding Adam's wife would enjoy. Although Hetty is presented as a superficial young woman, with 'a luxurious and vain nature' (p. 381), she is not entirely untypical of her class. Part of the problem lies in the related factors of education and opportunity. Hetty has been culturally influenced by certain attitudes to romance, marriage and social mobility. A stable and mature personality could accept that reality lies somewhere outside those culturally endorsed realms, but a shallow character cannot – nor is it just a matter of education, for an educated Hetty could at best cope with the reality, she would not be able to change the actual prospects of life.

Maggie Tulliver is from a slightly higher class, but nevertheless basically also 'a farmer's girl', she is more intelligent and has greater emotional depth than Hetty, but faces a very similar dilemma. Her father denies Maggie the education she is capable of intellectually benefiting from, but even if she had received it the lack of opportunity to use it remains. Almost the only careers open were those of teacher or governess. The former had neither public respect nor a decent income; the latter were often placed in the awful position of belonging neither to the family circle nor the servants' quarters. The employers treated them like servants, while the family's employees suspected them of being a form of spy or informer. The fictional ones, such as Charlotte Brontë's eponymous and popular heroine Jane Eyre, who achieved marriage with the master of the house were very much more plentiful in novels than reality. The opening of Helen Selina Hay's poem 'The German Teacher' captures the more prevalent mood:

> The long day's done and she sits still,
> And quiet, in the gathering gloom:
> What are the images that fill
> Those absent eyes – that silent room?[5]

The day's work was long, and the gloom and silence convey why the eyes are 'absent', for the teacher hardly exists as a woman in her own right. She is not performing a vital social function that earns her love and respect: when the schoolroom is empty so is she.

In *The Mill on the Floss*, despite Maggie having greater intelligence and moral perception than Hetty, she too falls into a romance that must inevitably end unhappily. Her response to Stephen Guest's covert attention throws her into confusion:

> Such things could have had no perceptible effect on a thoroughly well-educated young lady with a perfectly balanced mind. . . . In poor Maggie's highly strung, hungry nature – just come away from a third rate schoolroom, with all its jarring sounds and petty round of tasks – these apparently trivial causes had the effect of rousing and exalting her imagination.
>
> (p. 494)

Two features make Maggie vulnerable to the attractions of Stephen, a young man she knows is morally forbidden to her: her own 'highly strung, hungry nature', and the aridity of what might be called her career. Maggie's personality is in part sensitive and hungry because of the awfulness of the 'third rate schoolroom'. The 'jarring sounds' specifically contrast with the 'fine music sung by a fine bass voice' that Maggie has just experienced; and the schoolroom's 'petty round of tasks' sets into relief the singing's 'provincial amateur fashion' (ibid.), lending it a cultural depth it would not have enjoyed if Maggie's own circumstances had been less constrained. The juxtaposition of 'petty round of tasks' and 'trivial causes' might well have brought to the mind of a Victorian reader John Keble's very popular sentiment:

> The trivial round, the common task,
> Would furnish all we ought to ask;
> Room to deny ourselves; a road
> To bring us, daily, nearer God.[6]

This became part of a favourite hymn, and was one of the most well-known verses of Eliot's time.[7] It is an ironic association. In the context Keble's conventional religious sentiment is inadequate against the stifling deficiency of education available to Maggie, and the lack of opportunity for her to use and express her intelligence in ways that would both satisfy her as an individual and be socially productive. There is also an ironic prolepsis in that Maggie, partially under the influence of her sterile working life, will not 'deny' herself, but will seek escape with Stephen despite knowing the pain it will cause her cousin Lucy – taking herself, in practice, further from God.

The problem of the, even partially, educated female was that society as a whole did not take them seriously. Adam Bede, for instance, comments on the intellectually inclined Curate, Ryde: 'he wrote books; but as for math'matics and the natur o' things, he was as ignorant as a woman' (p. 226). Women do not understand the important aspects of life, even when they are admitted to be intelligent. Seth, for example, pays the curious compliment to Dinah Morris that 'she writes wonderful for a woman' (p. 372). In neither case is there any narrational commentary on the discourse of Adam and Seth – but the structure of the novel asserts Dinah's value. Adam recognizes it in marrying her, and Seth's own state of literacy in comparison with Dinah's graphically illustrates the patronizing nature of his remarks. The authorial restraint, and the fact that neither character means ill towards Dinah in particular, or 'woman' in general, but have simply adopted conventional social attitudes to the education and intelligence of females, makes the point with subtle emphasis.

The kind of half education that often passed for female learning is criticized in the character of Mrs Transome in *Felix Holt*:

> For thirty years she had led the monotonous narrowing life which used to be the lot of our poorer gentry.... When she was young she had been thought wonderfully clever and accomplished, and had been rather ambitious of intellectual superiority – had secretly picked out for private reading the lighter parts of dangerous French authors – and in company had been able to talk of Mr Burke's style, or of Chateaubriand's eloquence – had laughed at the *Lyrical Ballads*.
>
> (p. 104)

Despite the retrospective setting of the novel, 'life which used to be', Eliot always explored contemporary issues, and the experiences of the young Mrs Transome, in the early years of the nineteenth century, were in essence those of many young women of the 1860s. The class definitions had widened – the greater social mobility resulting from economic dynamicism, and the spread of education itself, had jointly broadened the base of female education beyond the narrow band of the 'gentry'. The emphasis, nevertheless, remained on being 'clever and accomplished', breeding an attitude 'rather ambitious of intellectual superiority'. The satiric tone is revealed by the practical extent of that intellectuality: a superficial acquaintance with 'the lighter parts of dangerous French authors'. This might be decoded as the romantic – and romanticized – episodes in novels that dealt with aspects of sexual passion, books thought of as 'wicked' and 'sinful' (ibid.). The veneer of culture is attained as a mere social adornment, to enable the woman to talk 'in company' of writers she had not understood. The clinching factor in the satire, despite there being no direct narrative comment on it, is the laughing at Wordsworth's '*Lyrical Ballads*', which Eliot herself held in enormous esteem.

The idea that much female education was designed solely to produce elevated drawing-room gossip is a recurring one. It is not that male education, or conversation, was very much better, but it had a slightly different form of superficiality – and on the whole Eliot dealt in more detail with, as it was known, the distaff side. This theme too is linked with the rural/urban dichotomy. An ideal Wordsworthian notion of rural education is that enjoyed by Effie in *Silas Marner*:

> she would turn her ear to some sudden bird-note, and Silas learned to please her by signs of hushed stillness, that they might listen for the note to come again ... the child's mind was growing into knowledge.... It was an influence which must gather force with every new year: the tones that stirred Silas's heart grew articulate, and called for more distinct answers.
>
> (p. 185)

This is true learning: of the immediate, not a theoretic, world; from genuine curiosity, rather than an enforced regimen; and with a teacher who is able to respond to specific questions, and has a personal delight in the process. It is a pre-literate stage, and not one a child may remain in '– but it is a more productive atmosphere in which to start learning.

The urban, if not urbane, drawing-rooms are represented in the novel by the visiting: 'Miss Gunns, the wine merchant's daughters from Lytherly, dressed in the height of fashion' (p. 145). Their middling-class education, as befitting a 'merchant's' daughters, causes them to be disappointed in the appearance, attitudes and behaviour of the leaders of rural society:

> The Miss Gunns smiled stiffly, and thought what a pity it was that these rich country people, who could afford to buy such good clothes (really Miss Nancy's lace and silk were very costly), should be brought up in utter ignorance and vulgarity. She actually said 'mate' for 'meat', ''appen' for 'perhaps'.... Miss Nancy, indeed, had never been to any school higher than Dame Tedman's ... yet she had the essential attributes of a lady – high veracity, delicate honour in her dealings, deference to others, and refined personal habits.
>
> (pp. 147–8)

This comprises a fair statement of Eliot's views on the attributes real education should imbue: 'veracity', 'honour', 'deference' and refinement. The Miss Gunns mistake fashion in dress and pronunciation, in which their education has dealt, for learning; and are confused because Nancy clearly comes from a background that could afford to buy a fashionable education.

The problem, Eliot realized, could not be solved easily and quickly by any particular system of education. The cultural factors were ingrained. The Miss Gunns are completely unable to appreciate Nancy's value, seeing it only as 'utter ignorance and vulgarity'. Even if a perfect educational programme could be constructed, for at least a generation it would be working against the mainstream culture. But whilst education is a commodity that has to be sold it will be bought only if it is offered in those terms currently acceptable. This meant a perpetuating system, in which when the Miss Gunns became wives and mothers themselves they would persuade their husbands to buy for their daughters the kind of education they had. The issue came to exercise the minds of many writers as it became increasingly obvious that the middling classes, and the females in particular, were responsible for the broad education of much of the populace at large. There were many novels during the period testifying to the importance of the subject, and to the fact that Eliot was in the mainstream of her society's concerns – although rather in advance of its thinking on most matters.

In 1865, for example, Charlotte Yonge's *The Clever Woman of the Family* was published. The Clever Woman, Rachel Curtis, is twenty-five years old and seeks to be a teacher. Unlike Maggie Tulliver, that is not some kind of necessity, for she and her sister Grace live in a household that boasts 'five maids, the coachman, and butler'.[8] Rachel deliberately rejects the normal paths of philanthropy:

> The quiet Lady Bountiful duties that had sufficed her mother and sister were too small and easy to satisfy a soul burning at the report of the great cry going up to heaven from a world of sin and woe.
>
> (p. 6)

Rachel Curtis, like Dorothea Brooke, looks for great issues. The tone, juxtaposing 'small and easy' duties with 'a soul burning', is amused and gently mocking, but that does not preclude the importance of the issue. The factor Rachel's mother and sister find too large to grapple with is education. Rachel bemoans the limited nature of her involvement:

> this is all I am doing for my fellow-creatures.... One class of half-grown lads, and those grudged to me! ... I have pottered about cottages and taught at schools in the *dilettante* way of the young lady who thinks it her duty to be charitable; and I am told ... that I may be satisfied.
>
> (p. 3)

She is not of the social class who were expected to become professional teachers, or indeed earn a living in any way at all. Such young ladies undertake 'charitable' tasks as a social function, but are not expected to become enthusiasts. Rachel is, however, given the opportunity to exercise her aspirations when less financially fortunate cousins arrive:

> It was not ameliorating the condition of the masses, but it was educating those who might ameliorate them; and Rachel gladly hailed the prospect of a vocation that might be conducted without pain to her mother.
> Young children of her own class were not exactly what her dream of usefulness had devised; but she had already a decided theory of education.
>
> (p. 7)

The difference between occupation and 'vocation' is crucial, for the former would cause 'pain to her mother', it would be stepping outside the class conventions that so clearly limited the horizons of young women with some education and a great deal of energy. There is also a recognition that 'children of her own class' do need educating, with the implication that the education they might expect would be inadequate, of the type, perhaps, with which the Miss Gunns were satisfied. Rachel's 'decided theory of education' suggests an independent approach that was not likely to consist of merely teaching fashion in dress and enunciation. Later Rachel writes an essay which she claims:

> is to be the beginning of a series, exposing the fallacies of woman's life as at present conducted; and out of these I mean

to point the way to more consistent, more independent, better combined exertion.

(pp. 51–2)

This seems to be a powerful feminist argument, and as it stands might have been linked with an editorial that appeared in a quarterly journal the following year. Under the title 'The Work We Have To Do' the argument runs:

> The truth is too often lost sight of, that the real interests of men and women are inseparable and identical, and that it is impossible to raise up a race of sober, well-conducted, self-respecting workmen, while their mothers, sisters, and future wives are left in poverty and degradation.
>
> (*The Englishwoman's Review*, October 1866)

An improvement in living and working conditions coupled with better education appears to be the answer, and the direction that Rachel's thought is taking her. That is all in the mainstream of feminist thinking in the mid-Victorian period, and easily accords with Rachel's views on social amelioration.

Ultimately, though, Charlotte Yonge draws back from the fundamental implications of her novel. Rachel encounters the great emotional force of love and is presented, in the text, with a choice between the satisfactions of a public and a private life. The early whimsical irony is turned against her, and her cleverness shown to be just that, rather than a deeper intellectuality:

> Rachel was constantly thrown with Mr Clare ... reaping much benefit from intercourse with such a mind. Many of her errors had chiefly arisen from the want of some one whose superiority she could feel, and her old presumptions withered up to nothing when she measured her own powers with those of a highly educated man ... unwilling as she would have been to own it, a woman's tone of thought is commonly moulded by the masculine intellect.
>
> (p. 337)

Being the clever woman of a fairly ordinary, squire's, family is not in the end much of an achievement. In the conclusion of the novel 'her errors' are not simply those of over-estimating her own intellect, but also include many of the views she had held. Those errors are shown to emanate from 'presumptions'. The emphasis here is not, as it might be in an Eliot novel, on the inadequacy of the woman's education, but only on the superiority of the 'highly educated man'. The narrational discourse, unlike those in the quotations from Eliot's work, draws a didactic generalization, acknowledging that Rachel would have disagreed, that 'the masculine intellect' moulds 'a woman's tone of thought'. Yonge offers no analysis as to why this, if true – and it is presented as such – might be the case. Yonge draws the reader into considering fundamental issues, and even into taking up radical stances, only to undermine them and re-position characters and readers alike happily within the status quo. Rachel the erstwhile radical concludes as contented wife and mother, admitting on the final page: 'Contact with really clever people has shown me that I am slow and unready' (p. 367). It is hardly a powerful resolution to the real dilemma of many earnest and ambitious young women, and leads to Rachel accepting her husband's opinion that she had a 'plodding intellectuality' (ibid.). Dorothea Brooke's marriage and motherhood, whatever self-abnegation they may be thought to have involved, do not end in such degradation, for it is never suggested that her mind is inferior to Will's – only her opportunities for using it.

Throughout the 1860s there was an increasing urgency in the education debate, and it was linked with the almost constant intellectual reappraisal of the questions of women's potential intelligence, education and general cultural, social and political status. Within that context the novels of Charlotte Yonge and similar writers tended to allow, or encourage, female readers a vicarious, fantasy rebellion against prevailing conventions only to more firmly assert by implication male hegemony. Mary Braddon's eponymous heroine Aurora Floyd, for example, sees her pet dog kicked by a male servant – and retribution is swift:

Aurora sprang upon him like a beautiful tigress, and catching the collar of his fustian jacket in her slight hands, rooted him to the spot upon which he stood. The grasp of those slender hands, convulsed by passion, was not to be easily shaken off ... she towered above him, her cheeks white with rage, her eyes flashing fury, her hat fallen off, and her black hair tumbling about her shoulders, sublime in her passion. The man

> crouched beneath the grasp of the imperious creature ... [she]
> rained a shower of blows upon his clumsy shoulders with her
> slender whip ... stinging like a rod of flexible steel in that little
> hand.

(p. 116)

Female dominance is played out here unambiguously, as 'The
man crouched beneath the grasp of the imperious creature'; and
perhaps even sadistically as she rained stinging blows on him
with her 'rod of flexible steel'. It is not impossible to see an
encoding of sexuality too in descriptions such as 'convulsed by
passion ... towered above him ... eyes flashing ... hat fallen off
... hair tumbling ... sublime in her passion'. It could be argued
that many female readers who felt oppressed and repressed are
being encouraged to enter a fantasy of release in this episode.

Braddon was a very popular novelist, and she was by no means
alone in this kind of writing. Aurora is to some extent throughout
the novel seeking a kind of independence. That was a recurring
feature of many popular heroines. The work of Ouida, another
extremely popular woman novelist, provides many examples.
Cigarette in *Under Two Flags*, which was published in 1867, the
year after *Felix Holt*, defies propriety by following the French
army in their colonial conquest of North Africa. She is a dancing
girl, performing for the delectation of soldiers:

> Her soft curls all fluttering, her cheeks all bright with a scarlet
> flush, her eyes as black as night, and full of fire ... Cigarette
> danced with ... wild grace ... as untutored and instinctive in
> her as its song to a bird ... Cigarette *en Bacchante* no man could
> resist.[9]

The denizens of the drawing-room could only dream of dancing
in this abandoned way. Again the sexuality is encoded in the
images of 'scarlet', 'fire', 'wild'; and is clinched in the final
sentence, which even has the French phrase to give it added
piquancy. Cigarette, however, is in control at this point, no man
could resist her, but the implication is that she can resist any man
she wishes to.

This independence is not thematically worked through to a
cultural analysis that allows the reader to understand the social
forces at play, and perhaps explore ways in which they can be

negotiated. Cigarette falls in love with a man who takes her for granted, hardly really noticing her, and literally sacrifices her life to save his. At that point he does notice her, and dying in his arms Cigarette is emotionally fulfilled by:

> the unconscious tenderness of his kisses that had the anguish of a farewell in them, the colour suddenly flushed all over her blanched face; she trembled in his arms; and a great shivering sigh ran through her. It came too late, this warmth of love. She learned what its sweetness might have been only when her lips grew numb.
>
> (p. 534)

The female reader has the pleasure of vicarious independence throughout the novel, and finally the consolation of knowing that she probably does not have to literally die in order to be noticed. Her life may be comparatively dull and constrained, but she is at least alive and materially relatively comfortable.

It seems hardly possible, yet is apparently true, that when in 1863 Ouida's first novel was published anonymously there was, according to her biographer Monica Stirling, speculation that its writer 'is said to be Miss Evans, the author of "Adam Bede"'.[10] Such a misunderstanding helps to illustrate why Eliot did not want to be published under a female name, or be associated with most women novelists. The stylistic differences alone are transparent, but more fundamentally Ouida, and Braddon, evade the central issues of oppression and repression. Their popularity with a mainly female readership is perhaps partly explained as a release of the tension caused by the debates about women's roles. The woman living in an uncertain cultural world, knowing that the past and present are coming under critical scrutiny from the feminism of the day – and from some non-feminist, even anti-feminist, sources too – and facing a future that may be different, that is exciting, but also potentially dangerous, and certainly unknown, may well need some reassurance that everything is ultimately for the best. Eliot does not provide such easy comfort as writers of the ilk of Charlotte Yonge, Mary Braddon and Ouida. Although the thematic problems are generally resolved in Eliot's novels, that is achieved in terms of the real, rather than a fantasy, world. She perceived that mere escapism did not confront the concerns, a central one of which remained education.

That education was a crucial matter is manifested by the passing of Forster's Education Act in 1870. In introducing his Bill to the House of Commons Forster claimed a dual impetus:

> We must not delay. Upon the speedy provision of elementary education depends our industrial prosperity. It is of no use to try to give technical teaching to our artizans without elementary education ... and if we leave our work-folk any longer unskilled ... they will become outmatched in the competition of the world ... I am one of those who would not wait until the people were educated before I would trust them with political power, now that we have given them political power we must not wait any longer to give them education.
>
> *(Hansard*, 17 February 1870)

The 1867 Reform Act had widened the franchise, and that is behind the statement concerning 'political power' – though in fact that is a hyperbolic phrase – but the other thrust picks up Ure's earlier argument, the rapidly changing industrial, commercial and mercantile worlds required an adaptive work force, capable of learning new skills. That argument emphasizes the economic and social dynamic of the period, and although the 1870 Act – which in fact covered girls as well as boys – was concerned with elementary education of the masses it was accompanied by a number of less spectacular, but nevertheless essentially radical, reforms in other educational areas.

Prestigious Royal Commissions were created to investigate some of the aspects of private education: for example, the Clarendon Commission of 1861, and the Taunton Commission three years later. Their reports were released through the decade, fuelling the debate about the nature of education and pedagogy in general. That official, as well as informal, interest continued is indicated by the fact that Oxford and Cambridge Universities were subjected to Commissions in 1872 and 1877. There was clearly a fear that private and higher education was not preparing Britain's young men – let alone its women – adequately for a dynamic world. In 1870 recruitment to most departments of the Civil Service was opened to competitive entry, which to some degree lessened the amount of nepotism that had had a debilitating effect on the efficiency of the national administration. From the following year it became no longer legally possible to purchase army commissions, so that military officers then had to have a measure of verifiable education. Two external catalystic events that helped to provoke these changes were the Paris Exhibition of 1867, in which British manufacturers were shown to be falling behind in new industrial processes, and the defeat of France in 1870 by a newly emergent German militarism. These were not phenomena from which the nation as a whole could retreat into escapism.

The roles and functions of women, although not generally considered central to this dynamism, were nevertheless caught up in the vortex. The Royal Commissions, with the exception of the Taunton Commissioners, specifically included the education of females in their terms of remit. There was also increased activity in the private sector, with the creation of Bedford College in 1860 opening up higher education facilities for women. They increasingly began to take public examinations, and in 1869 Girton College was set up at Cambridge as a women's college, with Newnham College following two years later. Two halls, which subsequently became full colleges, were created at Oxford the year before Eliot's death.

The feminists of the day were involved in some of this plethora of activity. The journal *The Englishwoman's Review* consistently recognized the importance of education. In 1868 it published an article 'On the Education of Young Servant Girls' by Julia Luard, 'a clergyman's daughter, experienced in parish work', in which she argued: 'One of the crying grievances of this our nineteenth century is the difficulty of meeting with good efficient servants, or of keeping them when once found' (*The Englishwoman's Review*, April 1868). In the article Luard equates loyal and 'efficient servants' with educated ones. This kind of sentiment reveals how close in some respects, although by no means all, feminist thought of the 1860s was to the moral – perhaps moralizing – sentiments of men like Colquhoun and Sharpe at the beginning of the century. Luard goes on to explicate the educated female employer's responsibility in steering the working-class girl away from vices: 'Many a girl has been influenced and saved by the friendship of one superior to her in rank and education, and has been able to protect herself from temptations' (ibid.). In this way the effects of a good education for middling-class women filter down the social hierarchy. Although Eliot was strongly in favour of a wider educational provision, and of improving the lot of women in general, she did have difficulty in accepting some of the arguments of feminists. She subscribed £50 to the Girton College fund, and took an interest in it, for example, but remained at a distance and was never personally involved in the project; just as she annually subscribed financially to *The Englishwoman's Review* but never contributed articles to it. The kind of – paradoxically – paternalism displayed by Luard was not something Eliot found easy to embrace.

Eliot's own attitude was expressed in a letter to John Morley in the year before Luard's article was published:

> If I were called on to act in the matter, I would certainly not oppose any plan which held out any reasonable promise of tending to establish as far as possible an equivalence of advantages for the two sexes, as to education and the possibilities of free development.
>
> (GEL, VIII, p. 402)

This displays Eliot's typical balance, her refusal to grasp at a single absolute solution to a complex problem, no matter how emotionally satisfying and mentally easy that might be. The extract is full of qualifications: 'If I were called on' carries the suggestion that she knows that is unlikely; she would 'not oppose', which is not the same as actively support; 'reasonable promise', 'tending', 'as far as possible', 'equivalence', 'possibilities' are all used as modifiers, avoiding direct polemic. This is not because Eliot did not know what she thought, but rather that she suspected her ideas were not necessarily exactly the same as other people's. Her educational ideal is 'free development' – of the individual.

It was partly out of this maelstrom that Eliot wrote her two great novels of the 1870s, although the discourse concerning education is never directly didactic. As usual, Eliot's style is to explore and analyse various aspects of the theme, showing the strengths and inadequacies of them all. The dialectical structure that is organized around the concepts of those forms of education that comparatively encourage 'free development', and those that positively inhibit it, being complicated by the fact that no form of education is shown as ideal.

The younger members of the Vincy family in *Middlemarch* to some extent parallel, although in a slightly higher social class,

Tom and Maggie Tulliver in regard to the theme of education. Just as it is attempted to force Tom into a form of learning he cannot manage Fred is pressured into a university, in order to qualify him for the clergy, despite his lack of interest and ability. Bulstrode chides Mr Vincy for the latter's attitude to Fred's education: 'It was entirely from worldly vanity that you destined him for the Church' (p. 156). Despite the Nonconformist bias in Bulstrode's position, many original readers would have accepted this as a valid comment on the motivation of the fathers of many young clergymen. The vanity consists in wishing to push the next generation into a higher sub-class, something more socially respectable than manufacturing. Fred predictably fails the examinations, but – like Tom Tulliver – displays intelligence and application when he is put into the right kind of milieu.

When an accident leads to Fred helping Caleb Garth the former has an insight into the meaning of work:

> I wish I had taken to it before I had thought of being a B.A. . . . Do you think I am too old to learn your business, Mr Garth? . . . I would work hard, I would deserve your good opinion. I should like to have to do with outdoor things. . . . a man ought to be allowed to judge for himself when he is four-and-twenty. How could I know when I was fifteen, what it would be right for me to do now? My education was a mistake.
>
> (pp. 606–7)

Work, or a career, is more than merely earning a living, although that is important, or holding a social status. Education that is designed purely towards those ends is likely to leave the individual undeveloped. This is not just a theoretic consideration, for when it becomes necessary to exercise rational decisions of choice the individual concerned has not been prepared for the eventuality. At the age of twenty-four Fred is ill-equipped to make decisions that will affect the rest of his life, although he knows they need to be made, and demands the right to make them. His mentor, Caleb, is virtually an autodidact: 'though he had only been a short time under a surveyor, and had been chiefly his own teacher, he knew more of land, building, and mining than most of the special men in the county' (p. 283). Fred too, despite his naivety in horse-trading, has some understanding of common matters, claiming to Caleb: 'I know a good deal about land and cattle already' (p. 607). These are practical matters of business, which BAs have been taught to denigrate. Indeed, previously Fred himself had: 'rather looked down on the manners and speech of young men who had not been to the university' (p. 268). He comes, however, to an appreciation of the real world of work, commerce and productivity. That Fred fundamentally has enough commonsense, even to overcome the disability of an inappropriate education, is shown by his choice of Caleb as his teacher.

Fred is, of course, ultimately helped by the more rational Mary, whose own education was basic and literally homely, yet who has more true intelligence and realistic judgement than most of the novel's characters. Mary's mother teaches her own children, and those of anyone else willing to pay a modest price, in a way that combines learning with life:

> She had sometimes taken pupils in a peripatetic fashion, making them follow her about in the kitchen with their book or slate. She thought that it was good for them to see that she could make an excellent lather while she corrected their blunders 'without looking', – that a woman with her sleeves tucked up above her elbows might know all about the Subjunctive Mood or the Torrid Zone.
>
> (p. 275)

This extract is followed by a scene in which Mrs Garth teaches her own children, Letty and Ben, whilst 'deftly handling her pastry' (p. 276). The episode also illustrates Eliot's concern that education, especially for females, should not be seen as necessarily divorcing them from domesticity. Most of Eliot's feminist friends had a tendency to correlate an opening up of education to women with a movement away from the home, and Eliot wrote to Barbara Bodichon in 1868 affirming her belief in the value of activities that had been designated humble, and were by implication of an inferior kind:

> No good can come to women, more than to any class of male mortals, while each aims at doing the highest kind of work . . . a more thorough education will tend to do away with the odious vulgarity of our notions about functions and employment, and . . . propagate the true gospel that the deepest disgrace is to

insist on doing work for which we are unfit – to do work of any sort badly.

(SL, p. 343)

This is a warning against over-ambition, against putting intellectuality above domesticity. Mrs Garth's knowledge of such diverse, and even relatively esoteric subjects, as 'the Subjunctive Mood' and 'the Torrid Zone' do not make her feel ashamed of washing clothes or cooking. On the contrary, they make her more of a complete woman than mere higher education would. If children initially learn in this kind of atmosphere they should grow up both educated and sensible, as the character of Mary Garth illustrates.

Unfortunately not all pupils do learn in the right kind of context, and in any event their later education can have a deforming effect. Fred's sister, Rosamond Vincy, is a clear indication of that process. The completion of her formal schooling is at the private establishment of Mrs Lemon: 'the chief school in the county, where the teaching included all that was demanded in the accomplished female – even to extras, such as the getting in and out of a carriage' (p. 123). The satire is expressed even in Mrs Lemon's name, with its associations of acidity and sourness, and in the descriptive phrase 'the chief school in the county'. That is later elaborated as being: 'close to a county town with a memorable history that had its relics in church and castle' (p. 190). Pretentiousness and pomposity appear to be indicated here, and the former characteristic, at least, refers back to the term 'the accomplished female'. The pretension is undermined by the specific nature of the 'extras' provided. Such activities as 'the getting in and out of a carriage' may indeed be important to the classes in society that regularly travel in carriages, but the text deliberately plays on a confounding of education and social training, between substance and periphery.

From a slightly more wealthy background Gwendolen, in *Daniel Deronda*, has a similar education, which: 'had no disturbing reference to the advancement of learning . . . but as to her "education" she would have admitted that it had left her under no disadvantages' (p. 69). In a society in which really educated and intelligent women could be considered something of an embarrassment there are 'no disadvantages' to relative ignorance. The typography draws attention to the concept of education being utilized. It has no relation to free development, but merely to superficial social accomplishments. Although Gwendolen actually knew very little: 'what remained of all things knowable, she was conscious of being sufficiently acquainted with through novels, plays, and poems' (p. 70). Like Mrs Transome she is 'sufficiently acquainted' with areas of knowledge to hold a drawing-room conversation on them.

Gwendolen is balanced in the novel by Mirah, who has had a sound education. Like Mary Garth she was taught largely by her parents: 'I gathered thoughts very fast, because I read many things – plays and poetry, Shakespeare and Schiller, and learned evil and good' (p. 253). Mirah actually understands what she reads, and her education is both aesthetic and moral. Partly because of this she has a powerful influence, helping Daniel to guide his dissatisfaction with a conventional upper-class education into positive avenues (cf. chapter 4 above).

The *Middlemarch* character of Dorothea Brooke is also in part involved in the discourse of education. Paradoxically her education was 'at once narrow and promiscuous', initially in England 'and afterwards in a Swiss family at Lausanne' (p. 30). Her search is partly for an intellectual life: 'Dorothea knew many passages of Pascal's *Pensées* and of Jeremy Taylor by heart. . . . The really delightful marriage must be that where your husband . . . could teach you even Hebrew' (pp. 30–2). It is this yearning, a theoretical approach to reality, that causes Dorothea to make mistakes commonsense would have avoided. Other characters perceive the unsuitability of Casaubon as a husband – Celia, for instance, had: 'begun to feel disgust . . . felt a sort of shame mingled with a sense of the ludicrous' (p. 71). Dorothea's reaching out beyond domesticity is positive, it takes her beyond the 'Bedlam' of 'the solicitudes of feminine fashion' (p. 30), but it is also destructive, alienating her from the common virtues of the home. Her natural intelligence, aided by her experiences of reality, eventually bring her to reconcile lofty ideas, that had in part been encouraged by her education, with ordinary day-to-day life, so that she finds happiness in 'wifely help' (p. 894). In the context this might be interpreted less as a compromise than as a fulfilment, a synthesizing of two roles.

Eliot's eventual husband, Cross, wrote of her:

She was keenly anxious to redress injustices to women . . . [but]

as a woman she wished to be, above all things feminine. . . . She was proud, too, of being an excellent housekeeper. . . . Nothing offended her more than the idea that because a woman had exceptional intellectual powers, therefore it was right that she should absolve herself . . . from her ordinary household duties.

(LIFE, p. 624)

These attitudes are revealed in the novels. Education of the right kind could open up career opportunities for women, might provide a degree of independence from the constrictions of socially-constructed gender roles, but being an independent woman did not mean, for Eliot, completely abandoning traditional female functions. After all, Eliot herself was both a professional writer and 'an excellent housekeeper'. She did not see education as a means of escaping from domesticity, but rather as a channel by which the domestic virtues could be augmented and opened up to wider horizons. Education that entailed the free development of the individual would lead her or him to greater sensitivity and sensibility in any role performed.

In 1863 a writer Eliot very much admired, and who helped to develop women's education, John Ruskin, claimed an aesthetic function for education. In his long essay *Munera Pulveris* Ruskin argued that the sensibility of the individual was being crushed:

By sensibility I mean its natural perception of beauty, fitness, and rightness; or of what is lovely, decent, and just: faculties . . . cultivable . . . by education, and necessarily perishing without it. True education, has, indeed, no other function than the development of these faculties. . . . You do not educate a man by telling him what he knew not, but by making him what he was not.[11]

Ruskin's own commitment to female education implicates women too in his final aphorism – which draws a vital distinction between mere knowledge and profound learning, or 'true education'. This is certainly a discrimination with which Eliot was also concerned. With their veneer of education Mrs Transome, Rosamond and Gwendolen all lack sensibility as Ruskin defines it. Their learning has not changed them, has not led to free development, but is simple knowledge that allows them to express opinions without having understanding.

Their education has not made them truly independent women, because they remain enmeshed in social conventions. It is significant that most of Eliot's female characters who are best educated, in Ruskin's sense, and who become most independent of social conventions in their judgement marry: Dinah to Adam Bede, Esther to Felix Holt, Mary to Fred, Dorothea eventually to Will, Mirah to Daniel Deronda. 'True education', in the novels, is generally presented in broad cultural, rather than narrow academic or vocational, terms. It does not necessarily take women away from the home, although it might help them earn an interesting living. Eliot is not concerned with merely substituting one role for women, that of the drudge, with another, that of what Victorians called the blue-stocking. Ideally education will give women a choice of roles, of which they may embrace, as Eliot herself did, more than one.

6

The Altar of Mammon

Only a few years before Eliot's birth Jane Austen began her novel *Pride and Prejudice* with the ironic sentence: 'It is a truth universally acknowledged, that a single man in possession of a good fortune, must be in want of a wife'.[1] The opening paragraph of her next published work, *Mansfield Park*, contained the axiom: 'there certainly are not so many men of large fortune in the world, as there are pretty women to deserve them'.[2] Austen's satire focuses on two aspects of life – wealth and marriage – that were not only central throughout the nineteenth century, but became more intensely so during the period of Eliot's lifetime. The balance of wealth gradually passed from the families of the traditional landed gentry, to the newer interests of manufacturing, trade and commerce. In effect this also meant a shift from rural and agrarian productivity to urban industrialism. The contrast is reflected in a speech from *Felix Holt* concerning the Transome estate: 'people who get their money out of land are as long scraping five pounds together as your trading men are in turning five pounds into a hundred' (p. 185). Although this should not necessarily be taken literally it does illustrate a general trait in economic change. As those processes gained momentum they led to the increasing financial power of the men involved in trade, commerce and manufacture. That was the foundation on which the subsequent political ascendancy of the middling classes was based. It is hardly surprising, therefore, that they were concerned, perhaps almost obsessed, with the concept, and accumulation, of wealth.

Marriage was a central concern because of the importance of family life, which became the backbone of the social system in, and by, which the new wealth was largely generated. For those people with wealth – which might constitute cash, property, shares, profit expectations – marriage was not a purely private act between two autonomous individuals. It entailed a public contract, a coming together of two sets of wealth; the couple may have been united at the altar in holy wedlock in the sight of God, but they were joined too in commercial transaction under the beneficence of Mammon.

It is, therefore, not possible to discuss Victorian notions of marriage without also considering money, or wealth in general. It was vital, for the middling classes, to have, and display, it. The great nineteenth-century municipal buildings of the industrial towns of Britain are ostentatious monuments of that idea, themselves altars to Mammon, emanating from the corporate feeling Briggs described as the: 'sense of civic pride which inspired the building of the imposing and often expensive Victorian town halls'.[3] They represented a public extension of the personal lives and attitudes of the middling-class men who controlled urban local government. Their aspirations were quite widely shared. One of the best-selling books of the period, for example, was Samuel Smiles' *Self-help*. Within a month of publication, in 1859, it sold out four editions, and was reprinted at least once annually for twenty-five of the following twenty-six years. It taught that all men were capable of gaining wealth and rising socially through their own efforts, by virtue of self-help. The achievement of social and financial mobility needed to be displayed, and in that context ostentation was not considered ill-mannered. It is not insignificant that Dickens' first novel of the 1860s was *Great Expectations*, in which the very title satirically summarizes the ethos of the age – all men could have expectations of great wealth. Silas Marner embodies one aspect of this spirit. When he worked in his earlier days simply in order to earn enough money on which to live, his little wealth had value only as a practical necessity. But once Silas begins to see the accumulation of capital as a purpose in itself his attitude to the hoarded coins changes: 'He handled them, he counted them, till their form and colour were like the satisfaction of a thirst ... he loved them all' (pp. 68-70). Silas worships his money, it fulfils the function of natural succour for him, being 'like the satisfaction of a thirst'. The affection which should be offered to another human is perverted into a love of the guineas. Silas' story is a parable for Eliot's society – worship of wealth isolates people from one another, and degrades natural feelings. The character realizes this when he is deprived of the money and receives the gift of the child.

A major practical problem of wealth was its vulnerability. Silas loses his because of robbery, but those who made money through commerce, investment or trade could also lose it by those means.

Whilst a few very exceptional, or lucky, men became self-made millionaires a great many more suffered bankruptcy and ruin. Palmer's Index to *The Times*, for instance, records over 1,000 bankruptcies reported in the newspaper in 1859, the year *Self-help* was published; and that was not untypical. In fact the number tended to increase, and in 1876, the year of Eliot's last novel, it had risen by almost 50 per cent.

Financial disaster of diverse kinds was a sufficiently recurring phenomenon in the economic culture for the popular female novelists to incorporate in their plots. A typical illustration occurs in Rosa Carey's 1871 novel *Barbara Heathcote's Trial*. Barbara's father is a doctor who takes on a relatively impoverished young assistant, Norman, with a widowed mother and persuades him to invest in shares:

> intoxicated with the success of his speculation, which was already repaying him far beyond his wildest hopes ... [he] spent his professional earnings in buying fresh shares. Dr Heathcote was doing the same, only more largely.[4]

Norman's mother is persuaded to cash in the last of her annuity, gambling her small financial security against the prospect of almost instant riches. It was a recurring situation in Victorian literature and life, fraught with both great expectations and even greater danger:

> The Spanish mines in which Dr Heathcote had so largely invested, and had persuaded Norman to take shares, had proved the bubble of a mock company, which had suddenly burst and engulfed them in ruin. Every penny of his hoarded savings, the remainder of his mother's annuity, even the accumulated dividends, had been swept away: the only difference between his ruin and his partner's was that Dr Heathcote's was more absolute.
>
> (p. 382)

This is not really investment, of course, but simple speculation. The images of 'bubble', 'burst', 'engulfed', 'swept away' and the reiterated 'ruin' emphasize the illusory, obsessive and unwise process into which the two men had been drawn. These are not evil characters, but have merely followed a Victorian dream of plenty to excess. But the punishment for their folly is suffered by the wider family circles.

When Barbara's father explains to his daughters the disaster he has caused he falls back on a typical Victorian stereotype: 'Your dear mother always said that she could not understand business, and I am afraid you all take after her ... I suppose all women are the same' (p. 387). There is no textual comment on the irony of this speech from a man whose own inability to 'understand business' has led to disaster, but the readers would no doubt have seen it. Barbara comes through her trial of the ruin – in addition to the general repetition, 'ruin' or 'ruined' are used four times in the space of twenty words (p. 387) at the crisis – despite her father's denigration of her comprehension.

Eliot too, although in her own distinctive way, uses that popular plot device in *Daniel Deronda*. But whereas Carey works towards it as the plot's catastrophe, in the more usual way, laboriously setting up the way of life and aspirations that are to be destroyed, Eliot virtually starts with the disaster, and then explores its consequences – although, of course, the novel as a whole is about considerably more than Gwendolen's life. The interest in the minor novelist's text is largely in the plot, the working up to a catastrophe, in *Daniel Deronda* it lies in the responses consequent to the misfortune. The former novel is based mainly on suspense, the latter on the exploration of themes.

The first image of Gwendolen is at the gambling table, and that serves as a metaphor of her social and financial position, for when she leaves the casino the letter from her mother awaiting Gwendolen informs her:

> You know nothing about business and will not understand it; but Grapnell & Co. have failed for a million and we are totally ruined. . . . All the property our poor father saved for us goes to pay the liabilities. There is nothing I can call my own.
>
> (p. 43)

Holding shares in companies and living off the income, at a time when personal and state pensions were unknown, was not uncommon amongst the classes who could afford the original capital investment. Although it was not the kind of speculation for quick gains that ensnares Dr Heathcote it was a form of gambling, based on the belief that apparently safe companies would not fail. Nevertheless, some did, no matter how carefully they were chosen – and in this case the efforts of the 'poor father' to provide for his family are thwarted by financial circumstances beyond any individual shareholder's immediate control. Like Barbara, and many of the initial readers, Gwendolen is expected to 'know nothing about business', although both her, and the readers', standard and style of living depends on the workings of commerce.

The shock to Gwendolen, as it would be to the reader in a similar situation, is great: 'The first effect of this letter on Gwendolen was half stupefying. The implicit confidence that her destiny must be one of luxurious ease . . . had been stronger in her own mind than in her mamma's' (p. 44). The assumed irrevocability of financial security was an 'implicit' aspect of the worship of wealth. There is no point in pursuing something that is material but transient – yet the dedication to great expectations showed no sign of being reduced, despite the evidence – in novels and newspapers – of the risks entailed. After all, those bankruptcies running at the rate of between twenty and thirty a week obviously affected at least tens, if not hundreds, of thousands of people.

Wealth was not solely connected with luxury, of course. In *Middlemarch* Bulstrode exercises *power* in his position as banker. He is able, for example, to command the loyalty of Lydgate – a situation he was able to achieve partly because of his wealth. He also has a certain amount of power that is based on his own financial standing. That status came from the illegal disinheriting of an innocent young woman, and the wealth becomes a moral canker as Silas' gold did. Bulstrode does not, unlike Silas, actually worship the money – but he does metaphorically erect an altar to its power, and the religious connotations are carried through his rationalizing of the original crime:

> Bulstrode's course up to that time had, he thought, been sanctioned by remarkable providences, appearing to point the way for him to be the agent in making the best use of a large property and withdrawing it from perversion. . . . It was easy for him to settle what was due from him to others by inquiring what were God's intentions with regard to himself.
>
> (p. 666)

Words such as 'sanctioned' and 'providences', presented almost as free indirect speech, indicate that the character sees the events as much more than mere material luck. 'God's intentions' are involved, and Bulstrode perceives himself as 'the agent' of them. He is able to worship God, and he is 'a Churchman' by dedicating his life to the best use of 'his hundred thousand' (p. 667). When faced with Raffles' blackmail Bulstrode seeks both a 'spiritual' and a 'material rescue' (p. 667). For him, as for many Victorians, there appears to be no dichotomy between wordly and other-wordly considerations. Yet the fact that Bulstrode has to rationalize his subjection to Mammon illustrates the unease with which the forces of spirituality and materialism live together. A society that demands both benefits for itself has to attempt to force a resolution of the conflict. Bulstrode ultimately fails to achieve a reconciliation, and as a representative figure of that nineteenth-century dilemma is, again like Silas, parabolic.

Bulstrode's original opportunity arose through a problem of inheritance. A woman made a will leaving: 'all the wealth . . . out of the magnificent trade, of which she never knew the precise nature . . . [to] her daughter, who had long been regarded as lost' (p. 665). The importance of wealth, coupled with that of family, made issues of inheritance extremely important. The story-line of *Felix Holt*, for instance, partly depends on the complexity and centrality of those concerns, yet the theme functions as more than an exigency of plot. Just as the theme of Reform is an allegory of contemporary interests, so that of wealth, family and inheritance serves as a metaphor for mid-Victorian obsessions.

The Last Will and Testament could itself be used as a form of power, exercised beyond the grave and therefore perhaps implying a kind of (economic) immortality. In *Daniel Deronda* Sir Hugo considers that Grandcourt's will comprises a 'kind of banishment' (p. 783) for Gwendolen, the final shot in their battle of wills. Nor is it presented as unusual Victorian behaviour, as Sir Hugo reveals:

> Even a wise man generally lets some folly ooze out of him in his will – my father did, I know; and if a fellow has any spite or tyranny in him, he's likely to bottle off a good deal for keeping in that sort of document. It's quite clear Grandcourt meant that his death should put an extinguisher on his wife.
>
> (ibid.)

Casaubon also attempts to do this in Book Five of *Middlemarch*, which is appropriately entitled 'The Dead Hand'. Dorothea learns that: 'he has made a codicil to his will, to say the property was all to go away from you if you married ... if you married Mr Ladislaw, not anybody else' (pp. 531–2). This is a crude attempt to influence the future behaviour of Dorothea through economic sanctions, nevertheless the importance of finance could give it a good deal of weight. The text evades this question by allowing Dorothea to have her 'own fortune ... seven hundred-a-year' (p. 870), which was indeed a 'fortune' in the early 1830s when the novel is set. Will is an important and complex concept and theme in *Middlemarch* and Casaubon's legal will is his way of exerting his willpower over Dorothea's will; and in order to attain her Will Ladislaw she has to find the willpower to renounce her dead husband's financial will and will to dominate from the grave.

Featherstone, too, uses his will to control the behaviour of his potential beneficiaries. He utilizes that power of dangling great expectations over them in order to buy a regard they would not give him naturally. Mary Garth's actions towards Featherstone's two wills serve as a test of her moral fibre. Fred Vincy is much weaker and, like many nineteenth-century young men, gets into serious debt by borrowing money on account of his great expectations from Featherstone's death.

Debt was another recurring Victorian theme: it was a form of spending money that was not actually available, and because of that could lead to bankruptcy, which might then – in the case of a company – involve a lot of innocent shareholders in financial hardship. Even the mismanagement of an individual could have an accumulative effect, as when Fred's borrowings threatened to ruin the Garth family in *Middlemarch*. Running into debt was seen as a manifestation of moral weakness. Lydgate's inability, in the same novel, to control his personal economy stems partially from his 'spots of commonness' (p. 179), a trait illustrated by his cavalier attitude to financing the marital home:

> he saw a dinner-service ... which struck him as so exactly the right thing that he bought it at once. ... The dinner-service in question was expensive, but that might be in the nature of dinner-services.
>
> (p. 387)

Lydgate acts on impulse because the article 'struck him as so exactly the right thing', although it was 'expensive' and his capital was beginning to run low. It is a thoughtless action by a character who cannot afford such luxury, and who then rationalizes his careless attitude by arguing that expensiveness 'might be in the nature of dinner-services'. The 'commonness' in this instance lies in not bothering to find out the nature of dinner-services, in adopting an unpractical approach to a practical problem, and persuading himself that he was justified. Lydgate, like most 'ordinary men' (p. 179), could not bring together different aspects of his personality: his 'distinction of mind ... did not penetrate his feeling and judgement about furniture, or women' (ibid.). Although not by inclination an immoral character Lydgate's attitudes to money, furniture and women are related, leading him into actions that are misguided, unperceptive, and create suffering. The accumulation and use of money are moral issues.

Eliot was by no means alone in this attitude. In one of the most popular mid-Victorian novels, Mrs Wood's *East Lynne*, Francis Levison not only seduces the formerly respectable and happy Lady Isabel into adultery and into leaving her husband and children for the transient joys of sexual passion, and then abandons her in France, but also runs up debts he has no intention of paying. Indeed, the two kinds of immorality are inextricably linked. Levison is the heir of a rich man, and like Fred Vincy – although on a greater scale – lives off his known, or anticipated, expectations of inheritance. A relative explains how Levison behaved towards innocents:

> I believe him to be a base and despicable man, both by nature and by inclination, and that he will remain so to the end of time.... They were simple, unsuspicious country people, understanding neither fraud nor vice, nor the ways of an evil world. Francis Levison persuaded them to put their names to bills, 'as a simple matter of form, to accommodate him for a month or so', as he stated.... They were not rich: they lived in comfort upon their own small estate, but with no superfluous money to spare, and when the time came for them to pay – as come it did – it brought them ruin, and they had to leave their home. He deliberately did it ... knowing what would be the end.

(pp. 225–6)

Levison persuades 'simple, unsuspicious country people' to underwrite his debts for a time, by putting 'their names to bills'. Fred Vincy involves Caleb Garth in a similar way, although he did have good intentions of finding the necessary money, and it was not an uncommon nineteenth-century practice. It worked in a practical way, in an age before more sophisticated types of credit had been widely evolved, as a form of money-lending without cash having to actually pass hands, since one person offered to stand security for another's debts over a specified period of time. However, if the debtor's money was not forthcoming the underwriter was legally bound to provide it. Levison 'deliberately' baulked his debts, and so caused 'ruin' and the loss of 'their home' to people who had trusted him. He flees the country, able to return only surreptitiously. All of this directly prefigures his actions towards, and with, Lady Isabel – taking advantage of her husband's trusting generosity in order to ruin the family's happiness. Seduction is both sexual and financial: and in this demotic moral scheme a man capable of one is not merely also capable, but is actually likely – almost certain – to undertake the other. Eliot's treatment of the theme of economic laxity, in both the cases of Fred and Lydgate, is much more complex than it was in popular literature.

If the heedless pursuit of wealth was seen as the worship of Mammon, it was nevertheless true that the good management of finances was a Christian, as well as secular, virtue. Although men had the opportunity to be virtuous or evil on a greater scale than women, females too had financial responsibilities. When an apparently respectable character in *The Clever Woman of the Family* runs her household accounts into debt shock is registered by Rachel:

> Even the direct evidence before her eyes would not at first persuade her that it was not 'all those wicked tradesmen;' she had always heard that fashionable shops were not to be trusted. 'I am afraid,' said Colonel Keith ... ' poor Bessie was scarcely free from blame in this matter.'
> 'Not paying! Going on in debt!' ...
> 'It is very sad and painful to make such discoveries,' said Colonel Keith; 'but I am afraid such things are not uncommon ... she must have greatly exceeded her means, and have used much cleverness and ingenuity in keeping the tradesmen quiet,

and preventing all from coming to light.'

(pp. 340–1)

The exclamation marks emphasize both the incredulity and horror at what can occur behind the facade of respectable housekeeping. Since many, perhaps most, of the novel's readers were in some way involved in similar responsibilities the trauma of 'Not paying! Going on in debt!' may have been very close to their own fears; and those would not have been lessened by the sensible Colonel's observation, and warning, that 'such things are not uncommon'. Exceeding 'her means' in expenditure was an act of irresponsible carelessness, but neglect is compounded into crime by 'cleverness and ingenuity'. One does not have to be actively evil to fall into debt, but since doing so is a manifestation of moral turpitude it can be the first step towards that state. Lack of requisite care may lead to the 'sad and painful' need for deceit, which is itself an uncontrollable vortex.

Despite Eliot's obvious moral concern with both the worship of the graven image of Mammon, and the real virtues of money-management, her novels never adopt quite such an overtly moralistic tone. In *Felix Holt* Mrs Transome rejects her son's advice, and offer, not to: 'worry yourself about things that don't properly belong to a woman. . . . You shall have nothing to do now but to be grandmamma on satin cushions', on the grounds that it 'is a part of the old woman's duty I am not prepared for. I am used to be chief bailiff, and to sit in the saddle two or three hours every day' (p. 95). Mrs Transome, the former adulteress, combines good financial management with a debilitated moral sense. Lydgate expects Rosamond 'would create order in the home and accounts with still magic' (p. 387), a standard nineteenth-century expectation of a wife in that class of society, and although he is disastrously wrong in his assessment of Rosamond's 'magic' the text makes it clear that Lydgate is also culpable in their financial catastrophe. In general Eliot's women characters are adept housekeepers: Mrs Poyser in *Adam Bede* and Mrs Tulliver in *The Mill on the Floss* are both scrupulous rather against the odds; Romola is an excellent manager; whilst Dorothea and the Garth women all perform that woman's role very well in *Middlemarch*. On the whole Eliot's novels might be seen as implying that women are not morally or practically inferior to men in matters of accountancy and management.

The deep concern of nineteenth-century society with wealth and family is further revealed in its attitudes to marriage. Legally, and financially, men were in a very much stronger position than women. A potential bride, for instance, was generally dependent on her father to provide a dowry. Lydgate hopes that Rosamond's father will help furnish their home as part of the marriage settlement: 'He was too proud to act as if he presupposed that Mr Vincy would advance money to provide furniture . . . he did not waste time in conjecturing how much his father-in-law would give in the form of dowry' (p. 389). Nevertheless he clearly expects Rosamond to come to him with a dowry. The fact that Lydgate does not wonder 'how much' it will be implies there will be something, he has no doubt of that – the dowry's existence is not a matter for conjecture. Romola hopes that a prospective husband will want to marry her so much the provision of a dowry could be overlooked. In the event she is attracted to a man who is sufficiently without friends, influence or position that he is willing to marry her, if for no other reason, in order to gain the patronage of a father-in-law with prestige.

It was perhaps partly because daughters cost fathers dowries that the latter sometimes looked rather more favourably on the birth of sons. Particularly in the mercantile, commercial and industrial classes sons could eventually enter business and become a source of productivity – a medium for generating wealth, rather than a source through which it was lost – and be someone to inherit the family prosperity. Of course, it was not the fault of daughters that they were excluded. Romola wished she were male so that her education would have enabled her to help Bardo more, and her father would take her scholarship more seriously; Maggie Tulliver has no desire to follow a conventional female direction, but has little choice; Gwendolen's Uncle Gascoigne in *Daniel Deronda*, following the conventional line, tells her 'Marriage is the only true and satisfactory sphere of a woman' (p. 180). On the other hand, Dinah is happy to give up a quasi-public life to marry Adam Bede; and Effie, surrogate daughter of Silas Marner, appears to have no other ambition than to marry Aaron. As usual Eliot presents an ambivalent, not doctrinaire, view of social practices, although she clearly exposed the abuses that were prevalent.

The subject of marriage was also important to the wider issue usually referred to at the time as the Woman Question. Early feminist campaigners such as Eliot's friend Barbara Bodichon brought together diverse areas of experience such as education, marriage and suffrage under the general concept of women's rights. An anonymous commentator observed:

> The subject of women's rights has of late occupied the minds of many people, the columns of some of our leading journals, and the speeches of more than one of our legislators. It is, truly, a vexed question.[5]

Eliot was clearly aware that women were discriminated against in the vast majority of social activities, but did not approach those experiences purely from the point of view of the 'vexed' Woman Question or 'women's rights' – tending, rather, to explore them from a broader perspective. Although, for example, she was centrally concerned with the limitations of Maggie Tulliver's education, that interest was presented within the framework of the educational experience of Tom too, and their father's social class' attitudes to learning and knowledge. In a similar way there is a deep involvement in the novels with the theme of marriage – as a financial agreement, a social institution and as a potential emotional haven or trap. The discourse is always pursued, though, in the broadest terms.

Although set in Renaissance Italy *Romola* certainly explores themes of profound importance to Eliot's initial readers. The 'Proem' makes this explicit, that in looking at Florence: 'in the mid spring-time of 1492 ... we are impressed with the broad sameness of the human lot' (p. 43). The historical hindsight is used to encourage the reader to bring a wider perspective to contemporary concerns. One of those is marriage.

A wedding, for Renaissance Florentines, as for socially-aspiring Victorians, was not simply a bringing together of two individuals, but also a public contract, a marriage of financial assets and expectations. In *Romola* the Florentine father in general: 'loved to strengthen his family by a good alliance, and went home with a triumphant light in his eyes after concluding a satisfactory *parentado*, or marriage, for his son or daughter' (p. 46). This presents, for the Victorian mind, an extremely formal process, suggesting that the people to be married had no voice at all – but it is an extremity of example close enough to practice for Eliot's readers to realize the connection with their own social attitudes and behaviour. The matter is expressed more in terms of emotion when Romola and her father, the blind scholar Bardo, discuss it:

> 'Romola ... thou wilt marry; Bernardo reproaches me that I do not seek a fitting *parentado* for thee, and we will delay no longer. ...'
>
> 'No, no, father ... wait till some one seeks me,' said Romola hastily.
>
> 'Nay, my child, that is not the paternal duty.'
>
> '... I will try and be as useful to you as if I had been a boy, and then perhaps some great scholar will want to marry me, and will not mind about a dowry.'
>
> (p. 100)

Romola expresses a desire that was probably not uncommon among intelligent, intellectually inclined, Victorian females. She sees fulfilment in male terms – serving her father by adopting a son's role. The alternative is simply to 'marry', which at that level of society would normally entail the complications of a financial settlement, the 'dowry'. Romola does not consider that she has a right to independence, and is prepared to wait passively for a husband, who will be 'a great scholar' and therefore able to satisfy her father's needs for an assistant. That is more important than any personal suitability as a husband. Bardo conceives 'paternal duty' as requiring him to follow the accepted modes of social behaviour, rather than pursuing the real emotional happiness of his daughter. The 'reproaches' of his friend Bernardo are more important than the wishes of Romola herself. Yet neither Bardo nor Bernardo are depicted as deliberately vicious or tyrannical men, they are, in a well-meaning way, merely following the conventions of the times, without realizing they victimize Romola.

In fact Romola is allowed to marry the man of her choice, because he is, conveniently, the scholar who is needed to help Bardo – but ironically the chosen husband, Tito, ultimately treats Romola with contempt and cruelty. The dialectic between parental choice and the freedom of the individual to choose is, through this structure, left unresolved. Marriage is always something of a lottery, whatever system of choices prevails. The importance for Victorians of getting it right was twofold: divorce was extremely difficult and very expensive indeed, so that a mistake could not

be easily remedied, but probably had to be lived with until the
death of one of the partners; and since marriage was a public
financial contract the ramifications of unravelling it were enormously complex, possibly affecting many more than the wife and
husband. Almost the only exception to these circumstances was
the clear adultery of the wife, as *East Lynne* illustrates; but even
then complications could arise. Eliot had personal experience of
marital ambiguity, since part of her earnings was contributing to
the adulterous household of Mrs Lewes, whilst Eliot herself was
unable to marry the legally hapless Lewes (cf. chapter 1 above).

The dowry system, for example, clearly equated women with
property: they were chattels to be traded. An implication of this
bride's status was that on becoming property themselves they
could not own it. In a society that regarded property, and wealth
in general, so highly, people who were debarred from having it
were naturally pariahs.

Unmarried women were allowed to own property, but lost
control of it to their husbands on marriage. This had been a cause
of controversy when Eliot was working regularly for the *Westminster Review*. An anonymous article from that period, entitled
'The Property of Married Women', argued:

> The attempt to maintain certain unjustly privileged classes has
> generally ended in evils far greater than those which were
> supposed likely to result from affording equal rights to all . . .
> the inequality of our social system . . . has had consequences far
> more serious than those who take a cursory view of it are at all
> aware of . . . without justice there can be neither prosperity nor
> happiness . . . an empire sinks into decay like a vicious man,
> from the very consequences of its own misdoings.
>
> (*The Westminster Review*, October 1856)

The nub of the argument is that men constitute the 'certain
unjustly privileged classes' in this case, especially in relation to
married women, who suffer the brunt of 'the inequality of our
social system'. This view, of course, is not concerned with other
social and economic privileges and inequalities. Ultimately injustice will destroy the very privileges it seeks to protect, 'without
justice . . . an empire sinks into decay'. The argument is powerfully expressed, and at a time when considerations of the larger

empire were becoming vital in political thinking it is articulated in appropriate terms.

It can be related to a slightly earlier booklet written by Barbara Leigh Smith, who has been quoted before, under the name Bodichon. She attempted to define 'in Plain Language ... the Most Important Laws Concerning Women': 'A man and a wife are one person in law; the wife loses all her rights as a single woman, and her existence is entirely absorbed in that of her husband. ... her condition is called coverture'.[6] Clearly marriage could entail, for women, an enormous material sacrifice. This was not only undignified, but could put a woman at risk too. The single woman with wealth who was unlucky enough to fall under the spell of a fortune-hunting husband suffered a treble misfortune: the trauma of knowing that she had been deceived; the loss of control over her financial assets, which would be squandered by the reprobate man; and she had to live a life of physical constraint and emotional unhappiness, without the possibility of ever being able to retrieve the situation.

Such circumstances could lead to a dull misery even if the man was not actually vicious. A fairly typical situation is outlined in *Barbara Heathcote's Trial*:

> Sir Geoffrey's father, having impoverished his estate, retrieved his fallen fortunes by a marriage ... with the only daughter and heiress of a rich London alderman; and though Lady Hunsden tried to raise herself to his rank, she somehow failed signally in winning either his affection or respect, so after some years she resigned herself to her position, and degenerated into a meek fussy little woman.
>
> (p. 24)

Lady Hunsden becomes the victim of her own apparent good fortune – being 'the only daughter and heiress of a rich' man. It is that status which attracts the upper class, but 'impoverished' suitor, who needs to retrieve 'his fallen fortunes'. It is incumbent on the woman to win the 'affection or respect' of her husband, and 'to raise herself to his rank'. The man is simply passive. Having provided the opportunity for the woman's social mobility he has no further responsibility to her. It is hardly surprising that the wife 'degenerated'.

A woman needed a very strong personality indeed to withstand the pressures exerted on heiresses. Eliot, although understanding the difficulties, illustrated that it could be achieved, through the character of Catherine Arrowpoint in *Daniel Deronda*:

> Heiresses vary ... but in every case it is taken for granted that she will consider herself an appendage to her fortune, and marry where others think her fortune ought to go.... She would not accept the view of her social duty which required her to marry a needy nobleman or a commoner on the ladder towards nobility.
>
> (p. 279)

Catherine refuses to be 'an appendage to her fortune', to risk degenerating into a meek and fussy woman in the asphyxia of a bad marriage in order to satisfy the requirements of 'social duty'. She determines to marry Klesmer the music teacher, following the path of true love and defying conventional expectations.

Not only women could suffer from the potentially repressive system of courtship and marriage. In the poem 'Forbidden Fruit' by TSS a male narrator describes his youthful hopes:

> I left her in a quiet country home,
>   Free from the taint of fashionable life, –
> A gentle, truthful, simple-hearted girl,
>   Fair promise of a loving, faithful wife.

He leaves to become a soldier, and by the time he returns the mother of the 'simple-hearted girl' has forbidden the promised marriage:

> She yielded to her mother's harsh command, –
>   . . .
> Alas, the world of fashion oft can tell
>   Of perjured vows and honest love denied,
> Of youth and beauty tied to feeble age,
>   To gratify a parent's selfish pride.
>
> (*Belgravia*, October 1867)

The juxtapositions – of 'gentle, truthful' with 'yielded', 'harsh command'; and 'loving, faithful' with 'perjured', 'selfish' – emphasize the feeling of conflict, the intensity of the betrayal, which in the social circumstances is irrevocable. There is no possibility of 'youth and beauty' overcoming the parental power of 'feeble age'. The daughter does suffer, of course, and the man too in this case. Although the injustices to women were more widespread and dramatic than those inflicted on men, the existence of this kind of fiction in popular culture indicates that the male was not immune to social iniquity, and the fact that it was published in a magazine edited by Mary Braddon suggests the poem was not merely an expression of male bigotry or prejudice, but the articulation of a genuine social problem.

The prohibition in this instance is in the interests of the 'parent's selfish pride', but parental protection could be exercised for valid reasons too. The handsome and apparently charming young man who was in reality an opportunistic fortune-hunter was not unknown in the conditions that prevailed. Although Romola does not have a fortune as such, and usually has an intelligent discernment of character, even she is deceived by Tito. Romola is so unused to handsome young scholars, 'she had hardly ever seen any but middle-aged or gray-headed men' (p. 105), their first meeting: 'seemed like a wreath of spring dropped suddenly into Romola's young but wintry life, which had inherited nothing but memories – memories of a dead mother, of a lost brother, of a blind father's happier time' (ibid.). The repetition stresses the deprivation of Romola's life, and although she is not dissatisfied the appearance of a personable young man 'was like the dawn of a new sense to her' (p. 111). It is partly an encoding of dawning sexuality:

> A girl of eighteen imagines the feelings behind the face that has moved her with its sympathetic youth, as easily as primitive people imagined the humours of the gods in fair weather: what is she to believe in, if not in this vision woven from within?
>
> (p. 115)

Since the fulfilment of sexual desire outside of marriage was considered socially unacceptable – although it occurred not infrequently – particularly for women, the rousing of those instincts would lead almost inevitably to marital union, if no impediment existed or was created. Part of the problem, though, was the possible transience of sexual feelings, as against the virtual permanence of the legal contract.

Mrs Wood forcefully reminded her women readers, in analysing a marriage in *East Lynne*, of the temporary nature of the
affections of many men:

> It was not that his love had faded, but that time and custom
> had wrought their natural effects. Look at children with their
> toys.... Are not the playthings kissed, and hugged, and
> clasped in arms, and never put down? ... But, wait a little time
> ... they are tired of them. ... Are grown children otherwise?
>
> (p. 201)

The transition from the particular, fictional case to a generalized
aphoristic implication – men are, after all, only 'grown children' –
about actual life leads to the female reader being invited to
confirm the truth of the text in terms of her own experience.
Women have to be very careful about entering into relationships
with men, even those who appear to be honest and sincere in
their protestations of love.

It was a recurring theme in the popular literature of Eliot's time,
and one that occurs in *Daniel Deronda*. Lydia Glasher describes to
Gwendolen her relationship with Grandcourt:

> 'I left my husband and child for him nine years ago. Those two
> children are his, and we have two others.... You are very
> attractive, Miss Harleth. But when he first knew me, I too was
> young. Since then my life has been broken up and embittered.'
> ... Gwendolen ... felt a sort of terror: it was as if some ghastly
> vision had come to her in a dream and said, 'I am a woman's
> life'.
>
> (pp. 189–90)

The similarity – although taking place over a longer period of
time, and dealt with in a very different manner (cf. chapter 3
above) – with the episode between Isabel and Levison in *East
Lynne* shows how Eliot used those common literary situations.
The very fact that they did recur in the literature tends to affirm
their likeness to life. The 'ghastly vision' suggests that all women
are vulnerable to the experience, the phrase 'a woman's life', with
its insistence on the indefinite article, is Eliot's way of generaliz-
ing the single fictional case, and relating it to actuality. Eliot's
method is more subtle, and perhaps more powerful, than Wood's

– their basic material came from the same source, a knowledge of Victorian female life.

Another result of the potential vulnerability encountered by women was undue timidity. Hester, in *Barbara Heathcote's Trial*, helps nurse a sick army officer:

> day by day, and hour by hour, Hester and Captain Mayhew were thrown together ... till her face became a necessity to him, and he forgot everything in the world but her. But the awakening came, all too soon. Summer and autumn had passed away, and with the new year he must return to his post ... he loved her, and he was sure she loved him, and she must come with him and be his wife. He spoke out suddenly and passionately. He was too hasty and proud.
>
> (pp. 20–1)

This is not a sudden sexual awakening, but an affection that grows over a period of time. The realization of the emotional feelings, the crisis, is precipitated by the necessary parting, 'he must return to his post', and the revelation is one of love. However, it is too sudden for Hester, who in the context is quite right to ask 'Did he really love her?', but ultimately is wrong to answer Mayhew's proposal, 'I cannot, I cannot; you ask too much' (ibid.). Hester's caution is entirely understandable, for acceptance would entail coverture and the loss of all her rights as a single woman. Yet on reflection, 'She loved him – yes, she was sure she loved him' (p. 22), and the repeated phrase expresses the genuineness of the emotion. Mayhew's 'calm steadfastness' (p. 21) of character ensures that he is neither rake nor fortune-hunter – but Hester's realization is too late, and the letter she writes retracting her refusal he never receives 'for six months after he reached Calcutta news came that Arthur Mayhew was dead; he had fallen a prey to a deadly fever' (p. 22).

Making the right judgement at the right time is crucial, the opportunity may arise only once and the odds are very great. A good marriage can bring a lifetime of happiness, as promised to Adam Bede and Dinah:

> What greater thing is there for two human souls, than to feel that they are joined for life – to strengthen each other in all labour, to rest on each other in all sorrow, to minister to each

other in all pain, to be one with each other in silent unspeak-
able memories at the moment of the last parting?

(p. 576)

The repetitions of 'each other' and 'all' emphasize the sense of
communion, of mutuality, to be enjoyed in a good marriage. But
this is not a wedding at the altar of Mammon, the emphasis is on
the conjoining of 'two human souls' rather than two financial
estates.

A bad marriage, however, may entail many long years of
emotional – and even physical – suffering, and perhaps the
exploitation of the woman's wealth by a reprobate husband. Even
Gwendolen's mother, in *Daniel Deronda*, although experienced in
the world, is taken advantage of in her second marriage: 'She
usually avoided any reference to such facts about Gwendolen's
step-father as that he had carried off his wife's jewellery and
disposed of it' (p. 319). The recurrence of the dilemma of marriage
in popular culture is evidence of its centrality in the lives of the,
mainly female, readers – and is the reason why Hester Heathcote's timidity and caution in regard to Captain Mayhew's proposal is understandable. Once again, of course, the man suffers
from the decision too. In this case he dies, and in any event Carey
was not interested in his reaction to being refused.

Eliot, as usual, took a broader gender perspective. She realized
the questions were more pressing for women, that they had more
at stake, but also that the wrong choice could trap the man. Mr
Transome of *Felix Holt* is by no means a stereotyped nineteenth-
century patriarch:

His threadbare clothes were thoroughly brushed; his soft white
hair was carefully parted and arranged: he was not a neglected-
looking old man. . . . But when Mrs Transome appeared within
the doorway, her husband paused in his work and shrank like a
timid animal looked at in a cage where flight is impossible.

(p. 88)

The man has a fundamental dignity, his 'clothes were thoroughly
brushed' and his 'hair was carefully parted and arranged', nevertheless the appearance of his wife has a dramatic effect. The
imagery – 'shrank', 'timid animal', 'cage', 'flight is impossible' –
carries the sense of entrapment: in a marriage that went badly

wrong a long time ago, in a life that has been mostly wasted. These impressions are confirmed later in the novel when the old man regains a good deal of liveliness under the influence of a child. Mrs Transome, who earlier refers to her husband as a 'distracted insect' (p. 95), expressing the unhuman way in which she sees him, also notices that the child 'makes quite a new life for Mr Transome; they were playfellows at once' (p. 178). It is typical of Eliot's open-minded, and compassionate, attitudes that she was able to embrace many points of view; and the whole exploration of the Transomes' marriage is another illustration of how Eliot wrote within the mainstream interests of her society and its popular literature, but simultaneously extended their moral and perceptive horizons.

This is not, of course, to argue that Eliot was unaware of specifically female concerns, especially as they related to the issues of marriage and wealth. Her readers were naturally deeply interested in those matters, and the concern of many women was not merely passive. Smith, for instance, concluded her argument on the 'Laws Concerning Women':

> Why should not these legal devices be done away with, by the simple abolition of a law which we have outgrown? We do not say that these laws of property are the only unjust laws concerning women . . . but they form a simple tangible, and not offensive point of attack.[7]

In the year of the Second Reform Act of the franchise, 1867, and when therefore the power of parliament was a matter of recurring discussion, some of these points were anonymously developed:

> all must allow that there is much room and scope for amendment in our Englishwoman's position. There are many ways in which she is oppressed, in which her position is still capable of much amelioration and improvement. There are men in the world who will oppress and tryannise over anything, any creature that is in their power, and to such men English law is a very tower of strength. . . . women need protection, protection from the laws and lawgivers of their country. This, of course, applies alone to married women. Single women can own money, houses, and land, and they do not risk ill usage; but once let a woman marry . . . these rights have vanished.[8]

A double paradox is exploited in the cause of this polemic: that women need 'protection' from the very factor of political and social life designed in theory to protect the vulnerable, 'the laws'; and those laws can be changed only by the 'lawgivers', who created them in the first place. Nevertheless, not all men 'oppress and tyrannise', and transformation was possible.

The groundswell that stemmed from the kind of publications quoted above eventually did lead parliament to the appointment of a Select Committee in 1868. One member of it, the Reverend Alfred Dewes, was reported to have commented on:

> the grievous hardships the law inflicts on widows, and the cruel change made in the law in 1833. . . . surely every lover of his country and his kind must long to see the time when there shall be no longer any variance between law and equity.
>
> (*The Englishwoman's Review*, October 1868).

Wider comprehension of the fact that the law was unjust, the 'variance', led to a legal change in the 1870 Married Woman's Property Act. During the parliamentary debates, and it was an extremely fiercely contested issue, Russell Gurney put the case strongly:

> the present state of the law is the cause of daily misery and almost daily crime . . . half the married people of this country are pronounced unfit to exercise any right of property . . . by the act of marriage a woman's property is at once forfeited . . . she forfeits what she previously possessed – she forfeits any which might come to her by gift or bequest – any which she might earn by her own industry or talent – all passes from her, and becomes at once and absolutely the property of her husband. . . . The wife's position formerly was far more favourable.
>
> (*Hansard*, 18 May 1870)

The original readers of *Middlemarch* may have made a connection between this kind of speech and Dorothea Casaubon's pre-1833 ability to retain some of her wealth, for the 1870 Act, because it was so bitterly contested, came into being in a compromised form. Rather than making real progress it at best gave married women back some of the rights they had held less than 40 years earlier. The unsatisfactoriness of the Act is indicated by the continuance of the debate, resulting in further Married Woman's Property Acts in 1882 and 1893. As usual Eliot did not use the past for merely nostalgic purposes, but in order to explore contemporary matters from a deeper perspective. She did not write directly about current affairs, but dealt rather with the analysis of the underlying concepts. Eliot was not concerned so much with the transient moment as with the fundamental, or recurring, state of things.

One aspect of the basic nineteenth-century relationship between marriage and money is that it could affect women without wealth too. When Doctor Heathcote ruins his family through foolish speculation his daughter Barbara receives a proposal of marriage from Nigel, a persistent suitor she has previously declined:

> you are not likely even now to marry me for your own sake, or mine either, though any other woman must be won by such devotion, but at least I can ask you to marry me for your father's sake. ... Only three words, 'I am yours, Nigel,' and every debt from these miserable shares shall be paid.
>
> (pp. 440–1)

Barbara does not sacrifice herself, although she feels the pressures to do so, and save the family, intensely. However immoral later ages may find such a proposition it was not entirely unknown in the Victorian period. Nigel partly bases his appeal on that aspect of life, pointing out to Barbara: 'Women make these sort of sacrifices every day' (p. 401).

Gwendolen is in basically similar circumstances in *Daniel Deronda*, except that she is expected, and expects, to make a brilliant rather than ordinary marriage in any event. Her Uncle Gascoigne comments, 'She ought to make a first-rate marriage' (p. 66) and Gwendolen herself has definite views on the institution:

> her thoughts never dwelt on marriage ... the dramas in which she imagined herself a heroine were not wrought up to that close. To be very much sued or hopelessly sighed for as a bride was indeed an indispensable and agreeable guarantee of womanly power; but to become a wife and wear all the domestic fetters of that condition, was on the whole a vexatious

necessity. . . . Of course marriage was social promotion . . . but promotions have sometimes to be taken with bitter herbs.

(pp. 68–9)

The single woman has many more rights, and less duties and responsibilities than her married sister who wears 'domestic fetters'. Yet Gwendolen is aware that the daughter of a financially ruined family needs 'social promotion', and that a desirable young woman's dowry, if she is impoverished, may be her very desirability, which is an aspect of 'womanly power'. Even before she sees the 'ghastly vision' conjured up by Lydia's life Gwendolen is aware of the transience of female attractiveness in her social context: 'I know that I must be married some time – before it is too late' (p. 179). Although Gwendolen sees herself as a romantic 'heroine' of fiction, she is also aware of the 'vexatious necessity' of practical considerations – which include the link between marriage and money.

That is ultimately the dichotomy – 'heroine'/'necessity' – that leads her to Grandcourt:

The prospect of marrying Grandcourt really seemed more attractive to her than she believed beforehand that any marriage could be: the dignities, the luxuries, the power of doing a great deal of what she liked to do. . . . Gwendolen conceived that after marriage she would most probably be able to manage him thoroughly.

(p. 173)

The flaw in Gwendolen's reasoning is simply that her desire to have reality exist in the way she would like it to entails a double misjudgement: of Grandcourt in particular, and marriage in general. At the moment of formally accepting his proposal, 'her vision was filled by her own release from the Momperts, and her mother's release from Sawyer's Cottage' (p. 348). The lure is partly that of the consequences of worshipping social promotion and Mammon, for Grandcourt is 'the almost certain baronet, the probable peer' (p. 177). If she had needed persuasion Gwendolen's uncle, the rector, had been ready with the relevant arguments in favour of accepting Grandcourt: 'You have a duty here both to yourself and your family' (p. 178). The stakes are greater than for Barbara Heathcote, but the guiding idea is the same.

Gwendolen pays dearly for her error, and in a sense her greed, and is saved from the full consequences of her action, like Dorothea Casaubon, and numerous other fictitious, and probably real, Victorian females only by the premature death of husband. The reasons for getting into bad marriages were diverse, and clearly Gwendolen and Dorothea differ very widely in those, but the result was always unhappiness for one or both of the partners. This was generally likely, although obviously not necessarily, to be worse for the woman, as Caleb warns Mary in *Middlemarch*: 'a woman, let her be as good as she may, has got to put up with the life her husband makes for her' (p. 290). This is axiomatic to nineteenth-century life, yet Gwendolen, reflecting many nonfictional women, fails to learn the full truth of it until it is too late.

Her case in particular illustrates Eliot's central contribution to her period's attitudes to those related obsessions – money and marriage. Gwendolen sacrifices herself at, and on, the altar of Mammon; and with the complaisant delight of most of her society, despite all the evidence that human souls are unlikely to find happiness in such circumstances. The difference in tone between Eliot and Austen on Mammon and the altar is not simply a question of their personalities. Both were concerned with the same problem, and no one explored it more finely than Austen, but because of the changes in the nature of society, by Eliot's time it had become very much more widespread and intense. The ranks of the middling classes had expanded enormously, they had established themselves as being much more important socially and politically, as well as in the field of economics, than they had been just before Eliot's birth. Whereas the old landed gentry had some stability of wealth in Austen's time, the financial foundation of individual members of the bourgeoisie by the latter part of Eliot's life could be unstable. New money could be lost more quickly than it had been gained. The relationship between marriage and money was, by the mid-Victorian period, no longer a subject for mocking irony, rather, it had become closer to tragedy.

7

Women, Jews and Bourgeois Hegemony

The increase in Britain's population and overall wealth that occurred in Eliot's lifetime meant the ranks of the middling classes, who formed the vast bulk of the readership and with which she was most directly concerned, expanded enormously. In effect this had at least two important consequences: people in those classes became much more conscious of, and anxious about, subtle demarcations between different levels of the broad social category Marx termed the bourgeoisie; and that group as a whole demanded greater political power than they had been previously granted. The expansion of industrialization, with its concomitant shift to urban living, was the mainspring of middling-class economic power – which itself created the motivation for political change.

In the 1830 parliamentary election less than 4 per cent of the population were entitled to vote. The middling classes felt that, on the whole, this caused the House of Commons to be dominated by the interests of the landed gentry, whilst the country's wealth was increasingly being generated by industrial and commercial forces which were excluded from political decision making. There was also a strong feeling amongst many of the lower, or labouring, classes that they too were producers of wealth, whilst being unrepresented politically. One aspect of the middling classes' tactics in the struggle for extension of the franchise in both the early 1830s and the mid-1860s was to mobilize the dissatisfactions of the lower classes in support of their own campaigns. In the latter period women also began to seek a vote, and the impetus of the twentieth-century suffragettes came largely from the frustrations of the 1860s pioneers.

The relationship between the classes in serious contention for political power in 1830 is graphically illustrated, in *Middlemarch*, at the burial of Peter Featherstone in Lowick churchyard. The rural characters 'watched old Featherstone's funeral from an upper window of the manor' (p. 359). Being in 'the manor' associates them with the traditional residence of authority, and from the advantage point of 'an upper window' they naturally, and literally, look down on the mainly urban mourners. That distance, and positioning, underlines the detachment of the upper rural classes from the characters who run the town. Dorothea observes, 'It seems to me we know nothing of our neighbours' (p. 360); and Vincy's family are not recognized by everyone, although he is the mayor of Middlemarch and therefore the most important civic figure in the town. The thematic and metaphoric value of this scene is explicated by the diegetic discourse: 'The country gentry of old time lived in a rarefied social air: dotted apart on their stations up the mountain they looked down with imperfect discrimination on the belts of thicker life below' (ibid.). The conflict over parliamentary reform that provides part of the plots in *Middlemarch* and *Felix Holt* stemmed partially from that rarefication, and the sense of exclusion it engendered amongst some of the 'belts of thicker life'. If the upper classes could not tell the difference between one group and another 'below' them, the groups themselves could certainly discriminate, not merely between classes, but sub-sections too. The 'imperfect discrimination' offended the middling classes' sense of self-importance, and when translated into the political arena was offensive to their aspirations of power.

Walter Vincy illustrates a fundamental bourgeois attitude: 'When a man . . . is ready, in the interests of commerce, to take up a firm attitude on politics generally, he has naturally a sense of his importance to the framework of things' (p. 156). An aspect of this is Vincy's insistence that his son Fred goes to, and remains at, the University of Oxford, despite the young man's lack of enthusiasm and aptitude for academic learning. Bulstrode is acerbic on the matter, arguing to Vincy:

> you will not get any concurrence from me as to the course you have pursued with your eldest son. . . . you were not warranted in devoting money to an expensive education which has succeeded in nothing but in giving him extravagant idle habits.
>
> (ibid.)

It is clear that Bulstrode sees Vincy's ambitions lying in the area of the subtleties of social class, that he is trying to buy a slight rise in status and esteem for the family through the means of 'an expensive education' for a son. This would be a movement up the sub-groups of the middling classes rather than a substantial change of actual class. Vincy's reply is also unequivocal: 'It's a good British feeling to try and raise your family a little: in my opinion, it's a father's duty to give his sons a fine chance' (pp. 156–7). Vincy repudiates Bulstrode's moral accusation of un-necessary extravagance with the pragmatic morality of 'a father's duty'. In any event to 'raise your family' socially is 'good'. Bulstrode, like most of the initial readers, is also middling class and so understands the argument very well. Indeed, Bulstrode and Vincy are related through marriage, as the former is married to the latter's sister, an aspect of the novel's central metaphor of the web. Although Bulstrode is speaking ostensibly in his profes-sional capacity as a banker, there is perhaps also a suggestion of family jealousy – since Bulstrode came from humbler origins than the Vincys, and background is not something easily out-lived.

Nevertheless the structure of the novel works against Vincy in this case, for Mary Garth sees that Fred has no vocation and provides the real opposition to Vincy's aspirations for his son. Fred could not 'imagine what he was to do, with his father on one side expecting him straightway to enter the Church, with Mary on the other threatening to forsake him if he did enter it' (p. 601). Mary's objection, that Fred would be an awful clergyman, is the one point of view that never occurs to Vincy. The ambition for social respectability was generally more important than the care of souls.

The Vincy family is not presented as particularly unusual, certainly not malicious or especially self-seeking within the ambi-tions of their class position. Yet they do appear to be obsessed with social status. The most common way for a young woman who was considered physically attractive to achieve class mobility was through marriage. Rosamond has a view of life that seems remarkably informed by the poorer kind of nineteenth-century fiction: 'a stranger was absolutely necessary to Rosamond's social romance, which had always turned on a lover and bridegroom who was not a Middlemarcher' (p. 145); but her perception of the new doctor is very much in keeping with the reality of the time and class:

here was Mr Lydgate suddenly corresponding to her ideal,

being altogether foreign to Middlemarch, carrying a certain air of distinction congruous with good family, and possessing connections which offered vistas of that middle-class heaven, rank.

(ibid.)

Lydgate is related to the aristocracy, 'good family' indeed for the daughter of a Midlands manufacturer. The word 'heaven' suggests the 'middle-class' worship 'rank', and the phrase adds up to sharp social satire of middling-class aspirations. Rank is a false idol, a graven image, that has replaced more profound values. In this context of the Vincy family it links with the disregard paid to Fred's lack of interest in a religious vocation. Bad clergymen hardly matter if heaven is conceived in terms of rank rather than soul.

These ideas recur a little later in the novel when Rosamond's perception is further explored:

the piquant fact about Lydgate was his good birth, which distinguished him from all Middlemarch admirers, and presented marriage as a prospect of rising in rank and getting a little nearer to that celestial condition on earth in which she would ... associate with relatives quite equal to the county people who looked down on the Middlemarchers.

(p. 195)

Ned Plymdale is the local suitor most likely, in tea-party speculation, to succeed, but Rosamond consistently refuses to acknowledge his claim even before she is aware of Lydgate. But none of the 'Middlemarch admirers' can match Tertius' appeal and therefore have a realistic chance of marriage. The reiteration of the concept 'rising in rank', and the diction of 'celestial condition on earth', emphasize the value of those features to the character and the narrational satire of them. Ultimately, though, there is some validity in Rosamond's class perception, for 'the county people' do literally look 'down on the Middlemarchers' who are members of her family, at Featherstone's funeral.

Rosamond is representative in respect of her attitudes. Her mother's only objections to the engagement with Lydgate, as she explains to Vincy, is that Rosamond might have done better by waiting, by giving herself the chance of meeting someone else: 'She might have met somebody on a visit who would have been a far better match; I mean at her schoolfellow Miss Willoughby's. There are relations in that family quite as high as Mr Lydgate's' (p. 377). Although Vincy himself complains, 'I don't want a son-in-law who has got nothing but his relations to recommend him' (ibid.), and sees Lydgate's comparative poverty as a disqualification – illustrating that middling-class worship of wealth at times competed with its adoration of the celestial condition of rank – he still responds to Lydgate within the limitations of his class: 'Vincy was a little in awe of him, a little vain that he wanted to marry Rosamond' (pp. 379–80). This way of thinking comprehends nothing wrong in social mobility through marriage, it is a way of attacking class privilege on an individual basis, but does not provide, of course, a collective middling-class route to the root of political power.

The rivalry between different sub-sections of the middling classes is also depicted in the relationship of the Vincys and the Garths, two families that are eventually united through the wedding of Fred and Mary:

> Even when Caleb Garth was prosperous, the Vincys were on condescending terms with him and his wife, for there were nice discriminations of rank in Middlemarch; and though old manufacturers could not any more than dukes be connected with none but equals, they were conscious of an inherent social superiority which was defined with great nicety in practice, though hardly expressible theoretically.

(p. 263)

The problem with analysing society in theoretic class terms is that the 'nicety' of 'discriminations' between sub-groups is 'hardly expressible'. The social theorists criticized by Eliot in her essay on Rheil (cf. chapter 2 above) would have been unable to distinguish between the two middling-class families, but the characters themselves were fully 'conscious' of 'inherent' matters of 'rank'. Eliot observes, records and – through the implied parallel with 'dukes' – satirizes the attitudes of 'superiority'. She is able to do so with such ease partly because of the prevalence of the distinctions in the society for which she was writing, and because of that the readers may be assumed to understand the significance, and terrible importance, of those niceties. Failure on the part of the reader to appreciate the differences, and their value to the characters, will lead to a misunderstanding of both the reality of the society the fiction records, and the artistic nature of the novel itself.

On the whole, women were more central in those kind of social distinctions than men. Males met usually on some kind of formal basis, even when meeting apparently informally. The banker, the manufacturer, the vicar, etc. all had fairly defined roles, and personal background may qualify those to some extent but the basic relationships were settled. The wives of those men, however, related to one another on a more personal basis – partly because they met much more frequently, and at one another's homes rather than in the formal settings of business. The intimacy that was generated meant almost every factor in the relationship gained significance:

Mrs Vincy had never been at her ease with Mrs Garth, and frequently spoke of her as a woman who had had to work for her bread – meaning that Mrs Garth had been a teacher before her marriage; in which case an intimacy with Lindley Murray and Mangnall's *Questions* was something like a draper's discrimination of calico trademarks, or a courier's acquaintance with foreign countries; no woman who was better off needed that sort of thing.

(p. 264)

Teaching is conceived of as a form of trade, and the popular textbooks by Murray and Mangnall as similar to 'draper's ... calico trademarks'. It is not the kind of familiarity with the world of common trade a 'woman who was better off needed', and therefore reveals an irradicable inadequacy in the background. The perceptive initial reader would have appreciated the ironic satire in Mrs Vincy, whose own position was essentially built on trade – although at the manufacturing end – adopting a supercilious attitude to that activity. Even if Caleb were to become very prosperous his wife's acquaintances would always be conscious of her need to have 'had to work for her bread'.

Mrs Garth herself is well aware of the distinctions, and the impossibility of their being ignored:

the passage from governess into housewife had wrought itself a little too strongly into her consciousness, and she rarely forgot that while her grammar and accent were above the town standard, she wore a plain cap, cooked the family dinner, and darned all the stockings.

(p. 275)

Mrs Garth really is a 'housewife', performing all the household tasks herself, rather than delegating them to servants. Even her superiority of education is unable to outweigh, in the practical niceties of social intercourse, the necessity of doing her own cooking and darning. It is an indictment of social attitudes, and female ones in particular, towards women's education. Ultimately it was not accorded a high status, which of course helped to keep it at at a generally poor standard.

Middlemarch deals more perceptively, and in greater detail, than any other novel of its time with the intricacies of bourgeois intra-class relationships. In the early 1830s, when the action is set, the middling classes were relatively small and in their political conflict with the ruling classes tended to present an homogenous identity. After 1867 they had gained political ascendancy, and general prosperity had widened their ranks considerably, so that the distinctions Eliot explores were vitally topical.

Inter-class differences were, of course, also important, although rather easier to see. The kind of observation Yonge made in her 1865 novel *The Clever Woman of the Family*, for instance, proliferated in popular fiction. When the aristocratic Keith family visit a bourgeois household in the country the diegesis records: 'Timber End was certainly a delightful place. Alick had called it a cockney villa, but it was in good taste, and very fair and sweet with flowers and shade' (p. 296). The term 'cockney villa' indicated a house built by someone from London who had made money in trade, it was a satiric appellation denoting the social superiority of the user against the pretension, and ostentation, of the cockney villa's owner. The satire is carried by the juxtaposition of the words: 'cockney' clearly refers to low birth, with its concomitant common habits and tastes; whilst the classical allusion of 'villa' connotes grandeur and high culture. The former can only aspire to the latter, and in the eyes of the governing classes if the bourgeoisie imagine they have really joined the ranks of the high born that denotes just how laughable they are. Whilst acknowledging that attitude the narrative voice in this extract re-establishes the validity of the house, for 'it was in good taste', not vulgar, as the aristocratic satire expects. 'Timber End' is 'very fair and sweet with flowers and shade', suggesting a real integration into rural life, not an imposition of city ostentation on the countryside, and also balance between the implied sunlight and shade. A nasty anti-bourgeois jibe is turned into a celebration of middling-class taste and sensibility. This, of course, does not challenge, but affirms the values of the bulk of the initial, middling-class, readership.

Carey's *Barbara Heathcote's Trial*, by way of variation, ontologically celebrates the middling class by presenting it in relation to the lower orders. Barbara and Hester:

> were just approaching the outskirts of the village, which, like most other English villages, was cleanly and cheerful.... A cleanly, and pretty little village ... where even the day-labourer touched his cap, and the children grinned and curtseyed, or pulled their sandy forelocks to the doctor's daughter as she passed.
>
> (p. 11)

The respectful 'day-labourer' and 'the children' behave normally in their subservience 'to the doctor's daughter', for this is specifically 'like most other English villages'. It is comforting to a middling-class readership, especially as many of them were in urban areas, in which the lower classes did not necessarily tug their forelocks in the street to their betters. Such a fictional scene reassures the reader that correct values do still exist, somewhere in England.

Adam Bede, a character set in a time before serious bourgeois aspirations for political power:

> was very susceptible to the influence of rank, and quite ready to give an extra amount of respect to every one who had more advantages than himself, not being a philosopher, or a proletaire with democratic ideas.... He had no theories about setting the world to rights.
>
> (pp. 208–9)

The time factor meant there was slightly less reassurance in this portrait, for his age had gone, but nevertheless the dismissal of the 'proletaire with democratic ideas' and 'theories', the 'respect' given to 'rank', would certainly have been comforting in the aftermath of Chartist disturbances. The later hero, Felix Holt, presents a more complex resolution of radicalism and conservatism, but that was written just at the point the bourgeoisie were about to attain parliamentary power, and is partly concerned with a warning about the duties and responsibilities entailed.

The story told in *Silas Marner*, set around the same period, satirizes middling-class social ambitions. Macey 'the old clerk' tells how Mr Cliff, 'a Lunnon tailor', bought up rural property and built 'stables four times as big as Squire Cass's' although he could not ride. This was partly a manifestation of ostentation, a crude use of wealth made in trade to appear more important than the local squire: 'Cliff, he was ashamed o' being called a tailor, and he was sore vexed'. His aim, like Walter Vincy's, was to raise his son, and to that end forced the boy, against the lad's natural inclination, to ride: 'it was a common saying as the father wanted to ride the tailor out o' the lad, and make a gentleman on him'. Macey's tale contains a moral ending: 'the poor lad got sickly and died, and the father ... died raving' (pp. 102–3). This is a view of middling-class pretension told from a lower-class perspective, and is a far from comfortable one for bourgeois readers. On a personal level it undermines their self-esteem, and in the 1860s, when the novel was published, was discomforting politically because the middling classes needed the support of the lower orders as part of the groundswell for further parliamentary reform.

Eliot rarely simply confirmed the validity of her readers' aspirations, and in *Silas Marner* the lost child of the gentry – the female who was offered without apparent cost the much coveted entry into the county set, the price for which was usually marriage – rejects that socio-economic mobility in favour of artisan life. When Eppie's natural father, Godfrey Cass, is appealing to Silas, her adopted father, to rescind his claim to her Godfrey does so in specifically class terms: 'she may marry some low working-man, and then, whatever I might do for her, I couldn't make her well-off' (p. 232). Eppie makes her own mind up, and replies on the same basis of her father's appeal: 'I can't think o' no other home. I wasn't brought up to be a lady, and I can't turn my mind to it. I like the working-folks, and their victuals, and their ways' (p. 234). Eppie confirms this by marrying Aaron the gardener, and her ideas are clearly the opposite of those of Cliff the tailor who thought he could turn his 'mind to it' to transform his class status, whatever he was 'brought up to be'. Esther in *Felix Holt* makes a similar decision, and 'resigned all claim to the Transome Estates' (p. 599). She too, by marrying Felix, accepts a much lower position in the social hierarchy. To some extent both characters are motivated by personal love, which they would have to forego in order to achieve socio-economic mobility, but the desire for that blessed state motivated many of the middling classes to all manner of sacrifices. Eliot demands of the reader that such factors are acknowledged, there is no easy affirmation of the sought-after values.

The political aspect of middling-class aspirations are epitomized in the two major struggles for parliamentary election voting rights, culminating in the Franchise Reform Acts of 1832 and 1867. Both were extremely hard fought, bitter events. In 1831 two attempts to achieve changes in the voting system were defeated in parliament, and the third Bill was successful only after widespread riots. Woodward has recorded the mood of the times when the third Bill was initially rejected:

> riots broke out almost at once in Nottingham and Derby ... there was trouble in Bristol on a [large] scale ... [demonstrators were able] to break into the old and new prisons and to burn the bishop's palace and a number of other buildings. Next day a cavalry charge restored order. ... there was, however, a danger that similar disturbances might break out in a score of towns.[1]

There was just not enough cavalry to contain countrywide mass arson and destruction of property. The extent of the rioting that did occur indicates how strong emotions had become, and how much the lower orders were involved in the issue.

Yet the degree of actual change brought about by the 1832 Reform Act was relatively small. Only adult males holding the requisite property qualifications were given a vote, and the electorate still constituted only about 5 per cent of the total population. The historian Anthony Wood has commented, 'The increase in the electorate had not brought the system much closer to anything resembling democracy. ... The power of the landlord was still considerable'.[2] Farmer Dibbs declares in *Felix Holt*: 'I don't care two straws who I vote for. ... It stands to reason a man should vote for his landlord' (p. 305). Even without such complacency because the ballot remained public bribery was widespread, and corruption of diverse forms occurred.

Elections under the new, Reformed franchise took place in December 1832, and the one described in *Felix Holt* was not untypical. To some degree Eliot drew upon her personal memory of the kind of mayhem that ensued in the first election after Reform. She witnessed the riots at Nuneaton, and Peter Coveney, in his Notes to the edition of the novel referred to throughout this book, quotes very interestingly from relevant documents (pp. 668–9). Perhaps the most important point, though, is that the novel was written when agitation for Reform had again built up, and in depicting the corruption of political life it demonstrates that increasing the ability to vote is not in itself a panacea for all ills.

One recurring problem was the mood of the mob. They had no votes, but in their numbers and their physical strength and potential ferocity there was power. Whenever violence was perpetrated in the name of Reform the leaders of that movement always denounced the perpetrators, but mass demonstrations undoubtedly did advance their cause, and some argument existed as to the extent they were deliberately used by Reformers. Once a mob was roused they could quickly get out of control. The Radical agent Johnson in *Felix Holt* certainly manipulates the voteless colliers into violence in the naive belief that it will serve their own political interests. Chubb, the publican of the Sugar Loaf, supports the Radical cause on the grounds that 'Chubb's notion of a Radical was that he was a new and agreeable kind of lick-spittle who fawned on the poor instead of on the rich, and so was likely to send customers to a "public"' (p. 222). With his cooperation Johnson treats the miners of the area to ale and so enlists their physical support on election day, and therefore both are in part responsible for the riot, and the consequent death of the constable. Neither character has any real interest in the political issues, both being motivated by a sense of self-importance and financial opportunism.

Although mainly set in 1832 *Felix Holt* is not strictly or merely a historical novel, at the time Eliot was writing it parliament was debating the Borough Franchise Extension Bill. The novel is a refraction of the topical issues being raised. Eliot was not against widening the suffrage as such, but she was wary of too much reliance on purely political solutions to deeper social problems, and her radicalism, like Holt's, was individualistic in nature. She did not agree with the kind of conservatism expressed by MPs such as Robert Lowe, but neither could she accept the simplistic axiom that if one side is wrong the other must inevitably be right. Eliot could agree with Lowe's analysis of the rhetoric of the Radical Reformers:

> One hon. Gentleman says the working classes are 'wrongfully' excluded from the exercise of the franchise; another describes their exclusion as 'unjust'; a third looks upon them as being in consequence 'degraded'; while a fourth speaks of them as being 'slaves'. So we go on until we have an accumulation of such terms.
>
> (*Hansard*, 3 May 1865)

The emotive language attributed, not unjustly, to the Radicals was dangerous because it used inaccurate terminology, and it was designed to lead the working classes to expect the vote to create a form of utopia. It was essentially dishonest, and Johnson's treachery, although repudiated by the Radical candidate – Harold Transome – himself, was a metaphoric extension of the linguistic deceit. Holt tells Transome:

> I'm a Radical myself, and mean to work all my life long against privilege, monopoly, and oppression. But I would rather be a livery-servant proud of my master's title, than I would seem to make common cause with scoundrels who turn the best hopes of men into by-words for cant and dishonesty.
>
> (p. 274)

It is the kind of speech that shows how Felix Holt is both an extension and development of Adam Bede. Holt has no respect for advantage, or 'privilege', as such, proclaiming himself 'a Radical', but he maintains a concept of pride in honourable service, 'proud of my master's title'. This extract also articulates the view that 'the best hopes of men' may be cynically manipulated by political 'scoundrels'.

Holt recognizes that working-class aspirations for parliamentary representation may indeed be amongst their 'best hopes', although as an individualist he is sceptical of collective panaceas. His own speech on election day is a reply to an essentially, although slightly anachronistic, Chartist who urges: 'universal suffrage, and annual parliaments, and the vote by ballot, and electoral districts' (p. 397). Holt's approach is more on the grounds of natural morality:

> the great question was how to give every man a man's share in life. But I think he expects voting to do more towards it than I do. . . . I hope there will be great changes. . . . The way to get rid of folly is to get rid of vain expectations, and of thoughts that don't agree with the nature of things. . . . all the schemes about voting, and districts, and annual parliaments, and the rest, are engines, and the water or steam – the force that is to work them – must come out of human nature – out of men's passions, feelings, desires.
>
> (pp. 399–400)

The 'hope' for 'great changes' expresses the radicalism, as opposed to the conservative desire to simply conserve the status quo, but the use of the concepts 'folly' and 'vain' carry a moral weight that is lacking in appeals for purely constitutional change. The metaphors of 'engines', 'steam' and 'force' suggest the inevitability of transformation, and 'the great question' is how that process may be channelled for the greatest good.

It is another instance of Eliot's prophetic vision that Holt's speech anticipates an essay by the political philosopher Thomas Carlyle. Within days of the eventual passing of the Reform Act in August 1867 Carlyle wrote in *Macmillan's Magazine* his essay 'Shooting Niagra: and After?', in which he questioned the value of an extended franchise:

> indeed your 'Reform' movement, from of old, has been wonderful to me; everybody meaning by it, not 'Reformation,' practical amendment of his own foul courses, or even of his neighbour's . . . but meaning simply 'Extension of the Suffrage'. Bring in more voting; that will clear away the universal rottenness, and quagmire of mendacities, in which poor England is drowning.[3]

Carlyle rejects the notion that life is essentially political and constitutional. He sees reform as a moral issue, as 'Reformation' of character, 'practical amendment' of 'foul courses', rather than 'more voting'. Ultimately, in this way of thinking, 'universal rottenness' and the 'quagmire of mendacities' will exist in any system which is not informed by moral decency, and a strong code of ethics. In the essay Carlyle goes further than Eliot, or any of her characters, in applauding the virtues of the aristocracy against the values of the bourgeosie, but the moral tone of the whole is close to that of the novel.

In so far as the fictional Holt's argument is basically optimistic it is different from those of the real Carlyle or actual Lowe. Holt's is something of an affirmation of radicalism, Lowe's speech in the House of Commons accepted none of that:

> I am inclined to think that democracy in the present state of things would be a great misfortune. . . . Look at Australia. There universal suffrage was conceded suddenly, and the working classes immediately availing themselves of it, became masters of the situation. Nobody else has a shadow of power. Does anybody doubt that in America the working classes are the masters? . . . [Reform is] a proposal to subvert the existing order of things, and to transfer power from the hands of property and intelligence, and to place it in the hands of men whose whole life is necessarily occupied in daily struggles for existence.
>
> (*Hansard*, 3 May 1865)

Whatever the validity of Lowe's unargued assertions about Australia and America, the main feature in this excerpt from his speech may be seen as fear of the lower orders. The reiterated juxtaposition of 'working classes' and 'masters' in the context of an inversion of power reveals Lowe's fears. He, and those he spoke for, did not conceive of 'democracy' as a sharing of power, which is Holt's term, but as an over-turning of the existing hierarchy. His linking of 'property and intelligence' was fundamental to mainstream Victorian political beliefs. Both the Reform Acts of 1832 and 1867 linked suffrage to property qualifications.

One reason for Lowe's fears was the behaviour of the mob when excited. The mid-1860s showed every sign of following the pattern of the early 1830s. Reform was first promised, then denied, and large sections of the population became agitated. In the month following the publication of the complete *Felix Holt* a large pro-Reform demonstration took place in London's Hyde Park, which was at that time enclosed by railings. A great many people arrived for the meeting, and the police attempted, very much against the odds, to restrict entry to the park. In the ensuing confrontation the constables were attacked, the cordon breached and the railings uprooted, as an eye-witness account recorded:

> vast crowds had collected in the neighbourhood of Hyde Park. A force of foot and mounted police, numbering 1,600 or 1,800, was here assembled. . . . The police, indeed, hastened to every point that was attacked, and for a short time kept the multitude at bay; but their numbers were ultimately insufficient . . . till in the end the crowd entered *ad libitum*. . . . The police brought their truncheons into active use, and a number of the 'roughs' were somewhat severely handled.
>
> (*The Times*, 24 July 1866)

It was a civil battle, as the euphemistic 'somewhat severely handled' indicates. The fact that at least part of the crowd were described as 'roughs' shows that people who were not politically sophisticated had been attracted to the event – a view supported by other sources – perhaps some of them like the colliers from the Sugar Loaf. That was certainly a suspicion the governing classes held. The uprooting of the railings became a metaphor for public disorder and anarchy for several decades. The Radical Reformers denied responsibility, but the newspaper's editorial put the establishment's perception of the matter:

> We trust that Mr Beales and his friends are satisfied with the success of their demonstration yesterday. They have succeeded in keeping the West-end of London in a state of disorder . . . in causing great damage to the Park, and in producing a dangerous riot, accompanied with serious injuries to several persons.
>
> (ibid.)

The mood of frustration, resentment and nervousness did indeed lead to the disturbances continuing through the week, although less violently. Later in that week, for example, 'John Nias, a member of the Council of the Reform League' was arrested in a street disturbance in which he was reported as shouting 'Never mind the police; we have got the matter in our own hands now, and can do as we like' (*The Times*, 27 July 1866). The kind of anarchy depicted in *Felix Holt* only a few weeks earlier achieved an immediacy of relevance:

> the main strength of the crowd was not on the side of sound opinion, but might come to be on the side of sound cudgelling and kicking. The navvies and pitmen in dishabille seemed to be multiplying, and to be clearly not belonging to the party of Order.
>
> (p. 413)

This was prophetic, and mainly the result of using the lower orders as a form of canon fodder, as muscular argument. It was effective up to a point, but ultimately unpredictable and liable to become uncontrollable, characteristics the riot in the novel develops. Eliot touches on a profound fear of the privileged classes in this respect.

An extension of the franchise was eventually achieved, but it still excluded, despite all the rhetoric, the majority of the working classes' males. The impetus had initially come from the growing number of the bourgeoisie who remained without a vote, but had gained even greater economic power and importance, as a result of the 1832 compromise. In 1867, with the suffrage being almost doubled, they at last gained parliamentary ascendancy. Nevertheless, it still meant that less than 10 per cent of the population were enfranchised. It was truly, however, many people contributed to it, in whatever ways, a victory for the middling classes. This was exactly the kind of outcome *Felix Holt* prophetically implies.

The hegemonic nature of the process was that the bourgeoisie had successfully articulated lower-class dissatisfactions. At no time in the period were the mass of the working classes realistically likely to have been given a vote, yet their support for the cause of Reform had certainly helped to bring it about – in the particular form, and at the time, it was achieved, as opposed to its inevitability later in the century, and then perhaps in a more dilute measure. In fact the lower orders did receive their reward in 1884, but Eliot's two last, great novels were written in the period of bourgeois hegemony, the one decade in which middling-class values and attitudes were supreme and fundamentally

unchallenged. That middling group held moral, economic, political and cultural leadership of the country and empire, linking the
interests of all other sections of that widespread community to its
own, and transforming others' aspirations into a framework that
coincided with bourgeois ambitions. In the 1880s that state of
hegemonic leadership began to break down, but by then Eliot
could no longer comment on it.

Although the middling classes enjoyed a decade without fundamental opposition there were voices of dissent. Carlyle's was
an important philosophical conservative voice affirming, in
'Shooting Niagra', the value of the old rulers: 'The Aristocracy, as
a class, has yet no thought of giving-up the game, or ceasing to be
what in the language of flattery is called "Governing Class"'
(p. 240). Matthew Arnold's *Culture and Anarchy*, two years later,
attacked both bourgeoisie and aristocracy in an intellectually
significant book that perhaps had greater affect in the long run
than in the years immediately following its publication. It must be
appreciated too that the term bourgeois hegemony is shorthand
for *male* middling-class leadership and supremacy. Although
women were not granted the franchise in 1867 the efforts of the
feminists of that period sowed the seeds for later victories, and
their active discontent eventually contributed to the undermining
of the status quo as it was constructed in that year. All these
rejections of the concept of bourgeois hegemony underlay the
surface stability of the last decade of Eliot's life.

Arnold divided the population into three major groups: Barbarians, Philistines and Populace. The Barbarians are 'our aristocratic class',[4] who 'care . . . for the body', which is a manifestation
of their 'exterior culture'. For Arnold this demonstrated a definite
inadequacy, for 'true culture teaches us to fetch sweetness and
light; but its hold upon these very studies appears remarkably
external, and unable to exert any deep power upon its spirit'
(p. 103). The Barbarians are distinguished from 'the Philistines', or
'middle class', who are:

> the enemy of the children of light or servants of the idea. . . .
> *Philistine* gives the notion of something particularly stiff-necked
> and perverse in the resistance to light and its children; and
> therein it specially suits our middle class, who not only do not
> pursue sweetness and light, but who even prefer to them that

sort of machinery of business ... which makes up the dismal
and illiberal life on which I have so often touched.

(pp. 101–2)

The 'Populace' are of course the remainder, 'half-hidden amidst
its poverty and squalor ... [but] beginning to perplex us by
marching where it likes, meeting where it likes, bawling what it
likes, breaking what it likes' (p. 105). The result of all this superficiality, concern with 'exterior' matters only, 'stiff-necked' and
'dismal' life, and merely hedonistic activity, will ultimately be
anarchy. Only a concern for real culture, the pursuit of 'sweetness
and light', can retrieve the situation.

In *Middlemarch* Dorothea does attempt to pursue sweetness and
light against the influence of the interested 'amiable handsome
baronet' Barbarian 'who said "Exactly" to her remarks even when
she expressed uncertainty' (p. 32), and in opposition to the stiff-
necked Philistinism of Casaubon who had 'a character as any
ruminant animal' (p. 227). The Populace is always likely to throw
eggs at any convenient target, as happens to Brooke at the
hustings: 'an unpleasant egg broke on Mr Brooke's shoulder ...
then came a hail of eggs' (p. 549). Anarchy reigns in the town, and
a kind of moral anarchism pervades the Lydgates' home; but the
cultured characters, such as Dorothea and Ladislaw, Mary and
Fred – under her influence – manage to make their own way, and
perpetuate the kind of social decency Carlyle recommended in
'Shooting Niagra': 'the talent of right conduct, of wise and useful
behaviour' (p. 233). Eliot too contributed to the underlying ques-
tioning of bourgeois hegemonic values.

Among those seeking extension of the franchise were a number
of women. The Kensington Group was formed in 1865 as an
organization to argue for female suffrage, using the MP John
Stuart Mill as their parliamentary spokesman. In fact the idea of
the franchise being extended to women was not absolutely new,
in terms of Eliot's lifetime dating back at least as far as 1842, when
The Westminster Review, the journal Eliot subsequently edited,
published an article advocating it. Many other articles and essays
on the subject appeared between then and the mid-1860s – but
the general impetus towards reform during the later time stimulated increased female interest.

Bodichon's magazine, which has been quoted from in earlier
chapters, had been founded in 1857 with the express purpose of

forwarding issues covered by the broad term The Woman Ques-
tion, so naturally it was in the forefront of the suffrage debate.
Under the title 'Some probable Consequences of Extending the
Franchise to Female Householders' it argued:

> To refuse the suffrage to educated women, while granting its
> extension to an increased number of uneducated men, would
> be to proclaim the superiority of physical force to intelligence;
> and it is certainly an anomaly to refuse the suffrage to women
> who pay income tax, yet grant it to men who pay none.
>
> (*The Englishwoman's Review*, October 1866)

As the title of the article reveals, voting is still being linked with
property and in this case the concern is mainly with 'Female
Householders' and 'women who pay income tax'. The petition
that Mill presented in the House of Commons was partly based
on the same argument: 'the possession of property in this country
carries with it the right to vote in the election of representatives in
Parliament ... the exclusion from this right of women holding
property is therefore anomalous ... [on] strictly constitutional
grounds' (*Westminster Review*, January 1867). It is mainly a technical point, and if accepted would have resulted in only a very
few – single and relatively wealthy – women gaining a vote. The
polemic, though, is typically based on a notion of natural justice,
that men less well qualified than women should not be constitu-
tionally more powerful. An important aspect of the argument was
that:

> One of the effects of admitting women to the suffrage will be,
> to lead them to read and think more about public events. The
> study of history and political economy will become more preva-
> lent among them, so that twenty years hence, women who
> possess what is called 'the education of a lady', will be very
> superior in mental acquirements to the same class at the pre-
> sent day.
>
> (*The Englishwoman's Review*, October 1866)

This again is very similar to the argument Mill had made in
parliament when attempting to enfranchise the male working
classes: 'If there was no reason for extending the franchise to the
working classes except the stimulus it would give to education ...

the reason would be more than sufficient' (*Hansard*, 13 April 1866). The connecting of those two vital issues, suffrage and education, continued into the twentieth century.

Since Eliot had no strong faith in political action she was not, despite her concern with the issues, an active participant in the movement for female suffrage. In 1869 she wrote to her friend Jane Senior:

> There is no subject on which I am more inclined to hold my peace and learn, than on the "Woman Question". It seems to me to overhang abysses.... Conclusions seem easy so long as we keep large blinkers on and look in the direction of our own private path.
>
> (SL, p. 367)

The journal she had once edited articulated the kind of involved detachment that characterizes Eliot's thinking: 'to seek the reform of existing evils rather in the development than in the overthrow of the present order' (*The Westminster Review*, January 1867). Eliot's ambivalence is illustrated in *Daniel Deronda* when the narrator describes Gwendolen's attitudes to social issues: 'she ... marked herself off from any sort of theoretical or practically reforming women by satirizing them' (p. 83). This was a common stance of many superficial young women, and men too of course, and it is the character herself who is being satirized in the passage as a whole: 'She rejoiced to feel herself exceptional; but her horizon was that of the genteel romance where the heroine's soul poured out in her journal is full of vague power, originality, and general rebellion, while her life moves strictly in the sphere of fashion' (ibid.). The juxtaposition of ideal and real here certainly offers a criticism of Gwendolen, and her type, and therefore seems to endorse the value of the 'practically reforming women' of whom the character is scathing. However, those women given to 'theoretical' considerations are proposing to enfranchise Gwendolen and her ilk, and it is difficult to see such people exercising rational judgement at the ballot box. In that respect the 'reforming women' are also being criticized for their 'theoretical' approach to problems.

As is clear from the previous chapters of this book Eliot was well aware of the complexity of the issues, that Gwendolen, for example, was in part the victim of her education, partly the dupe of social expectations and fashionable assumptions about life. The fundamental problem was the 'reform of existing evils' – which included education, social expectations and social assumptions, especially as they applied to women. Eliot was not against female suffrage as such, but did not accept it as a panacea for all women's legitimate grievances.

One of the features of the question was the emotion it raised. Purely rational discussion became impossible when prejudice met preconception in direct confrontation. The establishment responded to arguments about female education and franchise with entrenched views:

> Strong as the case may be, it only proves to us that women should be more cared for, not that they should be invited to care for themselves. A lunatic may be very ill used, but that is no reason for putting a sword in his hand.
>
> (*The Times*, 6 March 1867)

Whatever the arguments about the ethical value of paternalism in itself, the metaphor equating women with lunatics revealed the kind of attitudes that gave females no confidence in the men who claimed the right to 'care for' them.

Eliot was disdainful of *The Times'* kind of assertion, and although she did not argue in favour of suffrage neither did she specifically oppose it. Some women, however, were not receptive to the idea. An anonymous article entitled 'The Great Unrepresented' began 'The present writer has the disadvantage of being a woman' and concluded: 'we are women, not "lesser men". We are content with that place in the world's economy which God has given us ... all our powers are necessary for our own individual work' (*Blackwood's Magazine*, September 1866). It is extremely unlikely that a publisher, Eliot's own coincidentally, with the integrity of Blackwood would have published such an article as part of a male conspiracy. Its genuineness is also endorsed by a number of other similar articles. Those female authors felt that the attempt to gain a vote was simply the apeing of male life, the projection of women as 'lesser men', whilst they advocated concentration on the activities women did best, and uniquely, 'our own individual work'.

In 1868, the year after women had been specifically excluded – along with most men – from the franchise, Eliot wrote to the

feminist campaigner Emily Davies: 'The physical and physiological differences between women and men ... may be said to lie on
the surface.... But ... the differences are deep roots of
psychological development' (SL, p. 351). Eliot went on to celebrate
the 'spiritual wealth acquired for mankind ... that lies in
woman's peculiar constitution for a special moral influence'
(ibid.). For Eliot that influence was, paradoxically, more palpable
than a vote. It could be directed at individuals, whereas a vote
was merely one in several tens of thousands, with little concen-
trated effect.

Eliot's scepticism about the efficacy of suffrage in improving
the circumstances of women, and of social values and attitudes as
a whole, arose from the nature of politics and, in particular,
elections. In this respect Eliot's views were not far from those of
Carlyle and Arnold. The practices described in *Felix Holt* remained
current until after secret ballots were introduced in 1872, whilst
Middlemarch was appearing in serial form. At Treby Magna the
Tory supporters take a known Radical on his way to the poll, 'and
pushed [him] up an entry, where he remained the prisoner of
terror combined with the want of any back outlet, and never gave
his vote that day' (p. 412). Whilst potential Tory voters themselves
were also terrorized:

> a gentleman coming in on horseback ... to vote for Garstin had
> had his horse turned round and frightened into a head-long
> gallop out of it again.
>
> (p. 413)

It is typical of Eliot that both parties are presented as being guilty
of violence and intolerance. Eliot could see little real good emerging from such a system, therefore the possession or absence of a
vote seemed irrelevant.

She also recognized that influence, and even to some extent
power, was not necessarily entirely inscribed in formal institutions, such as parliament. Moral and cultural leadership, which
the later term hegemony came to cover, could be exercised, in
Eliot's view, by women without the benefit of franchise. At the
height of the Reform debate she wrote privately to John Morley,
editor of the influential journal the *Fortnightly*:

> It is the function of love in the largest sense, to mitigate the
> harshness of all fatalities ... through all transitions the goal

towards which we are proceeding is a more clearly discerned distinctness of function (allowing always for exceptional cases of individual organization) with as near an approach to equivalence of good for women and for men as can be secured by the effort of growing moral force.

(SL, p. 332)

The 'growing moral force' was, for Eliot, a powerful and positive female attribute, illustrating an entirely different view of womanhood from that manifested in *The Times* extract quoted above. Where that saw women as essentially passive recipients of male protection, Eliot depicts women as independently active – but in the moral rather than parliamentary sphere of experience. In this letter Eliot perceives the 'equivalence of good for women and for men' as progressing not through the sexes pursuing the same actions – such as voting – but by means of the 'distinctness of function', although she allows for the 'exceptional . . . individual' not fitting the general pattern. Against the tendency of her period's feminism, Eliot argued that if women were excluded from formal participation in the exercise of political power they must find some other form of contributing, and making their social presence felt. If men held the political arena women might still occupy the sites of moral and cultural discourse.

Eliot perceived that just as it was possible for an excluded group nevertheless to make a contribution, it was also in the nature of male bourgeois hegemony to exclude groups that were formally included. Many Jews, for instance, held the property qualifications that enabled them to vote, yet they were on the whole proscribed from occupying a central moral and cultural role in social life. The paradox was highlighted by the fact that although Disraeli, with his Jewish family background, held the prime ministership of Britain twice, a vein of anti-Semitism ran through British society.

This was not as virulent as the forms it took later under twentieth-century totalitarian regimes, but the anti-Semite strain was taken for granted in popular culture. It was by no means a Victorian phenomenon, for the most popular novelist of the early part of the century, Maria Edgeworth, displayed it. In her 1812 novel *The Absentee* 'Mordicai the Jew'[5] attempts to cheat a decent, although financially incautious, Englishman, and the physical description of the former indicates his moral state, for in:

his dark wooden face ... there was, altogether, something unnatural and shocking. ... When, at last, his eyes turned and his lips opened, this seemed to be done by machinery, and not by the will of a living creature, or from the impulses of a rational soul.

(p. 7)

The unnaturalness is linked to the character's Jewishness. He lacks basic human attributes, is not 'a rational soul'. Indeed, his Judaism may preclude him from having a 'soul' at all. Yet when Eliot came to write *Daniel Deronda* one of the emphases was the spiritual vitality of Jewish belief and practice (cf. chapter 4 above).

Eliot's last novel ran against a long tradition of suspicion and not a little contempt. Mirah expresses something of the Disraelian duality, 'I am English-born. But I am a Jewess'. Because of the latter state she expects to be discriminated against, asking Deronda directly 'Do you despise me for it?' (p. 234), and saying to Mrs Meyrick: 'I am a stranger. I am a Jewess. You might have thought I was wicked' (p. 241). In the reality reflected by demotic literature Mirah's expectations were quite valid.

In his 1839 *Oliver Twist* Dickens describes: 'a very old shrivelled Jew, whose villainous-looking and repulsive face was obscured by a quantity of matted red hair'.[6] This character is repeatedly referred to by the narrative discourse as 'the Jew' rather than his name, Fagin, as later: 'the Jew ... distorting every feature with a hideous grin' (p. 54), the technique echoing Edgeworth's – physical repulsiveness mirroring moral iniquity. Even the public house 'the Jew' visits is called 'The Three Cripples' (p. 157).

Fagin's trial is described as being a popular occasion:

The court was paved, from floor to roof, with human faces. Inquisitive and eager eyes peered from every inch of space. From the rail before the dock, away into the sharpest angle of the smallest corner in the galleries, all looks were fixed upon one man – the Jew.

(p. 339)

The audience have specifically 'human faces', implying that Fagin does not, and indeed he is being watched by 'Inquisitive and eager eyes' as though he were an animal, despite being described

as a 'man'. Ultimately, however, he is identified racially: 'the Jew'
– even the punctuation is used to emphasize that. In the original,
1839, version the chapter was headed specifically 'The Jew's Last
Night Alive' (ibid.), and it is interesting that Dickens' own
sensibilities changed sufficiently, after he was assured of his
reputation as a popular writer, for him to amend the heading of
the 1867 edition to 'Fagin's Last Night alive' (the version used in
the 1985 Penguin edition, p. 466). This was not a single change,
for as Kathleen Tillotson observes in her Introduction to the OUP
edition, based mainly on Dickens' 1846 text, referred to here: 'the
words "the Jew" were frequently eliminated in 1867' (p. xv).

Jews were mainly portrayed as being unscrupulous about
money. Edgeworth's Mordicai traps the extravagant Sir John
Berryl through 'an amazing amount of interest, and interest upon
interest' (p. 51) on his debts. When Sir John is dying Mordicai
forces his way into the house to collect in disregard of family
feelings: 'a debtor never yet escaped him, and never should; that
a man's lying upon his deathbed was no excuse to a creditor'
(ibid.). Mordicai's appearance again emphasizes his unhuman-
ness: 'livid with malice, and with atrocious determination in his
eyes ... grinning a horrible smile' (pp. 51–2). A man who would
badger someone on his deathbed is likely to be 'atrocious'.

The stereotype continued through the century. In Ouida's
Under Two Flags, for instance, a character faced by 'the falsehoods
of a Jew extortioner' feels 'a great horror, a loathing disgust'
(pp. 128–9). In that case the difference between the character who
is mainly identified by the term 'the Jew', and his English adver-
saries is stressed by their clean-cut nature. The 'malicious ... Jew'
(p. 130) is also provocatively insolent: 'with one moment more the
Jew would be dashed down at his feet with the lie branded on his
mouth by the fiery blow of a slandered and outraged honour'
(pp. 128–9). Whilst in Charlotte Yonge's *The Clever Woman of the
Family* an evil character naturally sends important documents to a
Semite: 'He is too cunning a scoundrel to tell unnecessary lies,
and very likely he may have disposed of them to some Jew
attorney' (p. 269). The use of 'some' suggests that every 'Jew
attorney' is willing to deal with 'a scoundrel' and it is unnecessary, therefore, to distinguish between individuals. It is implicit
that a 'Jew attorney' would be more devious and criminally
inclined than a Gentile. Writers such as Edgeworth, the young
Dickens, Yonge and Ouida were not necessarily themselves con-

sciously anti-Jewish, but were merely uncritically reflecting the common assumptions and attitudes of their day.

Eliot was never uncritical. *Daniel Deronda*, for instance, touches on the demotic Jewish figure when Gwendolen goes to a money-lender: 'these Jew dealers were so unscrupulous in taking advantage of Christians unfortunate at play!' (p. 48). But the Jew here is not described. There is no horrible grin or otherwise distorted features, and the observation on the 'unscrupulous' nature of 'Jew dealers' is not diegetic comment, as in the examples above, but Gwendolen's free indirect speech. It is the attitude of a character who is profoundly a product of social and cultural values which are fundamentally criticized in the novel as a whole. The context turns the thought into satire on Gwendolen, for she is raising money in order to gamble, an entirely immoral act in Eliot's canon, and not one sanctioned either by Christian theology. Gwendolen sees herself as merely 'unfortunate', but the reader might think her a very bad, rather than unlucky, Christian. The linguistic irony works against the character who is imposing the stereotyping. In this way Eliot perhaps challenges the reader's own assumptions about Jews, whereas the other writers simply, although unconsciously and without malice, confirmed prejudices.

Eliot's response, in her last novel, to the relatively recent triumphant emergence of bourgeois hegemony was not to storm its institutional fortresses, such as parliament. It was, rather, to suggest the development of other potential hegemonic spheres.

The working classes have their own value to exploit, and it is sometimes in a wider arena than that of their actual labour. When Rex is thrown from his horse in *Daniel Deronda*, for example, it is Joel Dagge who: 'on this occasion showed himself that most useful of personages, whose knowledge is of a kind suited to the immediate occasion' (p. 104). Despite his low social status Joel 'offered experienced surgical aid' (ibid.) in immediately resetting Rex' broken shoulder, and then attends to the general needs of the accident victim. The diegetic comment on the incident is satiric: 'Joel being clearly a low character, it is happily not necessary to say more of him to the refined reader' (ibid.). It is the readers who consider themselves 'refined' that are satirized, refined in this context meaning thinking the lower orders have no value. Real refinement had, for Eliot, nothing to do with mere snobbery. The lower orders themselves should not attempt to emulate, or envy, social pretension.

The members of 'The Philosophers' (p. 580) club of the *Hand and Banner* to which Deronda is invited have real refinement. They are 'poor men given to thought ... a company select of the select among poor men, being drawn together by a taste not prevalent even among the privileged heirs of learning and its institutions' (pp. 580–2). These characters' greatest delight is the discussion of ideas, not simply as practical measures but for their own sake, for the joy of intellectual excitement, 'the power of ideas' (p. 583). Since bourgeois hegemony had little philosophic depth Eliot saw the way forward for the working classes to lie in the direction of ideas. Votes may come eventually, but they, for Eliot, would be useless unless founded on a wider vision than mere materialism.

Women too should look beyond the suffrage into other spheres of influence. Eliot saw that process beginning with the establishment of a measure of personal, individual independence outside the confines set by the mores of the male middling classes. The potentially wealthy Catherine Arrowpoint defies her parents' wish for her to make a socially suitable marriage: 'I feel at liberty to marry the man I love and think worthy' (p. 290). She is willing to risk disinheritance to establish her independence of judgement and action. The impoverished Mirah Lapidoth also pursues her own vision, explaining to Mrs Meyrick 'I am come a long way, all the way from Prague by myself' (p. 242). The individual woman must assert her own identity, and will be able to despite the odds against her if she is sufficiently strong. A journey from Prague to London for a young woman alone in the mid-Victorian period manifests a great deal of resolution, challenging the cultural/gender norms of the hegemonic group by ignoring them. Both females eventually marry, but that, within the novel's structure, is not to imply they surrender their independence, for the husbands are men who encourage their wives to retain a personal identity.

In fact they are both Jews, and many Jewish men were in an ambiguous situation – part of the hegemonic order in having franchise, but outside the assumptions and attitudes of its social leadership. The political aspect of that order is partly represented by:

Mr Bult, an esteemed party man who, rather neutral in private life, had strong opinions concerning the districts of the Niger, was much at home also in the Brazils, spoke with decision of affairs in the South Seas, was studious of his parliamentary and itinerant speeches, and had the general solidity and suffusive pinkness of healthy Briton on the central table-land of life.

(p. 283)

The satire is expressed in part by the opposites. Bult's 'neutral . . . private life' contrasts with his being 'an esteemed party man', with its implication that he votes in parliament solely according to party dogma. His apparent neutrality covers an actual lack of thought and independence. Although he appears to know about circumstances all over the world the diversity of interests suggests superficiality, and certainly none of his knowledge pertains to situations at home, though critical issues were being debated. The final image of the extract, 'the central table-land of life', expresses the character's fundamental complacency. Mediocrity and self-satisfaction are not the province only of Bult, but of politicians in general. Deronda rejects Sir Hugo's suggestion that the young man 'might be in Parliament in no time' with the statement 'I cannot persuade myself to look at politics as a profession. . . . I don't want to make a living out of opinions . . . especially out of borrowed opinions' (p. 434). This directly rebuts, thematically, Bult's status as 'an esteemed party man', speaking and acting in an approved and unthinking manner.

Klesmer too, the character worthy of Catherine's love, rejects Bult's purely parliamentary approach to life, describing the 'creative artist' as being greater than a politician:

We help to rule the nations and make the age as much as any other public men. We count ourselves on level benches with legislators. And a man who speaks effectively through music is compelled to something more difficult than parliamentary eloquence.

(p. 284)

Creative vision is at least as, and perhaps even more, important than material interests. Bourgeois hegemony was based on the latter, and its cultural influence was materialistic. But of all the arts music is least palpable, and most concerned with harmony - in all that concept's senses – and Klesmer 'looks forward to a fusion of races' (ibid.), which is also a metaphor for the concord of all people.

The vision of Mordecai that Deronda ultimately rejects bourgeois hegemony in order to pursue is, 'A spiritual destiny embraced willingly' (p. 555). Although the action of an individual this is not a purely individualistic deed, just as music – or any art – has a communal life and function. In a somewhat mixed metaphor Mordecai impresses Deronda with the idea of 'a seed of fire that may enkindle the souls of multitudes, and make a new pathway' (p. 586).

Eliot's response to materialism, and the middling-class leadership that was confirmed in the 1867 Reform Act, was not to urge the excluded to become included, but to follow their own talents and vision. The expression of individual spirit, within responsible, not selfish or hedonistic, social attitudes was the greatest aspiration of which Eliot could conceive.

8

The Critical Crucible

Like some other great Victorian novelists Eliot's critical reputation was in her lifetime generally high, but after her death it went through a slough which lasted through the first half of the twentieth century. Her esteem was restored in the second part, and is now ambivalently poised between regard for her artistic achievement and dismissal of what is seen as her ideological conservatism. This pattern illustrates how difficult it is to achieve truly objective standards of critical judgement.

At a time when the conditions of publishing changed practice away from serialization over a long time, followed by the publication of a relatively huge volume, to the appearance of comparatively short novels directly in book form, Eliot's work seemed to much – although not all – critical and public taste, over-lengthy and ponderous, with plots on occasion melodramatic, and an intellectualizing and moralizing tone. After the trauma of the Second World War critics began to rediscover the qualities of moral concern – rather than didactic moralizing – and intellectual analysis in Eliot's work. These seemed to lead to a saner world than that experienced in general between the catastrophic two world wars. All these points are, of course, broad generalizations – and there are always notable exceptions to the overall trend, whether favourable or otherwise, in every period and phase.

Eliot's first fiction, the collection published as *Scenes of Clerical Life*, was very well received. Dickens wrote to Eliot in January 1858 of the stories:

to express my admiration of their extraordinary merit. The exquisite truth and delicacy, both of the humour and the pathos of these stories, I have never seen the like of ... I have observed what seemed to me such womanly touches in these moving fictions, that the assurance on the title-page is insufficient to satisfy me even now.

(GEL, II, pp. 423–4)

Receiving a letter of this kind from the most famous, and popular, of contemporary novelists was obviously extremely encouraging for someone who had only just begun to write fiction. Eliot's comment to her publisher, Blackwood, affirms her pleasure: 'There can be hardly any climax of approbation for me after this, I am so deeply moved by the finely-felt and finely expressed sympathy of the letter' (SL, p. 183). Dickens' perceptive remarks on the gender of the author illustrate that his was no superficial reading, which obviously reinforced the power of the compliment.

After Eliot's first novel, *Adam Bede*, Dickens again wrote to her in glowing terms:

> Every high quality that was in the former book, is in that, with a World of Power added ... if you should ever have the freedom and inclination to be a fellow labourer with me, it would yield me a pleasure that I have never known yet and can never know otherwise.
>
> (GEL, III, pp. 114–5)

Again the compliment is given substance by the suggestion that Eliot should be 'a fellow labourer', in effect an offer to publish her future work in the journal Dickens was editing, *All the Year Round*. Although Eliot was not a young writer as such, she was approaching 40 when this letter was written, it nevertheless provided a necessary encouragement. The letter represents a genuine appreciation of a first novel, and considerable confidence, from the leading novelist of the day, in Eliot's ability and potential. Eliot never in fact wrote for Dickens, but her subsequent development certainly validates his critical judgement.

Indeed, *Adam Bede* was generally very popular with both the reading public and reviewers in newspapers, magazines and journals. A typical response to the novel was that made by an anonymous reviewer who recommended: 'Persons who only read one novel a year – and it is seldom that more than one really good novel is published in a year – may venture to make their selection, and read *Adam Bede*' (*The Saturday Review*, 26 February 1859). The dry dismissal of almost all other novels published in any year suggests a parsimonious approach to reading, which gives the praise even greater weight in this case. The novelist Geraldine Jewsbury, in a reputable journal appearing on the same day, began her review under the heading 'New Novels' with a general aesthetic statement: 'The works of true genius seem the most natural things in the world, – so right, that one cannot imagine them different, – so exactly what is needed, that they come as matters of course' (*The Athenaeum*, 26 February 1859). She went on to include *Adam Bede* in this category of 'works of true genius', claiming that it: 'is a novel of the highest class. Full of quiet power, without exaggeration and without any strain after effect' (ibid.). Since one of the subsequent criticisms of the novel, and Eliot's work in general, has been that it is exaggerated and strained it is interesting to perceive her achievement through the intelligence of a contemporary novelist. Jewsbury concluded her appreciation by, like the reviewer quoted above, asserting the novel's uniqueness: 'it is very seldom we are called on to deal with a book in which there is so little to qualify our praise' (ibid.). This was the tone of the vast majority of reviewers. Indeed, later in Eliot's career *Adam Bede* was sometimes the novel critics referred back to as her greatest achievement. The critics John Holmstrom and Laurence Lerner laconically observe that by the 1870s some critics were using *Adam Bede* 'as a stick to beat the later novels'.[1]

Even so, no novel has ever gained absolutely universal acclaim, and there were a small minority of dissenting voices. The Reverend J. C. Robertson, a notable religious academic, for instance, complained:

> She delights in unpleasant subjects – in the representation of things which are repulsive, coarse, and degrading. . . . The idea that fiction should contain something to soothe, to elevate, or to purify seems to be extinct. In its stead there is a love for exploring what would be better left in obscurity; for portraying the wildness of passion and the harrowing miseries of mental conflict; for dark pictures of sin and remorse and punishment; for the discussion of those questions which it is painful and revolting to think of . . . we do not believe that any good end is to be effected by fictions which fill the mind with details of imaginary vice and distress and crime.
>
> (*The Quarterly Review*, October 1860)

Robertson was including the recently published second novel, *The Mill on the Floss*, in this condemnation. His is a classic illustration of the critic who judges books by their moral, or ideological, soundness. Our own society may find his objections banal – although there is still a group of potential censors who think fictional characters should set only approved examples of behaviour. On the whole, however, art must deal with the 'dark' side of life on occasions, and to do so does not automatically mean it cannot 'elevate'. However, ideological objections – which is where Robertson's essential position rests – are not confined to the Victorian era, although their parameters may have changed.

In fact *The Mill on the Floss*, despite its initial commercial success, was not generally as enthusiastically reviewed as its predecessor. The critic E. S. Dallas, in a prestigious two and half column review found himself in something of a minority in declaring: '"George Eliot" is as great as ever. She has produced a second novel, equal to her first in power' (*The Times*, 19 May 1860). Even he, though, thought it not as interesting a book as *Adam Bede*. An anonymous reviewer had already made the point: 'The first great fault . . . is want of interest in the story or in any of the principal characters' (*The Atlas*, 14 April 1860). Another unsigned review praised the novel in general, but modified it with two serious qualifications. One anticipates, although more openmindedly, Robertson's wider-sweeping moral objections:

> Passion is one of the legitimate materials of the novelist. But he incurs deep responsibility by the way in which he treats it. And we cannot think that he does good service by bringing into clear and powerful light its perverted and unwholesome growths.
>
> (*The Guardian*, 25 April 1860)

The particular problem here is Maggie's abortive elopement with Stephen, although this writer – unlike Robertson – displays no objection to Hetty's illegitimate pregnancy in the previous novel. Perhaps the issue is partly that Hetty, though important, is less absolutely central as a character than Maggie. This relates to the reviewer's other criticism of *The Mill on the Floss*, which is of the 'structure':

> Nobody who reads it can, we should think, avoid the feeling that in the last volume he passes into a new book. There is a

clear dislocation in the story, between Maggie's girlhood and Maggie's great temptation.

(ibid.)

This writer is clearly reluctant to see that the frustrations of Maggie's early life may have contributed thematically to that appalling error of succumbing to the temptation, that a development of subtle cause and effect exists rather than a fracture in the conception of the character. Maggie, for instance, is an extremely intelligent girl denied a proper education because of her gender; she suffers the denial of her feelings towards Philip through the tyranny of the male members of her family; she is constrained into a narrow drudgery of school teaching when she longs for her life to open up to greater horizons.

A slightly earlier anonymous reviewer did make the connections in praising the characterization of Maggie:

A woman's natural impulses; all the wild fancies and self-torturing thoughts of a young girl vivid in imagination ... obliged to live a life at first very narrow, and then very mean – are described exactly as they might happen, as they do happen, in thousands of English homes. The novelty and interest lie in the fact that in very few works of fiction has the interior of the mind been so keenly analyzed.

(*The Spectator*, 7 April 1860)

The character of Maggie is both specific, accredited with individual attributes, and yet is representative of 'thousands' of young women. For this reviewer the continuity of characterization lies in the presentation and analysis of Maggie's mind. If there is a 'perverted and unwholesome' growth it does not emanate from the 'woman's natural impulses', but the way in which society constrains them. Responses to the novel tended to divide between those two poles: of moral distaste, and intellectual and aesthetic admiration.

The publication of *Silas Marner* in the following year restored Eliot's moral standing with the reviewers, and continued her commercial popularity. As the critic David Carroll has put it: 'Sighs of relief were mixed with the paeans of praise'.[2] *The Saturday Review* expressed the mood unequivocally: 'It is as good as *Adam Bede*' (13 April 1861). The theologian and mathematician

Richard Hutton drew the comparison in more balanced terms: 'It does not approach in tragic power some parts of "Adam Bede" ... but it is a more perfect whole' (*The Economist*, 27 April 1861). Hutton perceptively identified the emergence of a central strength in Eliot's novels:

> One of the most striking features in this striking tale is the strong intellectual impress which the author contrives to give to a story of which the main elements are altogether unintellectual, without the smallest injury to the verisimilitude of the tale.
>
> (ibid.)

This is a shrewd recognition that Eliot is not simply a teller of interesting tales, or an astute observer of the human psyche, although she is both of those – but is an intellectual writer grappling with the fundamental ideas and issues of her day.

Another critical admirer of Eliot's, Dallas, concluded his assessment, which ran for over two columns, in a similar tone:

> The moral purpose which is evident in her writing is mostly an unconscious purpose. It is that sort of moral meaning which belongs to every great work of art, and which no elevated mind can get rid of. She tells a simple story without the least idea of inculcating any copy-book lesson, but by merely elevating the reader to her mount of observation she cannot fail to suggest to the mind some profound reflections.
>
> (*The Times*, 29 April 1861)

Dallas is aware that moral ideas impregnate the work, and are in turn permeated by Eliot's own thought – so that the fiction does not merely mirror intellectual life, but expands it, encouraging the reader to new mental perceptions. There were extremely few hostile reviews of *Silas Marner*, but a typical complaint echoed those made of earlier novels: 'If George Eliot has a special taste for low life, she might surely pick out scenes better worth recording than most of those which here greet us' (*Dublin University Magazine*, April 1862). For this unidentified writer there is, in contrast to Dallas, no elevation, and there cannot be because of the nature of the 'low life' subject matter. Any artist who wants to concentrate on common, as opposed to socially and economically privileged, lives faces the same problem with readers who simply bring preconceptions about art into their reading.

The next novel, *Romola*, with its Renaissance Florentine setting, became in the opinion of Carroll:

> an important turning-point in George Eliot's career: it divided her reading-public into those who welcomèd the latest unfolding of her genius and those who persisted until the very end in their nostalgia for the world of the early novels. The critics were caught awkwardly between the two.[3]

Hutton was in the former group, referring to the novel as: 'one of the greatest works of modern fiction ... probably the author's greatest work' (*The Spectator*, 18 July 1863). As every good critic should, he went on to explicate his reasons for these assessments. One factor to strike Hutton particularly was that:

> The greatest artistic purpose of the story is to trace out the conflict between liberal culture and the more passionate form of the Christian faith in that strange era, which has so many points of resemblance with the present.
>
> (ibid.)

As in the review of *Silas Marner*, quoted above, Hutton recognized the intellectual power of the work, and the fact that Eliot's 'greatest artistic purpose', no matter when the novels are set, is to explore the contemporary issues, the 'many points of resemblance with the present'. Exactly the theme, of course, of the central chapters of this book.

Eliot herself confirmed the validity of Hutton's judgement. Lewes tried assiduously to shield her from reviews, especially hostile ones, but on this occasion the reviewer wrote to Eliot about his opinions, drawing attention to *The Spectator* article. She replied to Hutton:

> I find nothing fanciful in your interpretation. On the contrary, I am confirmed in the satisfaction ... at finding that certain chief elements of my intention have impressed themselves so strongly on your mind.... That consciousness makes me cherish the more any proof that my work has been seen to have some true significance by minds prepared not simply by instruction, but

by that religious and moral sympathy with the historical life of
man which is the larger half of culture.

(GEL, IV, pp. 96–7)

Eliot's intellectual belief that is expressed here may be referred
back to her article 'The Natural History of German Life' (cf.
chapter 2 above). History was never merely something in the past
for Eliot, it was always part of a continuing stream of process that
helped in providing an understanding of the present.

Hutton, even whilst lauding its qualities in the article quoted
above, was perceptive enough to recognize that *Romola*, 'will
never be George Eliot's most popular book'. An anonymous
reviewer, whilst acknowledging its strengths, also focused on
elements that were seen as the novel's faults:

> The conclusion of the story is its weakest point, because here, if
> anywhere, there was need of action. Few, we think, can be fully
> satisfied with the manner of Tito's death. . . . Romola's history
> after her second flight is strangely disconnected with the rest of
> the tale . . . another of those extravagantly fortuitous circum-
> stances of which the author makes such free use. All sense of
> probability is here sacrificed for a moral effect, which yet jars
> upon us.
>
> (*The Westminster Review*, October 1863)

This is a long way from Hutton's perceptive reading, and is the
kind of criticism that gave Eliot actual headaches when they
slipped through Lewes' censorship net. It approaches the fiction
as though it were a documentary account of life in northern Italy
400 years previously, with no relation or relevance to the reader's
own time and society.

Felix Holt, Eliot's next novel, returned in setting to familiar
ground, England in the 1830s. The moral and overtly political
nature of the story caused many reviewers to react in very
subjective terms. Holmstrom and Lerner have observed: 'no previous novel of George Eliot had so complex and interesting a
reception'.[4] The novel's full title, *Felix Holt: the Radical*, itself
appeared to trigger an automatic response. The writer in the
journal which Eliot herself had once edited wrote irritatedly of
Felix' practical radicalism, and also attacked the attitudes seen to
be embodied in another character:

how far is he right in his deliberate choice of poverty? ... [to] demand, as Mrs Transome does, sacrifice only from the man, is ... misleading ... such teaching countenances the worst error of the day with regard to women. Women can never rise until they become self-dependent.... Women must depend more on the intellect than the feelings.

(The Westminster Review, July 1866)

The nervousness of a journal that considered itself radical illustrates how close the novel was to some raw political nerves. The reviewer clearly recognized the contemporary relevance of the issues, and was unwilling to go as far along the democratizing processes as they thought the author was suggesting.

An even stronger repudiation of the radicalism was expressed by the lawyer and journalist George Venables:

Eliot finds in the absence or narrowness of education a sufficient explanation of sluggish understandings and of inconsecutive arguments ... her untaught or half-taught personages set logic at defiance. Her zeal for the elevation of the humbler classes is the more laudable because she has an extraordinary relish for the picturesque results of satisfied ignorance.

(The Edinburgh Review, October 1866)

This is asserted, rather than argued, criticism. No detailed analysis of the text occurs to substantiate these views, although the article takes up almost fifteen pages of the journal. The tone expressed by words such as 'zeal', 'laudable', 'relish' appears superciliously mocking – not only the author, but also the characters; and perhaps by implication actual 'untaught or half-taught personages'. The very use of the term 'personages' dehumanizes such people, perhaps putting them in the category of baggages or packages. There seems to be an assumption behind the comments that being taught entails an education at university. Although neither Felix, nor Esther who ultimately fundamentally shares his ideas, have been formally educated in that manner it is hardly possible to describe them as 'untaught or half-taught' in any real sense. Eliot may well have argued that the 'satisfied ignorance' emanated from the complacency of the reviewer rather than the book.

If Venables had been shocked, possibly even a little frightened, by the prospect of a Radical hero, another reviewer was relieved by Felix' restraint:

> We are little likely ... to adopt Radicalism of any shade; but if we ever see reason to change our political colours, we shall certainly follow Felix Holt rather than John Bright. When the 'demagogue' shall appear on the platform who will teach the unenfranchised classes that the first step towards political freedom is to free their own minds from ignorance and prejudice ... and when they have learnt to listen patiently to such teaching, we think the question of fitness to exercise political power will have pretty well been answered.
>
> (*Blackwood's Magazine*, July 1866)

There is a sense of relief here, a satisfaction that Radicalism is not necessarily a force that will destroy the constitution. By comparing the fictional, and historic, character of Felix with the living Radical politician Bright, the critic implicitly recognized that the novel was concerned with contemporary issues. The attitudes of this reviewer are not unlike those of others quoted above – essentially conservative, wanting to slow down the pace of change, or even delay it on the argument of 'fitness'. Their different responses to the novel are determined simply by whether or not they see its fundamental doctrine as recklessly or cautiously radical. It was the agitation, at the time of the novel's publication, for further reform of the franchise, which was achieved in the following year, that made it particularly politically contentious.

There was also a, perhaps not unrelated, moral objection. This is typified in the reaction to the character and story of Mrs Transome, which was considered unnecessary. In comparing it with Hetty's experiences in *Adam Bede*, which were just about acceptable as fiction, one reviewer wrote:

> In proportion as a writer of fiction holds a high and commanding place in influencing the public, does that writer owe it to the public not to outrage decency.... The story, in all its main features, would remain the same, if the dark blot on Mrs Transome's character had never occurred.
>
> (*The Contemporary Review*, September 1866)

There was a feeling that Eliot had included the adultery simply to 'outrage decency'. In some minds the overthrowing of the British political constitution and the affronting of sexual moral values appeared to be synonymous. *Felix Holt: the Radical*, more than any other of Eliot's works, was a novel that stimulated either fear or relief.

That book was followed by the longest prose fiction interregnum between any of Eliot's novels. In the following decade the work most generally considered her masterpiece, if not the greatest of all nineteenth-century English novels, appeared. *Middlemarch* was accepted by some reviewers at the time as a work of great genius, although as always there were dissenting voices. Many journals, magazines and newspapers published reviews whilst it was being serialized, but the full force of the work rested in the strength of its entirety.

Some of the adverse comments were of a trivial nature: 'many of the characters of the drama are uninteresting, Lydgate, Rosamond, Ladislaw, Bulstrode, Chettam, and Cadwallader, for example' (*The Standard*, 4 December 1872). The limitation of this kind of interpretation is that it tends to approach characters in fiction as though they were real people. The above reviewer was not alone in this: 'it is not easy to like young Ladislaw; one is tempted to think that, in marrying him, Dorothea makes nearly as great a blunder as she did in marrying Mr Casaubon' (*The Examiner*, 7 December 1872). Dissatisfaction with the character of Ladislaw has been an enduring response, but it is absurd to write of him and Dorothea as though they had an independent existence outside the text. They function within the novel's artistic structure, and if there is an aesthetic flaw it must be explored in terms of the work's themes. The text is clear that Dorothea did not make 'a blunder': 'They were bound to each other by a love stronger than any impulses which could have marred it' (p. 894). Interpretation based solely on the critic's own expectations and preconceptions is seldom helpful.

A more serious form of reservation about *Middlemarch* concerned doubts about the way its central dialectics were argued. In the conflict between individual personality and social constraints, for example, is there an authorial bias in either direction, or a clear resolution of the dichotomy? Many reviewers thought Eliot came down too harshly against society, absolving her characters too easily from their own errors. A typical reaction of this kind concluded:

> The key-note, then, is that of Comtism, – that in an organised society, where each of us finds his place, mistakes such as those of Dorothea and Lydgate would be impossible, or, at any rate, less sadly possible than they are now. And yet it is hard to see that a faith such as this is more than a vague ideal. The errors of life are due fully as much to ourselves as to the medium which surrounds us.
>
> (*The Athenaeum*, 7 December 1872)

This is an interestingly balanced response, although perhaps putting Eliot rather closer to the Comtist fold than she would liked to have been placed. The novel is structured partly on a reworking of the very old nature/nurture debate, and this critic does perceive that.

Another, and very topical, aspect of the dialectical conflict concerned the role of women in nineteenth-century society. The critic of *Felix Holt*, quoted above, who objected to what he/she saw as the bias in the character of Mrs Transome found an echo in the views of Frederick Broome, diplomat and minor poet. Broome's overall view of the novel was almost eulogistic: 'There are few novels in the language which will repay reading over again so well as *Middlemarch*' (*The Times*, 7 March 1873). It demands, he argued, a lot more of the reader than the ordinary novel, but does reward the persistent and intelligent mind. One of the features of the novel that many reviewers remarked is noted by Broome too, even in his praise of it:

> No one can close *Middlemarch* without feeling that he has read a great book. He is impressed, and, perhaps, depressed, by its cruel likeness to life . . . nothing happens merely in order that the curtain may fall pleasantly . . . sober happiness and length of humdrum days . . . scarcely lighten the general gray of sky which novelists usually make it a point of honour to flood with sunshine at the final hour.
>
> (ibid.)

Eliot's stance was felt by many contemporaries to be too uncompromising, and the challenge to conventional literary norms too severe. But Broome's fundamental reservation concerns the recurring women's issue:

> There is a certain school which will find satisfaction in thinking that Dorothea's story involves some special impeachment of the fitness of the present female lot. We do not think this is at all intended, and if it be intended it is certainly not justified. George Eliot gives us a noble portrait and an affecting history of a woman who nearly spoilt her life by attempting to rise above her opportunities, but her failures and mistakes are not due to the fact of her being a woman, but are simply those which belong to the common lot of human life. Just as she married a husband who did not suit her, so a man may marry a wife who does not suit him. . . . The fetters she wore are too common to humanity, but the weight of them is felt far more by men than by women.
>
> (ibid.)

The very insistence of the argument appears to betray the real fear behind it, that women did have a 'justified' complaint. In the novel's thematic structure Lydgate obviously parallels Dorothea, and he does suffer both social and matrimonial 'fetters', without the privilege of being freed by the convenient death of his spouse. Broome, however, confounds the concepts of marriage and 'opportunities' in his haste to deny firstly the intention of Eliot to impeach 'the present female lot', and secondly her justification for having done so. Dorothea hardly conceives of having any opportunity outside of marriage – and 'no one stated exactly what else was in her power' (p. 894) – which in itself may well be a valid point of 'impeachment'.

Broome's review ran to over three columns, and was on the whole a very appreciative assessment. He displayed, though, a not uncommon yearning backward glance. In comparing *Middlemarch* with the first great success, *Adam Bede*, he concluded:

> As a novel proper it is inferior to the early work; its plot is not exciting; it has not the liveliness, variety, and picturesqueness of its great predecessor ... but it is its philosophical power which is its distinctive and supreme excellence.
>
> (ibid.)

The earlier novel was maybe a little easier to live with. It raises pertinent issues, but there are sufficient distractions of plot and character to diffuse them to some extent. *Middlemarch*, as Broome's own review reveals, is an uncomfortable book for the Victorian establishment; the questions are asked more uncompromisingly.

The astute critic, and Cambridge's Slade Professor of Fine Art, Sidney Colvin, praised the novel fulsomely:

> In the sense in which anything is called ripe because of fulness and strength, I think the last of George Eliot's novels is also the ripest. 'Middlemarch' is extraordinarily full and strong. . . . There is nothing in the literature of the day so rousing. . . . What she writes is so full of her time . . . saturated with modern ideas, and poured into a language of which every word bites home with peculiar sharpness to the contemporary consciousness.
>
> (*The Fortnightly Review*, 19 January 1873)

Colvin recognizes the novel's immediacy, its 'rousing' quality, that although it is set back 40 odd years in time it 'bites home with peculiar sharpness to the contemporary consciousness'. He also appreciates that *Middlemarch* is not merely a tale of an enormous diversity of characters, but primarily an intellectual novel, 'saturated with modern ideas'.

He saw too that Eliot had expanded the boundaries of the novel. In comparing *Middlemarch* with other 'English tales and the manner of their telling' he argues:

> Plenty of other writers have taken humdrum and narrow aspects of English life. . . . But this procedure of George Eliot's is a newer thing in literature, and infinitely harder to judge of, than the gray and tranquil harmonies of that other mode of art.
>
> (ibid.)

There is a shrewd realization here that new critical horizons are required, that the broad, and profound, intellectual approach of the novelist demands more of the reader than paltry judgements on whether or not a certain character is likeable.

The shrewd Hutton wrote 33 pages on Eliot, and also perceived that she had expanded the novel form beyond its previous boundaries, commenting, ambivalently, that *Middlemarch* was:

> the most remarkable work of the ablest of living novelists ... those old-fashioned and simple novels were more perfect and complete. ... They gratified and invigorated. ... [now] It is the darkest of prospects which is conjured up.
>
> (*The Quarterly Review*, April 1873)

It is a similar point to Broome's, but Hutton tends to see the difference more positively. For him the point of comparison is *Silas Marner*: 'the most poetical ... the most hopeful of all her books' (ibid.). The bleaker vision of the later novel disturbed a number of readers, including, such as Hutton, some of Eliot's admirers.

Henry James, writing in the journal *Galaxy* in 1873, decided that *Middlemarch*: 'is a treasure-house of details, but it is an indifferent whole'.[5] Nevertheless, he too recognized that the novel had irrevocably drawn new parameters: 'It sets a limit, we think, to the development of the old-fashioned English novel. ... If we write novels so, how shall we write History?'[6] It was a question that recurred for James as he sought new ways of his own to reach beyond Eliot's achievement. As Klingopulos has observed, James was one of 'The main inheritors from George Eliot'.[7]

Daniel Deronda, Eliot's final novel, was a disappointment to many readers, and a puzzle to a number of reviewers. The novel's intellectual power was recognized, but objections to it as a whole fell into two, sometimes overlapping, camps: that it was actually two stories indifferently stitched together; and that it presented an uncritical, even glorified, view of Jews and Judaism.

A typical response mixing praise and reservation came from the anonymous reviewer who after some reluctant, but severe, criticism wrote:

> All this is very painful to say, for it is a disturbance of the sentiments which we have ourselves shared with all the rest of the English public; but there is a time when dissent must find a voice. ... 'Nobody except George Eliot could have written it, but –,' has become the formula with which even the boldest preface their faltering disapproval. ... How much more truly

great was the broad and noble expanse, the spontaneous eloquence, the simple insight of 'Adam Bede', and 'Silas Marner'!
                              (*The Edinburgh Review*, October 1876)

There is here the recurrence of the complaint that Eliot – or
perhaps, by implication, any writer – should not engage in
international, inter-racial issues. The reviewer's confusion seems
evident in the potentially paradoxical terms of the compliments to
the earlier works: that they had both 'broad and noble expanse'
and 'simple insight'. It is *Daniel Deronda*, surely, that exhibits
'noble expanse', and that is, ironically, one of the contemporary
objections to it.

The publisher and editor, Richard Bowker, observed a discrepancy of view between writer and reader:

The novel has two centres, Gwendolen and Mordecai, between
whose circles the author's hero is the connecting link. The
evident difference of opinion between the author and her
readers, as to which is the leading person of the story, grows
out of the conditions of this pervasive problem.
                              (*The International Review*, January 1877)

The criticism that *Daniel Deronda* is actually two novels which are
only loosely connected was, and has persisted in being, a recurring one. It is based on the, possibly fallacious, idea that Eliot, in
her final novel, did not have control of its conception or structure.

The most virulent criticism, however, was caused by the novel's
Jewish elements. Eliot records an inkling of this potential hostility
in her journal during the text's serialization: 'What will be the
feeling of the public as the story advances I am entirely doubtful.
The Jewish element seems to me likely to satisfy nobody' (SL,
p. 470). In the belief that she might encourage a wider vision
among her readers Eliot persisted, and was rewarded by a very
enthusiastic response from many Jews. After publication in
volume form Eliot wrote in her journal: 'Words of gratitude have
come from Jews and Jewesses, and there are certain signs that I
may have contributed my mite to a good result' (SL, p. 478). But
the objections to the Jewish theme remained, sometimes expressed as genuine bewilderment about its artistic and intellectual
functions in the book, occasionally as thinly veiled anti-Semitic

prejudice. One anonymous reviewer, for instance, condemned the novel in terms of:

> a falling off from *Adam Bede*, and *Middlemarch.* . . . What can be the design of this ostentatious separation from the universal instinct of Christendom, this subsidence into Jewish hopes and aims? . . . [it] may be defined as a religious novel without a religion . . . when a young man of English training and Eton and University education, and, up to manhood, of assumed English birth, so obliging also as to entertain Christian sympathies, finishes off with his wedding in a Jewish synagogue, on the discovery that his father was a Jew, the most confiding reader leaves off with a sense of bewilderment and affront.
>
> (*The Saturday Review*, 16 September 1876)

It is as though the provincial settings of the earlier novels limited them to mere provinciality, that the wider issues overtly taken up in *Daniel Deronda* did not appear in the previous books. The reader displays a personal narrowness of interpretation in this respect, and a prejudice in such assumptions that the 'instinct of Christendom' is 'universal', which clearly runs against the evidence to the contrary. An interest in 'Jewish hopes and aims' is considered a 'subsidence', presumably a lowering of intellectual and religious values, which makes it a 'novel without a religion'. Whatever the comparative merits and deficiencies of Christianity and Judaism, the latter has at least to be recognized as a religion.

Although they were less numerous than for the early books the novel had its unstinted admirers:

> Eliot has invaded the province of the novelist of fashionable life. As long as she described the ways and doings of Silas Marner and Seth Bede, and such people, the fashionable novelist felt safe. But now Park Lane has found a chronicler . . . [we] express a hope that it may be the beginning of a fresh series of tales which must entirely revolutionise the tone of novels of fashionable life.
>
> (*The Westminster Review*, October 1876)

The novel is certainly satiric of the lack of virtues and values, and the vacuous nature, of fashionable society – but to describe it as a novel 'of fashionable life' seems to misrepresent the book as a whole. Some of its defenders, even, appeared to misunderstand the novel's true range.

Eliot's general standing as a novelist started to decline towards the end of her life. The minor novelist William Mallock wrote: 'Eliot might have been a second Miss Austen, and has failed to be so' (*The Edinburgh Review*, October 1879). There is a tone of regret here, but the judgement sets the general critical scene for the following decades. The academic George Saintsbury recorded in 1895, and reiterated in 1918, that 'a considerable reaction ... has set in against her since her death'.[8] The historian Jonathan Rose remarks on how many Edwardians found her novels written in 'ornate, decorated language'.[9]

Readers such as Woolf continued to acknowledge Eliot's talent – 'That greatness is here we can have no doubt'[10] – but its status was not fully restored until 1948. The influential critic F. R. Leavis included Eliot as a central writer in his definition of the great tradition of English literature, celebrating her 'distinctive kind of greatness'.[11] More recent post-structuralist, and post post-structuralist, theorists have examined the novels with a different critical perception. In his influential Marxist criticism Terry Eagleton, for example, sees Eliot attempting: 'to resolve a structural conflict between two forms of mid-Victorian ideology ... Romantic individualism ... and ... corporate ideological modes'.[12] He concludes that she fails because the two forces are in reality irreconcilable, and that by the last novel: 'The voice of liberal humanism has become the voice of jingoist reaction'.[13] As the extracts from the reviews above illustrate, this is a quite different interpretation from that of many of Eliot's contemporaries – which does not, of course, invalidate either response. The grounds of both need to be understood.

Feminism's problematic relationship with Eliot has been touched on in chapter 1 of this book, and the apparent paradox is perhaps best summarized by Beer's judgement that Eliot: 'persistently worked at the central dilemmas of feminism in her time without setting out to write feminist novels'.[14] This fact in itself has outraged those critics who see Eliot, although perfectly capable of confronting the real issues, deliberately avoiding them, or sublimating their reality into fantasy situations and 'ideologically insufficient'[15] resolutions.

Examining *The Mill on the Floss* in particular Tony Davies, for instance, finds:

certain contradictions in George Eliot's own history and predicament. There is a persistent, mawkish nostalgia for what she
calls the 'golden gates of childhood', and a patronising face-
tiousness in the rendering of the petit-bourgeois ... house-
holds. But these are far outweighed ... by the clarity with
which the ideological purposes and limitations of education are
realised; a clarity available to this text by virtue of its *feminism*.[16]

The notion that Eliot sees 'ideological purposes and limitations'
with 'clarity', yet refuses to attack the political and social roots of
the problems is the cause of Davies' anger. He is not alone, and
the concepts at play here have been applied in diverse ways to all
the novels. To a large extent the validity of such interpretations
depends on the definition of *'feminism'*. Eliot herself refuted the
categorization, and perhaps the argument is that the text *should*
have been feminist given what is seen as 'Eliot's own history and
predicament'.

A reaction against the theories of more recent critical schools is
provided by the judgement of the novelist and critic David Lodge,
who has argued that Eliot was not only aware of stresses and
possible contradictions in society, and the relationship between
art and reality, but actually used them constructively:

she was well aware of the indeterminacy that lurks in all efforts
at human communication, and frequently reminded her readers
of this fact in the very act of apparently denying it through the
use of an intrusive 'omniscient' authorial voice.[17]

This attributes Eliot with a very considerable talent – the ability to
simultaneously use and question the dominant literary forms of
the time – and the elusiveness of the fiction, which has been
recognized by some readers over the years, but missed by others,
partly emanates from it.

All of her novels utilize some degree of historical perspective,
and as readers get further away from the mid-Victorian era the
difficulties of truly appreciating the work become greater. The
original readers knew their own times, of course, and the perceptive ones realized that the novels were not simple exercises in
nostalgia, or historical reconstructions, but were a view of the
present in the light of the past. Unless current readers understand
both the time in which Eliot was writing, and something of how

that period perceived its own past, they are likely to fall into error – to assume she was attempting to achieve a different effect from that Eliot actually intended, and must therefore judge the work at least a partial failure, although the flaw actually lies in the false assumption applied to the fiction. The novels must be comprehended as products of the time in which they were written, as criticisms of those times, and as positive contributions to that culture. Because of the subtlety of her craft Eliot's work will continue to create interpretive controversy, and to generate enormous pleasure.

Chronological Table

Unless otherwise stated publication dates refer to the year in which works appeared in complete volume form.

1819   Eliot born (22 November).
       (The future Queen) Victoria born.
       Peterloo massacre in Manchester.
1825   Stockton-Darlington railway opened.
1828   Test and Corporation Acts repealed, allowing Nonconformists to hold public office.
1829   Roman Catholics given vote and allowed to hold public office.
1830   Accession of William IV.
       Foundation of Positivism with the commencement of publication of Comte's *Course of Positive Philosophy*.
1831   Reform Bill crisis.
       Faraday develops electromagnetic induction.
1832   Reform Act extends franchise.
       Scott dies.
       Morse invents telegraph.
       First railway in continental Europe opens.
1833   First government grant for education.
       Grand National Consolidated Trades Union formed.
       Tracts for the Times begin to be published.
1834   McCormick develops a reaping machine.
1837   Accession of Queen Victoria.
1838   Cobden founds Anti-Corn Law League to further free trade movement.
       People's Charter demands fundamental political reform, inaugurates Chartism as a political movement.
1839   Chartist agitation.
       Beginnings of photography.
1840   Eliot's first published work, a poem, appears in the *Christian Observer*.
       Hardy born.

Zola born.

Penny post introduced.

1841 Carlyle's *On Heroes* published.

Satirical magazine *Punch* founded.

1842 Rejection of Chartist petition precedes further agitation.

Mudie's circulating library founded.

1843 James born.

Carlyle's *Past and Present* published.

Ruskin's *Modern Painters* published.

News of the World founded.

1844 Co-operative Society founded.

Turner's painting *Rain, Steam, and Speed*.

1845 Disraeli's *Sybil* published.

1846 Eliot's translation of Strauss' *Life of Jesus, Critically Examined* published.

Dickens' *Dombey and Son* published.

Corn Laws repealed.

1847 Brontës' *Wuthering Heights* and *Jane Eyre* published.

Chloroform first used as an anaesthetic.

1848 Thackeray's *Vanity Fair* published.

Gaskell's *Mary Barton* published.

Newman's *Loss and Gain* published.

Severe national cholera epidemic.

Public Health Act introduces new standards of sanitation.

Chartism finally collapses.

Revolutions attempted in many European countries, all of which fail.

Marx and Engels compose the *Communist Manifesto*.

1849 Bedford College for Women founded in London.

Eliot travels to the continent, staying alone in Geneva for several months.

Froude's *The Nemesis of Faith* published.

1850 Wordsworth dies.

Tennyson's *In Memoriam* published.

Public Libraries Act.

1851 Ruskin's *Stones of Venice* published.

Eliot published in *Westminster Review* for the first time.

Eliot domiciled in London as lodger in Chapman's house.

Eliot begins editorial work on *Westminster Review* and meets Lewes.

Great Exhibition held in London.

1852   Eliot's close, rumouredly romantic, friendship with Spencer ends.

The term 'evolution' introduced by Spencer.

1853   Dickens' *Bleak House* published.

Lewes' essays *Comte's Philosophy of the Sciences* published.

1854   Eliot's translation of Feuerbach's *The Essence of Christianity* published.

Eliot and Lewes leave for a working trip to Germany, and begin their life together.

Lewes' *The Work and Life of Goethe* published.

Eliot begins translating Spinoza's *Ethics*.

Dickens' *Hard Times* published.

Working Men's College founded in London.

Crimean War, in which Britain and France are engaged with Russia, and in which Florence Nightingale comes to public prominence, begins.

1855   Gaskell's *North and South* published.

1856   Flaubert's *Madame Bovary* published.

Bessemer's new, and cheaper, steel-making process introduced.

Crimean War ends.

1857   Eliot's first fiction, *Amos Barton*, published in *Blackwood's Magazine*.

Trollope's *Barchester Towers* published.

The Englishwoman's Journal founded.

Conrad born.

Matrimonial Causes Act, setting up divorce courts allowing men to obtain divorce on the grounds of the adultery of a wife.

Indian Mutiny in which Sepoy troops revolt.

1858   Eliot's *Scenes of Clerical Life* published.

Lewes' *Physiology of Common Life* published.

1859   Eliot's *Adam Bede* published.

Darwin's *The Origin of Species* published.

Smiles' *Self-help* published.

The Society for Promoting the Employment of Women formed.

First oil well, in US, drilled.

Wagner's *Tristan and Isolde* performed.

1860   Eliot's *The Mill on the Floss* published.

Eliot and Lewes travel extensively in Europe.

1861   Eliot's *Silas Marner* published.
       Eliot re-visits Italy.
       Dickens' *Great Expectations* published.
       Wood's *East Lynne* published.
       First all iron warship, *HMS Warrior*, launched.
       Siemens' steel-making process further reduces manufacturing cost.
       US Civil War begins.
       Russian serfs emancipated.
       Pasteur develops the germ theory of disease.
1862   Braddon's *Lady Audley's Secret* published.
       Gatling gun invented to facilitate rapid fire.
1863   Eliot's *Romola* published.
       Braddon's *Aurora Floyd* published.
       Oliphant's *Salem Chapel* published.
       Thackeray dies.
1864   Eliot visits Italy again.
       International Working-Men's Association founded in London.
       First national Trade Union Conference held.
       Pasteur invents the process of pasteurization.
1865   Dicken's *Our Mutual Friend* published.
       Yonge's *The Clever Woman of the Family* published.
       Carroll's *Alice in Wonderland* published.
       Irish Fenian movement founded against British rule.
       Bicycle invented.
       Mechanical dishwasher invented.
       Lister develops antiseptic surgery.
       Cable laid across the Atlantic.
       End of US Civil War.
       Lincoln assassinated.
1866   Eliot's *Felix Holt* published.
       Dostoevsky's *Crime and Punishment* published.
       Eliot and Lewes visit Spain.
       Mill presents first Women's Suffrage Petition to parliament.
       Mendel begins to establish the laws of heredity.
1867   Second Reform Act increases suffrage.
       Royal Commission on Trade Unions.
       First volume of Marx' *Das Kapital* published.
       Lewes begins his five-volume *Problems of Life and Mind*.
       Ouida's *Under Two Flags* published.

University extension movement introduces lectures for working men.

1868 Eliot's long narrative poem *The Spanish Gypsy* published.
Eliot and Lewes travel in Europe.
Trade Union Congress meets for first time.

1869 Arnold's *Culture and Anarchy* published.
Mill's *On the Subjection of Women* published.
Tolstoy's *War and Peace* published.
Eliot travels to Italy.
Eliot meets John Cross.
Labour Representation League founded.
First woman admitted to classes in medicine at a British University (Edinburgh).

1870 Dickens dies.
Eliot and Lewes again travel extensively in Europe.
Forster's Education Act extends the provision of elementary education.

1871 First residence for women students established in Cambridge.

1872 Eliot's *Middlemarch* published.
Eliot and Lewes visit Germany.
Hardy's *Under the Greenwood Tree* published.
Ballot Act creates secret voting.

1873 Eliot and Lewes travel to Germany again.

1874 Eliot's *The Legend of Jubal and other Poems* published.
Hardy's *Far from the Madding Crowd* published.
First Trade Union Members of Parliament elected.
Women's Trade Union League founded.
Lawn tennis invented.

1875 James' *The American* published.
Medical School for Women founded in London.

1876 Eliot's *Daniel Deronda* published.
Bradlaugh and Besant prosecuted for publishing a manual giving advice on contraception.
Wagner's *Ring* cycle first performed.
Bell invents the telephone.
Edison invents the phonograph.

1877 Eliot and Lewes gain ultimate social approval when they dine with royalty.
Ibsen's *Pillars of Society* first performed.

1878 Lewes dies.

Hardy's *The Return of the Native* published.
James' *The Europeans* published.
Tolstoy's *Anna Karenina* published.
Women admitted to degree courses at University of London.
Electric street lighting introduced in London.

1879 Eliot's essays *Impressions of Theophrastus Such* published.
Eliot completes Lewes' unfinished *Problems of Life and Mind*.
Problems of Life and Mind published.
Eliot founds Lewes studentship at University of Cambridge.
James' *Daisy Miller* published.
Ibsen's *A Doll's House* first performed.
College for women established at University of Oxford.

1880 Eliot marries John Cross (6 May).
Eliot dies (22 December).
Flaubert dies.
James' *Washington Square* published.
Dostoevsky's *The Brothers Karamazov* published.
Mundella's Education Act makes elementary education compulsory.

1881 Dostoevsky dies.

1882 Married Women's Property Act establishes right of married women to independent ownership of property.
Daimler constructs first petrol engine.

1884 Third Reform Act extends suffrage to virtually all adult males.

1885 Cross edits *George Eliot's Life* ... which is published in three volumes.

1887 Cross revises the *Life* ... and it is published in a single volume.

Notes

CHAPTER 1   OBSCURITY TO EMINENCE
1. Gordon S. Haight (ed.), *George Eliot: A Biography* (Oxford: Clarendon Press, 1969), p. 2.
2. Quoted in ibid., p. 410.
3. Leon Edel (ed.), *Henry James Letters*, I (London: Macmillan, 1974), p. 116.
4. Herbert Spencer, *An Autobiography*, I (London: Watts and Co., 1926), pp. 394–5.
5. ibid., p. 399.
6. Jennifer Uglow, *George Eliot* (London: Virago Press, 1987), pp. 246–7.
7. *James Letters*, pp. 116–7.
8. Mark Rutherford, *Last Pages From a Journal* (Oxford: Humphrey Milford, 1915), p. 132.
9. *An Autobiography*, p. 395.
10. ibid., p. 396.
11. Gillian Beer, *George Eliot* (Brighton: Harvester Press, 1986), p. 3.
12. Kate Millett, *Sexual Politics* (London: Virago Press, 1981), p. 139.
13. ibid.
14. Ludwig Feuerbach, *The Essence of Christianity* translated by Marian Evans (New York: Harper and Row, 1957), p. 271.
15. ibid.
16. Michael Peled Ginsburg, 'Pseudonym, Epigraphs, and Narrative Voice: *Middlemarch* and the Problem of Authorship', *ELH* [*Journal of English Literary History*], XXXXVII (1980), p. 546.
17. Marilyn Butler, *Maria Edgeworth: A Literary Biography* (Oxford: Clarendon Press, 1972), p. 1.
18. David Grylls, *Guardians and Angels* (London: Faber and Faber, 1978), p. 13.
19. John Bunyan, *The Pilgrim's Progress* (Harmondsworth: Penguin, 1987), p. 102.
20. Uglow, *George Eliot*, p. 9.
21. G. D. H. Cole and Raymond Postgate, *The Common People 1746–1946* (London: Methuen and Co. Ltd, 1968), p. 226.
22. Thomas Hutchinson (ed.), *Shelley: Poetical Works* (Oxford: University Press, 1990), p. 338.
23. ibid., p. 341.

CHAPTER 2   THE FEMALE THINKER
1. Sally Shuttleworth, *George Eliot and Nineteenth-Century Science* (Cambridge: University Press, 1984), p. 18.

CHAPTER 3   THE FEMALE NOVEL
1. J. H. Clapham, *An Economic History of Modern Britain 1820–1850* (Cambridge: University Press, 1950), p. 460.
2. Frank L. Huggett, *Life Below Stairs* (London: Book Club Associates, 1977), p. 72.
3. Peter Keating, *The Haunted Study* (London: Secker and Warburg, 1989), p. 24.
4. Pauline Gregg, *A Social and Economic History of Britain 1760–1980* (London: Harrap, 1982), p. 258.
5. Charles Dickens, *Great Expectations* (Harmondsworth: Penguin, 1985), p. 74.
6. Philip Collins, *Dickens and Education* (London: Macmillan, 1965), pp. 94–7.
7. Sir Llewellyn Woodward, *The Age of Reform 1815–1870* (Oxford: Clarendon Press, 1962), p. 483.
8. G. D. Klingopulos, 'The Literary Scene', in Boris Ford (ed.), *The New Pelican Guide to English Literature*, VI (Harmondsworth: Penguin, 1990), p. 100.
9. Michael Wheeler, *English Fiction of the Victorian Period 1830–1890* (London: Longman, 1985), p. 120.
10. F. R. Leavis, *The Great Tradition* (Harmondsworth: Penguin, 1966), p. 41.
11. Henry Fielding, *The History of Tom Jones* (Harmondsworth: Penguin, 1985), p. 253.
12. ibid., p. 122.
13. Mary E. Braddon, *Aurora Floyd* (London: Virago Press, 1984), p. 95. All subsequent references are also to this edition.
14. Charles Dickens, *Hard Times* (Harmondsworth: Penguin, 1985), pp. 58–9.
15. E. T., *D. H. Lawrence: a Personal Record* (Cambridge: University Press, 1980), p. 105.
16. Virginia Woolf, *Collected Essays*, I (London: Hogarth Press, 1971), p. 201.
17. Mrs Henry Wood, *East Lynne* (London: J. M. Dent and Sons Ltd, 1984), p. 215. All subsequent references are also to this edition.
18. Thomas Hutchinson (ed.), *Wordsworth: Poetical Works* (Oxford: University Press, 1989), p. 164. All subsequent references are also to this edition.

CHAPTER 4   TOWARDS A GODLESS SOCIETY
1. A. N. Whitehead, *Science and the Modern World* (Cambridge: University Press, 1932), p. 120.
2. Asa Briggs, *The Age of Improvement 1783–1867* (London: Longman, 1979), p. 480.
3. Mrs Lyell (ed.), *Life, Letters and Journals of Sir Charles Lyell, Bart.*, I (London: John Murray, 1881), p. 168.
4. ibid., p. 328.
5. Charles Darwin, *The Origin of Species* (Harmondsworth: Penguin, 1982), p. 54. All subsequent references are also to this edition.

6. Christopher Ricks (ed.), *The Poems of Tennyson* (London: Longman, 1969), p. 912. All subsequent references are also to this edition.
7. John Lubbock, *The Origin of Civilisation and The Primitive Condition of Man* (Chicago: University of Chicago Press, 1978), p. 256.
8. Francis Darwin (ed.), *The Life and Letters of Charles Darwin*, II (London: John Murray, 1888), p. 357.
9. Hutchinson, *Wordsworth*, p. 462.
10. Asa Briggs, *Victorian Cities* (Harmondsworth: Penguin, 1975), p. 63.
11. Joan Bennett, *George Eliot: Her Mind and Her Art* (Cambridge: University Press, 1974), pp. 148–9.
12. Elizabeth Furlong Shipton Harris, *From Oxford to Rome* (New York: Garland Publishing Inc., 1975), p. 1. All subsequent references are also to this edition.
13. John D. Baird and Charles Ryskamp (eds), *The Poems of William Cowper*, I (Oxford: Clarendon Press, 1980), p. 174.
14. John Henry Newman, *Loss and Gain* (Oxford: University Press, 1986), p. 296.
15. James Anthony Froude, *The Nemesis of Faith* (New York: Garland Publishing, Inc., 1975), pp. 226–7.
16. Briggs, *Victorian Cities*, pp. 68–9.
17. Mrs Oliphant, *Salem Chapel* (London: Virago Press, 1986), p. 2. All subsequent references are also to this edition.
18. Valentine Cunningham, *Everywhere Spoken Against: Dissent in the Victorian Novel* (Oxford: Clarendon Press, 1977), p. 25. Chapter 2 of this book is especially detailed in its information about, and understanding of, the diversity of sects.
19. ibid., p. 27.
20. Thomas H. Huxley, *Collected Essays*, V (London: Macmillan, 1894), p. 239.
21. ibid., p. 310
22. T. R. Wright, *The Religion of Humanity* (Cambridge: University Press, 1986), pp. 189–90. This is an excellent book for anyone who would like to understand Comte's influence in the nineteenth century as a whole.
23. Auguste Comte, *System of Positive Polity* translated by Edward Spencer Beesly and others, III (London: Longmans, Green and Co., 1875), p. 345. [First published in French 1853.]
24. ibid.
25. William Baker, *George Eliot and Judaism* (Salzburg: University of Salzburg, 1975), pp. 176–7.
26. Comte, *Positive Polity* translated by Richard Congreve, IV (1877), pp. 48–9. [First published in French 1854.]
27. ibid., p. 27.
28. Wright, *Religion of Humanity*, p. 85.

CHAPTER 5   EDUCATION AND WOMEN'S ROLES

1. Patrick Colquhoun. *A New and Appropriate System of Education for the Labouring People* (London: J. Hatchard, 1806), pp. 11–3.
2. Hutchinson, *Wordsworth*, p. 692.

3. ibid., p. 733.
4. Andrew Ure, *The Philosophy of Manufacturers* (London: H. G. Bohn, 1861), p. 404.
5. Helen, Lady Dufferin, *Songs, Poems & Verses* (London: John Murray, 1894), p. 206.
6. John Keble, *The Christian Year* (London: Church Literature Association, 1977), p. 4.
7. Words and music are reproduced in *Hymns Ancient and Modern* (London: William Clowes and Sons Ltd, 1909), p. 8.
8. Charlotte M. Yonge, *The Clever Woman of the Family* (London: Virago Press, 1985), p. 3. All subsequent references are to this edition.
9. Ouida, *Under Two Flags* (London: Anthony Blond, 1967), p. 196. All subsequent references are to this edition.
10. Monica Stirling, *The Fine and the Wicked: The Life and Times of Ouida* (London: Victor Gollancz Ltd, 1957), p. 57.
11. John Ruskin, *Munera Pulveris* (London: George Allen, 1904), p. 130.

CHAPTER 6   THE ALTAR OF MAMMON
1. Jane Austen, *Pride and Prejudice* (Oxford: University Press, 1991), p. 1.
2. Jane Austen, *Mansfield Park* (Oxford: University Press, 1991), p. 1.
3. Briggs, *Victorian Cities*, p. 52.
4. Rosa Nouchette Carey, *Barbara Heathcote's Trial* (London: Macmillan, 1899), p. 340. All subsequent references are to this edition.
5. Anon, *A Woman's View of Woman's Rights* (London: Edward Bumpus, 1867), p. 3.
6. Barbara Leigh Smith, *A Brief Summary, in Plain Language, of the Most Important Laws Concerning Women* (London: John Chapman, 1854), p. 6.
7. ibid., p. 18.
8. *A Woman's View . . .*, p. 16.

CHAPTER 7   WOMEN, JEWS AND BOURGEOIS HEGEMONY
1. *The Age of Reform*, p. 83.
2. Anthony Wood, *Nineteenth Century Britain 1815–1914* (London: Longman, 1984), p. 85.
3. Thomas Carlyle, *Critical and Miscellaneous Essays*, VII (London: Chapman & Hall, 1888), p. 207. All subsequent references are to this edition.
4. Mathew Arnold, *Culture and Anarchy* (Cambridge: University Press, 1971), p. 102. All subsequent references are to this edition.
5. Maria Edgeworth, *The Absentee* (Oxford: University Press, 1988), p. 62. All subsequent references are to this edition.
6. Charles Dickens, *Oliver Twist* (Oxford: University Press, 1990), p. 50. All subsequent references are to this edition.

CHAPTER 8   THE CRITICAL CRUCIBLE
1. John Holmstrom and Laurence Lerner (eds), *George Eliot and her readers* (London: Bodley Head, 1966), pp. 15–6.

2. David Carroll (ed.), *George Eliot: The Critical Heritage* (London: Routledge & Kegan Paul, 1971), p. 85. Both the above books are extraordinarily rich in contemporary reviews and criticism. This chapter is deeply indebted to the above editors, and some of the quotations used here are also reproduced in these books.

3. ibid., p. 19.

4. Holmstrong and Lerner, *George Eliot*, p. 73.

5. Henry James, *The House of Fiction* (London: Rupert Hart-Davis, 1957), p. 259.

6. ibid., p. 267.

7. Klingopulos, *Guide to English Literature*, p. 104.

8. George Saintsbury, *A History of Nineteenth Century Literature* (London: Macmillan 1918), p. 333.

9. Jonathan Rose, *The Edwardian Temperament* (Athens, Ohio: Ohio University Press, 1986), p. 146.

10. Virginia Woolf, *The Common Reader* (London: Hogarth Press, 1975), p. 216.

11. Leavis, *Great Tradition*, p. 25.

12. Terry Eagleton, *Criticism and Ideology* (London: Verso, 1990), p. 111.

13. ibid., p. 125.

14. Beer, *George Eliot*, pp. 1–2.

15. Eagleton, *Criticism and Ideology*, p. 121.

16. Tony Davies, 'Education, Ideology and Literature', in Tony Bennett, Graham Martin, Colin Mercer, Janet Woollacott (eds), *Culture, Ideology and Social Process* (London: Batsford Academic and Educational Ltd, 1981), p. 258.

17. David Lodge, '*Middlemarch* and the Idea of the Classic Realist Text' in K. M. Newton (ed.), *George Eliot* (London: Longman, 1991), p. 184.

Select Bibliography

ELIOT'S NOVELS

These are available in many different editions. For the sake of consistency references in this book are to the Penguin versions, published (Harmondsworth) on the following dates.

Adam Bede (1985)
Daniel Deronda (1986)
Felix Holt (1987)
Middlemarch (1985)
Romola (1980)
Silas Marner (1985)
The Mill on the Floss (1985)

OTHER MAIN WRITING

William Baker, *Some George Eliot Notebooks* (Salzburg: Universität Salzburg, 1976)

A. S. Byatt and Nicholas Warren (eds), *George Eliot: Selected Essays, Poems and Other Writings* (Harmondsworth: Penguin, 1990)

J. W. Cross (ed.), *George Eliot's Life as Related in Her Letters and Journals*, new edition (Edinburgh: William Blackwood and Sons, 1887)

George Eliot, *Brother Jacob* (London: Virago Press, 1989)

George Eliot, *Impressions of Theophrastus Such* (Edinburgh: William Blackwood and Sons, 1879)

George Eliot, *Scenes of Clerical Life* (Harmondsworth: Penguin, 1985)

George Eliot, *The Lifted Veil* (London: Virago Press, 1992)

Ludwig Feuerbach, *The Essence of Christianity* translated by Marian Evans (New York: Harper and Row, 1957)

Gordon S. Haight (ed.), *The George Eliot Letters*
  I–III (London: Oxford University Press, 1954)
  IV-VII (London: Oxford University Press, 1956)
  VIII-IX (New Haven: Yale University Press, 1978)

——, *Selections from George Eliot's Letters* (New Haven: Yale University Press, 1985)

Lucien Jenkins (ed.), *George Eliot: Collected Poems* (London: Skoob Books Publishing Ltd, 1989)

Thomas Pinney (ed.), *Essays of George Eliot* (London: Routledge & Kegan Paul, 1963)

Spinoza, *Ethics* translated by George Eliot (Salzburg: Universität Salzburg, 1981)

David Friedrich Strauss, *The Life of Jesus Critically Examined* translated by George Eliot (London: SCM Press, 1972)

Joseph Wiesenfarth (ed.), *George Eliot: Writer's Notebook 1854–79* (Virginia: University Press of Virginia, 1985)

CRITICAL WORKS

There are a great many critical books relevant to Eliot's work, many of which are devoted to single novels. This is necessarily a very brief selection, and one criterion has been to omit all books that deal with only one novel.

Rosemary Ashton, *George Eliot* (Oxford: University Press, 1987)

William Baker, *George Eliot and Judaism* (Salzburg: Universität Salzburg, 1975)

Gillian Beer, *George Eliot* (Brighton: Harvester, 1986)

Joan Bennett, *George Eliot: Her Mind and Her Art* (Cambridge: University Press, 1974)

Kristin Brady, *George Eliot* (Basingstoke: Macmillan, 1992)

Mary Wilson Carpenter, *George Eliot and the Landscape of Time* (Chapel Hill: University of North Carolina Press, 1986)

David Carroll (ed.), *George Eliot: The Critical Heritage* (London: Routledge & Kegan Paul, 1971)

Valentine Cunningham, *Everywhere Spoken Against: Dissent in the Victorian Novel* (Oxford: Clarendon Press, 1977)

Deirdre David, *Intellectual Women and Victorian Patriarchy* (London: Macmillan, 1987)

Valerie A. Dodd, *George Eliot: An Intellectual Life* (Basingstoke: Macmillan, 1990)

erry Eagleton, *Criticism and Ideology* (London: Verso, 1990)

Boris Ford (ed.), *The New Pelican Guide to English Literature*, VI (Harmondsworth: Penguin, 1990)

Richard Freadman, *Eliot, James and the Fictional Self* (Basingstoke: Macmillan, 1986)

Suzanne Graver, *George Eliot and Community* (Berkeley: University of California Press, 1984)

Gordon S. Haight (ed.), *George Eliot: A Biography* (Oxford: Clarendon Press, 1969)

Gordon Sherman Haight and Rosemary T. Van Arsdel (eds), *George Eliot: A Centenary Tribute* (London: Macmillan, 1982)

Timothy Hands, *A George Eliot Chronology* (London: Macmillan, 1989)

John Holmstrom and Laurence Lerner (eds), *George Eliot and her readers* (London: Bodley Head, 1966)

Linda C. Hunt, *A Woman's Portion* (New York: Garland Press, 1988)

F. R. Leavis, *The Great Tradition* (Harmondsworth: Penguin, 1966)

Jane Miller, *Women Writing About Men* (London: Virago Press, 1986)

Ellen Moers, *Literary Women* (London: The Women's Press, 1986)

K. M. Newton, *George Eliot: Romantic Humanist* (London: Macmillan, 1981)

K. M. Newton (ed.), *George Eliot* (London: Longman, 1991)

Barbara Prentis, *The Brontë Sisters and George Eliot* (Basingstoke: Macmillan, 1988)

John Purkiss, *A Preface to George Eliot* (London: Longman, 1985)

Elaine Showalter, *A Literature of Their Own* (London: Virago Press, 1991)

Sally Shuttleworth, *George Eliot and Nineteenth-Century Science* (Cambridge: University Press, 1984)

Julia Swindells, *Victorian Writing and Working Women* (Cambridge: Polity, 1985)

Ina Taylor, *George Eliot: Woman of Contradiction* (London: Weidenfeld and Nicholson, 1990)

Jennifer Uglow, *George Eliot* (London: Virago Press, 1987)

Alexander Welsh, *George Eliot and Blackmail* (Cambridge, Mass.: Harvard University Press, 1985)

Michael Wheeler, *English Fiction of the Victorian Period 1830–1890* (London: Longman, 1985)

Virginia Woolf, *Collected Essays*, I (London: Hogarth Press, 1971)

T. R. Wright, *The Religion of Humanity* (Cambridge: University Press, 1986)

SELECTED BACKGROUND BIBLIOGRAPHY

Rosemary Ashton, *G. H. Lewes: A Life* (Oxford: Clarendon Press, 1991)

Asa Briggs, *The Age of Improvement 1783–1867* (London: Longman, 1979)

——, *Victorian Cities* (Harmondsworth: Penguin, 1968)

J. H. Clapham, *An Economic History of Modern Britain 1820–1850* (Cambridge: University Press, 1950)

G. D. H. Cole and Raymond Postgate, *The Common People 1746–1946* (London: Methuen and Co. Ltd, 1968)

Auguste Comte, *System of Positive Polity* translated by Edward Spencer Beesly and others, III (London: Longmans, Green and Co., 1875)

Auguste Comte, *System of Positive Polity* translated by Richard Congreve, IV (1877)

Charles Darwin, *The Origin of Species* (Harmondsworth: Penguin, 1982)

Pauline Gregg, *A Social and Economic History of Britain 1760–1980* (London: Harrap, 1982)

Mrs Lyell (ed.), *Life, Letters and Journals of Sir Charles Lyell, Bart.*, I (London: John Murray, 1881)

A. N. Whitehead, *Science and the Modern World* (Cambridge: University Press, 1932)

Sir Llewellyn Woodward, *The Age of Reform 1815–1870* (Oxford: Clarendon Press, 1962)

Index